Leading International Projects

Leading International Projects

Diverse strategies for project success

Bob Dignen and
Peter Wollmann

KoganPage

Publisher's note

Every possible effort has been made to ensure that the information contained in this book is accurate at the time of going to press, and the publishers and authors cannot accept responsibility for any errors or omissions, however caused. No responsibility for loss or damage occasioned to any person acting, or refraining from action, as a result of the material in this publication can be accepted by the editors, the publisher or the contributors.

First published in Great Britain and the United States in 2016 by Kogan Page Limited

2nd Floor, 45 Gee Street	1518 Walnut Street, Suite 1100	4737/23 Ansari Road
London	Philadelphia PA 19102	Daryaganj
EC1V 3RS	USA	New Delhi 110002
United Kingdom		India

© Bob Dignen and Peter Wollmann 2016

ISBN   978 0 7494 7686 1
E-ISBN 978 0 7494 7687 8

British Library Cataloguing-in-Publication Data

A CIP record for this book is available from the British Library.

Library of Congress Control Number

2016953529

Typeset by Graphicraft Limited, Hong Kong
Print production managed by Jellyfish
Printed and bound in Great Britain by CPI Group (UK) Ltd, Croydon CR0 4YY

CONTENTS

07 An iterative evaluation of an online class to increase inclusion of international learners in an online forum 91

Sharon Lalla

08 Implementation of a global performance management system 109

Volker Hische

09 Global Offensive: project management within 150 days 124

Frank Kühn

10 A tale of David and Goliath: storytelling in projects   142

Bob Dignen

11 Setting up a RTGS (Real Time Gross Settlement) system in a Latin American context   156

Alberto Casagrande

12 Strategic business expansion   177

Nathan Lamshed

ONLINE RESOURCES

The following supplementary materials are available to download at www.koganpage.com/LIF

- Bibliography
- Literature review
- Miscellaneous research papers into international project management
- PowerPoint slides for team development

ABOUT THE CONTRIBUTORS

Abhijit Dey is currently working for Sodexo Asia Services Pte Ltd (BRS) as the VP – IT, Operations and Service Delivery for Asia Region. He has over 16 years of experience with almost 10 years of senior management experience in the sphere of IT in the consumer foods, chemical, FMCG and services industries. Abhijit has a strong background in programme management and governance, along with extensive experience of IT change management during mergers and acquisitions. and working in international teams on global projects.

Donato Nitti is founder and partner of Studio Legale Nitti & Associati with offices in Florence, Italy, and Shanghai, China. As a lawyer, Donato specializes in intellectual property, international commercial law and networks between enterprises, and in the fields of intellectual property law, arbitration law, EU law and international contracts. He is a guest professor of EU intellectual property law, IP Institute, Tongji University, Shanghai, China (2015), an Honorary Consul of the Kingdom of the Netherlands in Florence, Avvocato (Italian Bar, 1998, Italian Supreme Courts, 2011) and Arbitrator at Shanghai International Economic and Trade Arbitration Commission (2015).

Stefan Pap is a management consultant based in Switzerland. Having begun his career at Deloitte Consulting and later joining McKinsey & Company as a Project Manager, he now focuses on supporting clients in financial services, telecommunications, consumer goods and the non-profit sector design and implement business transformation initiatives. Stefan has led change efforts across different continents and is experienced in managing complex multi-stakeholder engagements.

José Moreno Codina is currently president of the consulting firm Applied Viability (AV Group) which is in the process of becoming a full member of the Transformation Alliance. For the last two years although still to a lesser extent at this stage, he has served as an internal consultant for Zurich Insurance Company (General Insurance) for the Latam Region. In his career he has held C-levels positions for multinational corporates in international contexts. He has also held high-profile appointments in professional institutions including the vice-presidency of the UK Chamber of Commerce in Barcelona and president of the International Insurers Club.

Rana Sinha is a consultant with a strong background in planning, organizing and providing human resource development functions in diverse cultural settings with a rich experience of over 30 years. Of Indian and Finnish parentage, he was born in India and has lived in many countries. Currently living in Finland, he runs his own consultancy, which specializes in inter-cultural business consulting, presentation skills, working and managing in an Indian context, as well as helping foreigners working with Finnish companies.

Peter Wollmann has been the responsible manager of a complex global programme at Zurich Insurance Company since 2013, located at its headquarters. Additionally, he is in charge of strategic change management at the German business unit, as well as additional headquarter projects. Prior to this, he worked within Zurich as the German head of project portfolio management and strategic business development from 2005 on, having worked as head of strategic planning and controlling in Zurich's German business unit.

Sharon Lalla has managed large and small-scale projects in both industry and academia for 15 years. After earning a doctorate in education technologies from Pepperdine University, she took a leadership role in administration of education technologies at New Mexico State University (NMSU). Her current focus is on improving the quality of online teaching grounded by measurable assessment, instructional design, and pedagogy. Sharon is also college assistant professor in the Education department.

Volker Hische has been managing director of CSC Akademie in Wiesbaden, Germany since 2014. He was director of human resources development and chief learning officer at CSC EMEA Aldershot, UK, and managed a number of major projects including a global performance management review system, succession planning, talent management and global career framework. He is an associate professor in human capital management MBA at Lake Constance Business School, and a certified international project manager, International Project Management Association, and certified international project management trainer (IPMA).

Frank Kühn co-founded ICG (Integrated Consulting Group Germany) in 2008. He is currently a Business Partner of ICG, and is networked with a wider circle of management consultancies and expert communities. Frank supports executives, management teams and change teams in strategic projects, change processes and excellence programmes. He is a writer and public speaker with a multitude of publications, and lectures on project management with progressive project management as a focal point.

Bob Dignen specializes, as a director of York Associates, in supporting international leaders, international teams and networks to become high performing, delivering a broad range of training programmes worldwide which drive international collaboration. He also coaches professionals in senior leadership positions, supporting the transition to a global or international C-level role. Bob specializes in international project management, coaching those leading complex project environments, facilitating international project (kick-off) meetings and team-building sessions. He is also a keynote motivational speaker for leadership event professional conferences.

Alberto Casagrande is an active managing director of The Core Inc., a boutique firm devoted to strategic, ICT and economic advisory for the last 15 years. During this period, Alberto has advised both the World Bank and several central banks across the world on financial infrastructural reforms and SME finance. He was senior advisor for several banking sector restructuring projects across the world, and has advised several global players in the insurance sector on strategic issues, also supporting various countries' economic ministries on growth strategies and debt management. Project locations include North and Latin America, Europe, Middle East and North Africa. Alberto was previously project manager at McKinsey in Italy.

Nathan Lamshed is a project and programme manager with 15 years of experience delivering business and technology projects for some of the world's largest global investment banks as well as the airline and education industries. Nathan has experience delivering strategic business expansion programmes, organizational transformations as well as software and infrastructure technology initiatives. Nathan has experienced the project lifecycle from executive intent to business as usual and has worked closely with C-level executive sponsors and stakeholders around the globe.

Bernadette Cass works with people and organizations who want to create change, often through challenging circumstances. She has a strong business and change delivery background, having held posts as IT director and programme manager for organizations including Gillette International, London Underground Limited, HM Treasury and BP. Her experience includes implementing major business systems implementations, including on one occasion new sales and financial reporting systems across 56 countries. Bernadette now works as an organizational change facilitator and executive, board and team coach.

Dagmar Boersch is a project, programme and consultancy professional with her own company. As graduate molecular biologist and certified project manager she was involved in numerous projects with a focus on pharma and medical device development. She is very well known within the German Project Management Associations and is a jury member of the German Project Excellence Award.

Mike Hogan is a director of York Associates, and is specialized in international team and leadership development and coaching, with a very strong interest in the dynamics of working in cross-cultural working and virtual teams. Additionally, he has many years' experience in e-learning development, virtual training and live event streaming.

Christal Lalla has been working as a certified sommelier in Italy, Germany, France and the United States since 2012, and has built up a fast developing innovative business around wine, wine services and wine education under the name VinAuthority. Based on her extensive travels, Christal has developed a broad understanding of the cultures of the world, and the diverse understandings and interpretations of the project of wine making and wines in different countries and regions.

Introduction

Making a case for creative thinking about international projects

In the last couple of years, the world of large, global companies has changed significantly for different and relatively well-documented reasons. Chief among these are the acceleration of globalization and an associated intensification of competition, particularly driven by new market entrants from developing economies. Digitalization is placing many established business models under pressure, especially in consumer retail. Additionally, global crises relating to finance infrastructure or regional wars are increasingly affecting enterprises by creating an environment of higher uncertainty and volatility than known previously.

International programmes and projects in globally acting enterprises are strongly impacted by this environment. Higher uncertainty and volatility necessitates acting in flexible and agile ways, with readiness to recalibrate direction, scope and proceedings of projects or portfolios. At the same time, there are increased governance-related pressures to produce ever-more detailed and solid plans from the beginning, and to respect quality, time and budget targets, particularly with programmes or projects with commercial significance for enterprises.

The commercial and strategic significance of programme and project management is also increasing, with studies indicating that the share of programmes and projects in an enterprise's total value creation has significantly increased over the last couple of years, and can be up to 40 per cent in some industries. This is crucial in two respects. On the one hand, an enterprise as a whole can fail if its 10 largest and most important programmes and projects fail, with the many consequences this implies. On the other hand, the ability to select and exercise effective supervision over decisions on the right programmes and projects, and the ability to run them successfully, becomes a competitive advantage for enterprises and a unique strategic success factor. In other words, the enterprise that manages to design the right project portfolio with a perfect mix of the right long-term strategic and short-term operative programmes and projects, and runs the selected programmes and projects in the most effective way, flexibly calibrating the whole setting in case of environmental change, is a business champion. Indeed, if this enterprise has this ability globally, which means across regions and countries, across cultures and languages, across roles and functions, it become a global champion. Such an enterprise has the best strategic alignment and the lowest waste of energy, so creating the highest value from its invested equity.

In fact, this perspective on project was understood by industries and enterprises some decades ago. The consequence was a high investment in project and portfolio management systems in terms of concepts, methods and tools. This is a quite predictable reaction from a systemic point of view: an organizational system with defined beliefs, rules, procedures, methods and tools should minimize threatening levels of uncertainty and volatility and any dependency from single persons. Unfortunately, efforts to standardize and professionalize programme and project management – and also project portfolio management – were not as successful as expected. The failure ratio regarding projects and portfolios is testament to this, if we look at the results of many professional studies. The trend is curiously worrying, with PMI stressing recently that the success ratio of programmes and projects is becoming even lower.

This statement does not imply that efforts to improve the concept of and approaches to project management were in vain. On the contrary, many improvements in process and practice have been made. However, what is obvious is that historical efforts have not been sufficient to change the game. Something is lacking.

The question, therefore, arises as to what is lacking. The answer lies in the nature of complex and highly differentiated systems, namely large global organizations, which defy management according to standardized categories and processes. By definition, a project is a unique setting of political, economic, historical, sociological, structural, technical and also very human and personal factors which only can partly be mapped to a conceptual category such a 'project management'. This means that even very well-developed global project and portfolio frameworks, methods, tools, and procedures have to be mapped in detail in order to decide what can best be applied, to which depth, and in which manner, assuming hybrids or derivations from the standard have to be developed. Put simply, the uniqueness of complex situations involving multiple variables, particularly the human factor which includes the cultural and sociological backgrounds and beliefs of key agents, prevents the successful application of standard recipes.

We should not conclude that it makes no sense to further develop programme and project management frameworks and their associated sets of methods and tools. But the key leadership challenge now and in the future is attentiveness to developing the art of the right application, tailoring or calibration of standard frameworks to unique contexts, and on the use of learning from real cases to do so. In other words, a learning-based approach where project and programme practitioners learn from other project and programme practitioners in a virtuous circle. With this ambition and mindset, we convinced a large group of very experienced professionals – all very busy people – to contribute. The joint idea is to achieve a book beyond the normal textbook pattern, based on case studies from different industries and different parts of the world.

Leading International Projects, therefore, offers a diverse range of experienced programme and project managers from all over the world, from different industries, engaging in different types of international projects, offering a broad range of potential learnings. No author has a final truth, but all have interesting topics to regard and discuss. Ultimately this book is an encouragement for you to find your own, reasonably tailored way to run your unique project – or at least to prepare for it. The right way to read these case studies is, therefore, to try to understand each case holistically in its unique environment, and to view its initial situations, proceedings, experiences and learnings primarily within its own context first, before trying to generalize to your own.

There will be some 'eternal' recommendations – tips or tricks – in relation to key areas such as sponsor management, project manager attitudinal and behavioural profile, and situation scoping with an eye on cultural differences. But these will be what can be termed 'high-level' reflections. Unfortunately, on this level nearly everything can be held to be true. Your challenge will be to extract something meaningful for your own unique project undertaking, which requires your own effort, curiosity and decisions.

So you should regard the cases as an encouragement for creativity, to think out of the box in new ways. This is exemplified in the inclusion of a very different case study from another industry – Christal's wine-making case – which lets you explore potential similarities between international projects and the alien environment of wine production, as alienation is a key driver for creativity and personal development. While we do not expect you to become wine experts, we want to offer you insight and impulse into other worlds, which might help to give you some additional ideas for your own creative project world.

Peter Wollmann

International leadership

As internationalization continues its relentless progress, impacting so many walks of professional life and general society, project professionals, as with so many others, are increasingly stopping to ask themselves a question: whether there exists a specific set of skills which will enable them to succeed in this rapidly and unevenly globalizing context.

It's a reasonable question but one which, quite naturally, carries a number of assumptions: that 'international', or 'international project' in this case, can be seen as a single entity or experience, which embodies specific challenges requiring skills proven to help to navigate the related challenges successfully. Beginning with the first assumption, of course 'internationality' is not a single phenomenon. For example, the phenomenon of international projects is immensely diverse, sometimes with the 'light' touch of a 'foreigner' joining a predominantly domestic team in a small-to-medium enterprise, stretching all the way up to a multinational team dispersed across the globe deploying project deliverables in several local business units and even regions.

To which degree is it then possible to identify generic international challenges if the notion itself is so broad? Interestingly, most professionals will claim to 'know' these international challenges, categorizing them as threefold: first, language (which often implies, *'I don't speak good enough English'* (non-native English speaker) or *'They don't speak good enough English'* (native English speaker); second, culture (meaning national culture); finally, distance and those annoying time zone differences and the fact that other people send too many e-mails. Yet these intuitious may be misleading. For example, we know that speaking perfect English cannot be said to define international communicative competence, or native English speakers would be the best international communicators, when they are actually often the worst. As for culture, well, what isn't culture? The term is so huge, so complex, and moves so quickly to damaging forms of national stereotyping that it becomes useless as an organizing principle to understand other individuals. As for the virtual problem of time and distance, research provides no conclusive evidence that proves virtual is more 'difficult'; indeed, it may even have advantages.

Internationality is a multi-layered phenomenon, and can be experienced as a minor or major impact, as exhilarating or deeply problematic. Yet for those working in large corporates today and leading international projects, to focus on this specific target group, a common landscape of experience has emerged presenting four broad challenges, which in turn demand a particular mindset, a specific approach to communication, and the strategic deployment of project management practices. While this might seem prescriptive at first glance, it is precisely the opposite, predicated as it is on the recognition of the diversity of international project and a plurality of potentially successful project leadership strategies available in any given situation.

The four challenges mentioned above which seem common to those leading projects in many of the larger corporate animals of today can be summarized: high levels of uncertainty, complexity, paradox and diversity. Uncertainty comes in many shapes and sizes. Working across borders with colleagues and consultants in other countries presents the challenge of working with people we don't know very well. Not knowing often means not understanding the approach of the other: their logic, their skills, their way of thinking, and the priorities of their local environment which may corrupt their commitment to the project. There are many other uncertainties, but relationship uncertainty is corrosive, and can diminish the ability of international project teams to establish trust quickly. Throughout the cases that follow, there is regular reference to the need to make the other knowable by building relationships, by making communication more transparent.

Complexity is also high in many international projects, operating as they do across different legal and regulatory contexts, seeking to implement, construct and even align new or complex technologies. The experience of complexity seems part of large international projects. The competence to be expert with that complexity, to realize it may be a different complexity to the one experienced before, and to keep a project moving and delivering visible wins – all of these are picked up in the cases.

Diversity is perhaps obvious when working internationally; at least, it is often more visible and often more unfamiliar than the everyday diversity we face at home with the different psychologies of our colleagues, friends and children. 'Culture' is the term most favoured by project professionals for the experience of diversity in an international project, judging from the cases in this volume. Whatever the term, there is a consensus that managing diversity (cultural and individual) must figure high on the radar of an effective international project leader.

Finally, there is paradox; the often untold reality that many organizations running international projects are highly immature international entities, and struggle to live their own declared international model due to inadequate budgets, non-aligned and competing global-local roles that drive political behaviours, a lack of skills in critical parts of the organization, and short-term pressures to deliver some form of result when longer-term planning would actually make more sense. The 'system' challenges are highlighted in so many of the cases that it challenges our common sense of organization, as it seems that so much of what we thought was organization is actually 'disorganization'. Those leading international projects need to understand and then engage with and steer this disorganized reality.

Those working in the larger projects in global corporates will quickly realize this landscape and will already be executing a range of relevant actions: to build relationships quickly; to simplify complexity to retain project momentum; to establish a clear and common modus operandi for the team; and to build stakeholder relationships that help to navigate organizational politics and dysfunctionality. However, many struggle, not least due to a lack of time.

The pressure and range of challenges on those in the international project world are high. Unfortunately, lessons from the past can prove both a benefit and a burden. Expertise brings with it insight, but also the risk of assumption and generalization, application of a past solution to a potentially very different current problem. Whilst expertise is valuable, cognitive flexibility may be the real gem: the ability to use expertise intelligently in novel contexts; to understand the presence and role of assumption in project analysis and decision making; to manage the emotions that face us when dealing with those who reject our very definitions of professionalism; to stay curious, open and collaborative. The growth of mindfulness – a Western offshoot of Buddhism – in leadership training is testament to the fact that managing mindset is a key success factor.

Beyond openness of mindset and thinking, international project professionals also have to decide on how best to behave and how best to communicate. Is there a way to communicate which guarantees success in complex environments where a lingua franca such as English is often in play (compromising clear communication from the start, many would argue)? Challengingly, as we work across the world we discover that there is little consensus on what constitutes effective or professional communication: direct or indirect; analytically oriented or action oriented; quick decision or slow decision; task first or relationships the priority? The list of opposing dimensions is bewildering, which may be why some statistics indicate that over 80 per cent of professionals characterize the internal cross-border communications in their own organizations as *often* failing, leading to a clearly negative cost impact. Most of the cases in this book cite communication in some form as a critical success factor. Most indicate that international project professionals need to work harder to be clear what they say, to listen effectively (ask more questions) and to be as excellent in relationship management as in task management. It's simple but still difficult.

In terms of actual project practice, it seems that planning and structuring have strong opponents today in the name of flexibility and creativity. Naturally, no one wholly disputes the traditional powers and rationale of classical waterfall design and its host of useful methodologies. Unfortunately, with high levels of uncertainty, complexity, paradox and diversity in play, it is evident that agility in some measure is required; the challenge is to know when and how to deploy structure, and to which degree. There are no models that will always accurately predict that ratio; it seems international project management may sometimes be as much art as science.

My own practice as a trainer, coach and facilitator for international project leaders and teams is defined very much by the above insights, developed over 25 years of literally thousands of conversations with professionals working internationally. In many ways, the book was stimulated by a frustration with confident leadership and project management discourses and mythologies, which offer metrics and templates in a universalist fashion onto a dynamic and shifting reality; which showcase 'best practice' and claim to guarantee success. It seems to me that there are few models and methodologies that guarantee anything in today's unique project environments. So for international project life, with its high levels of uncertainty, complexity, paradox and diversity, perhaps it comes down to simple human basics: a resilient and mindful thinking style which challenges assumption and manages emotions well; clarity of speech and deep listening; and then a smart deployment of own and others' technical abilities. And somehow, all this has to be calibrated to the people around you, the dynamics of the broader environment, and to the talent at your disposal. It means that continuous learning, keeping an eye on an ever-shifting project reality, really matters, not the blind application of past or even present expertise.

The cases in this book provide some excellent learning opportunities, insights into other realities and successful solutions, which can complement your own reservoir of knowledge, helping you in the end to manage your own international project realities more effectively.

A brief introduction to the cases

1 *Consumer insights* | Abhijit Dey
A global project which expanded way beyond its original scope, led by an inexperienced project leader, yet was highly successful.

Finally, a huge thank you to the contributing authors. I hope their cases and experiences provide both insight and practical guidance to help create more successful international projects everywhere.

'Expertise is my greatest handicap.'

A participant in a recent training course to promote international skills

Consumer insights

01

ABHIJIT DEY

Profile

Abhijit Dey is currently working for Sodexo Asia Services Pte Ltd (BRS) as the VP – IT, operations and service delivery for the Asia region. In this role, his primary responsibility is to engage with business and align and integrate the IT and operations strategy with the business strategic initiatives, to bring about operational efficiencies, thereby supporting the organization's growth objectives and complementing its effort as a leading provider of quality of life services. Abhijit has over 16 years of total work experience, with almost 10 years of senior management experience in the sphere of IT in the consumer foods, chemical, FMCG and services industries. He has a strong background in programme management and governance, along with extensive experience of IT change management during mergers and acquisitions, and working in international teams on global projects. Abhijit also takes keen interest in and works very closely with the teams from D&I, CSR and crisis communication, and was also part of the core investigation committee (ICC) for prevention of sexual and workplace harassment (POSH).

Abhijit, who has an MBA in IT, is also an IRCA Certified ISO 9001:2008 lead auditor and is trained in project management, based on PMBOX and ITIL v3.

Foreword

This case describes an international project to develop higher quality and more unified processes for collecting customer feedback across corporate operations in a number of business segments in a number of countries. The project is an interesting project on a number of levels.

First, the case highlights the manner in which an originally relatively simple domestic project scope can grow into a more complex cross-border and cross-function project, presenting a series of new and unexpected challenges to the project leader.

Second, the case throws up insights into the challenge for organizations to appoint leaders with the capability to manage challenging cross-border projects, with insights into the value of using experienced internal coaches as a support mechanism to grow individual capability and ensure project success.

Third, the project illustrates the value of a supportive organizational culture as a foundation to drive strategic change via international projects.

Before reading on, reflect on a number of key questions addressed in the case. Then compare your experience and answers to the ideas in the case itself and the final commentary.

1 Which KPIs are important when leading international projects? Why?

2 How important is it for organizations to select experienced project managers to be the leaders of a strategic international project? Why?

3 How useful are coaches and mentors (internal and external) in supporting those leading international projects? Why?

PART 1: CASE STUDY   Consumer insights

Introduction

My organization is a global leader in the services industry and has a range of services that have given it the unique positioning as the pioneer in quality of life services in all industries across the globe. These services make a noticeable and appreciable difference to the lives of people, from children to seniors, making every day a better day.

In its effort to continually improve its services across all segments and set a new benchmark for customer satisfaction, the organization initiated a project in India to better capture consumer feedback in real time and generate data trends and analysis which would provide insights to improve still further our service delivery and offers to clients and consumers globally.

The original impulse for this project was a conversation with a key client in which he expressed a degree of uncertainty about our service level, specifically around the feedback that we provided him on our quality of service. From the client point of view, the problem was that there was actually no real way for him to validate the numbers we were giving him. In fact, our processes were quite old, and collected a variety of data in a number of ways, so the comments were quite fair in a way. It wasn't a trust issue, just a demand for more transparency.

Project overview

The project was very much a local project in India originally, one that focused on core operations but with a strong component of marketing and IT. This is seen in the steering committee for the project, as there were strong representations from operations, marketing and IT.

At the beginning, we started thinking about a project that could automate the whole feedback and data collection process, making things faster and more transparent. We wanted to be able to collect more real-time data on customer satisfaction at the point of consumption. A lot of feedback processes have a time lag; we run interviews days or weeks after events to find out about the client experience of a service. We wanted a business IT solution to speed that up. The idea actually came from someone's experience in an airplane washroom, where there was the opportunity to press a button on a screen and give immediate feedback on whether you were happy or not with the quality of service experienced. So the project was designed to design and deploy an app to collect feedback in a similar way: how happy are you with the quality of food, the ambience of the meeting room etc? The project created different sets of data for the different lines of business – food, facility management – and these were loaded onto tablets and placed at strategic places in a lobby, in the restaurant etc. And all this feedback data was transported to a central server and at any time you could drill down to look at the feedback, by client, by site, by country, whatever, and analyse the data.

While the original purpose and goals remained the same throughout the life cycle of the project, the scope changed substantially because the project became adopted as a regional solution, cross-border and multi-lingual, as most countries in Asia had similar requirements. And at the same time, as the organization was undergoing a huge transformation structurally to move more to a truly global model, with transformation of structures and reporting lines, the project scope expanded to incorporate new global hierarchies and reporting lines which were emerging at the same time. This meant that key stakeholders from Asian countries became part of the project team; there were also senior marketing leaders from group level, representing different global segments, who were pulled into the steering committee to ensure that the newly restructured organization transformation was correctly aligned into the solution design for reporting purposes.

Key challenges

So, handling the unexpected internationalization of the project was the main challenge in a way. This had a number of sub-challenges. First, we had to build a project solution that was more generic and global in nature than originally intended, and yet still catered to local specific requirements. Local meant the demands of different segments of the business rather than simply geographical segments. So this balancing of global and local needs became a central challenge.

Second, as we were in the middle of an organizational transformation that was not finished, we had the challenge of aligning ourselves as a global project with a structure that was not finalized. The project had started in the context of having business units with reporting lines up to country CEOs, who could ultimately use this data to drive strategy. We were now seeing the removal of CEOs – in fact we don't really have country CEOs any more – and the creation of global segment heads, across countries, with their own responsibility. We were in the middle of this transformation and had to align to it.

Third, the project leader was someone who had been hired to lead a domestic project, and he had done so successfully several times before. But he now had to lead a much more complex international project with very different and more senior stakeholders. This was a challenge for the project leader; someone senior locally had to get involved, and so it was decided that I join the project as a coach and mentor to guide the project manager on the communication, planning and overall governance.

Project results

The project ran for almost a year, and delivered on two very critical aspects:

1 Consumer insights – it helped to improve our existing services and build new offers for our clients and consumers.

2 Consolidation and reporting – from the global segments to the smallest unit of the organization, we had more and better quality data which we could leverage to improve, ultimately, internal decision making.

The project is now implemented successfully across all countries in Asia and also in the business in the Gulf of Mexico. It has high visibility globally within the organization and is today one of the examples of the organization's digital journey. In the end, as the project became more international, the app proved to be an incredibly flexible tool and it was easy to make it multilingual and configurable for multiple countries. Interestingly, the project wasn't even in the top 50 in terms of budget but it proved to be top 10 in terms of innovation. It was just a small tool but it really provided us with the commercial perspective to better steer the business. We have a new range of KPIs looking at how many devices are online, how well they are used, when the data is being collected, and whether enough data is being collected. These kinds of dashboards really help to ensure we get adoption of the project solution.

Overall, business at the local level has much better real-time insights into consumer expectations and is working closely with the clients to enhance consumer satisfaction and thereby improve employee motivation and retention for our clients. We have the data to make meaningful inferences and develop global standard offers for clients and consumers, all of which supports our global strategy. The timing of the project couldn't have been better as it really supported the global transformation journey the organization had embarked upon.

For the project manager involved, he really grew. Today this guy is a very well-known and highly confident project manager. As an appreciation of his professional growth, he has been nominated to lead the Global CRM project for Asia. It was a great outcome for him.

Lessons learned

Some of the key lessons I learned personally are below:

1 First, on the leadership issue, one big learning for me was that we need to stop overthinking project leadership competence. In reality, nobody is fully ready to take the next big steps; it's hard to be fully prepared for such a role. It would have been easy to replace the manager who was originally appointed but the organization and I decided to support him, and he was very successful. I'm not sure we always need to wait or look for the most experienced manager; a person with potential is good enough.

2 Second, and maybe this is nothing radically new, but the steering committee has a huge role in these projects. It needs to be asking relevant questions, probing but also guiding and supporting, particularly to navigate through the higher level organizational challenges such as we had with global transformation.

3 Involvement of local stakeholders is always critical. So many projects fail to do this and the deployment phase of projects – often good projects – fails.

Summary

It was a landmark project for the organization, one that exemplified collaboration, working in international teams and cultures and a very transparent communication. The project has been handed over to the regional application team for support post-deployment. It has been now moved from project to business as usual.

Part 2: Interview

Q: I see a lot of these cross-border projects implementing globally strategic solutions running into resistance at a local level. Did this project generate or experience conflict?

A: Not really. The whole thing scaled from domestic to international very easily.

Q: **How did you achieve this?**

A: A couple of reasons. First, the organization as a whole had been well groomed in global strategy – we were working towards a clear global operating model of business segments rather than country business units – for a long time, so thinking was aligned and the logic was clear. We didn't have to make the global case. I think another critical factor was that when we scaled to go more international, we hadn't actually completed the technical solution for India yet. So our first task was simply to share our work, our specifications, and ask countries to validate, to share their needs. And we found that the needs were very similar, and that the countries were really looking for this kind of solution. So the process became very bottom up and collaborative early on. And there was a clear need in the different countries for this kind of solution.

Q: **OK. So you reached out really at a good time?**

A: Yes. And I had the benefit of being a member of the senior leadership in the country, and had recently been to Berlin to discuss the future operating model. I knew what was coming and that we had to align with it. And coming from global IT in other countries, this whole global model was really ingrained in me, so it triggered me to involve others and to check our solution as early as possible – the same with my manager. So this reaching out to the countries and not developing a standalone country solution, well, it was pretty obvious to me. And in fact, this kind of 'glocal' thinking is pretty deep in the organizational culture anyway in many ways.

Q: **You mentioned global IT. IT is often more global than the business, isn't it? Was that an advantage too?**

A: I have to correct you there. We are not IT; we run business IT projects. The only pure IT projects in the company are to change a server or network provider, or something like that. Our philosophy is very much that we support the business. We are not internal consultants, but business partners. It's a philosophy that really drives our projects, which don't end at deployment, only when we have 100 per cent adoption in the organization. I know it's maybe unusual; in other companies, I see that they tend to organize themselves with a segmentation of duties, with IT only to develop and deploy, and no more responsibility. We've discussed this a lot in our executive committees, that we need an integrated approach. Otherwise, you create a lot of nice solutions that don't get used, which are idle investments in the end.

Q: So does this reflect in how projects are driven in the company; do you lead them in a different way, for example, with different KPIs?

A: Absolutely. In this project, for example, we worked with two types of KPI. First, we had the usual project ones around timeliness and budget. And then we had KPIs around deployment and adoption of the project inside operations. So we had kind of post-project KPIs looking at how many devices collecting data were online, how they were being used, and even using this data to change operations. For example, in staff restaurants, trying to collect feedback on quality of food, we found that we got more feedback during breakfast and dinner than for lunch. We assumed that people worked to tighter timeframes at lunch, so were more in a hurry, and didn't stop to give feedback at the terminals. So we had tablets held by people at lunchtime at the exits of the restaurants, to make it easier and faster for people to stop and give quick feedback. And we saw an immediate benefit it this. And this is all embedded in the project.

Q: Can you tell me about your coaching process and experience? What exactly did you support with?

A: One of the main things I did was to groom the project manager for the international environment. I helped him to understand the different cultures, even the accents in the conference calls, to appreciate the time zone impacts, and to not get worried about working with very senior people involved in strategic projects, just understand how to communicate with them as it's a little different.

Q: How different exactly?

A: I think senior management wants a kind of, how to say it, crisp communication. Those without experience tend to go too detailed too early. I think you need to summarize things into clear bullet points, give people the overview and high-level perspective, and if they get curious about something, you need to be able to answer and give more detail. And beyond that, it is just confidence, which you need when talking to guys five or so levels above you. So we would do mock presentations, go through things in advance, and they found this very useful, particularly to prepare for the steering committee meetings. So a lot of support with comms.

Q: What did you yourself learn as a coach in this process? Was it two-way learning?

A: I think to be a good coach you really need to get involved, you need to give feedback but don't stop there; you need to look at how people take feedback, how they learn, how they come back to you, and be there to really help them develop. It's quite consultative. I would take my slides to the steering committee and show how I did it and just ask, 'What do you think? Can you take anything from this?' You need to devote time. Just telling people what to do won't achieve the final process. You need to somehow become part of the process. And help people to believe in their own potential to be successful.

Part 3: Commentary

Here are some reflections on Abhijit's case and interview.

This case contains a number of important perspectives. One of the most interesting is Abhijit's claim that we need to stop overthinking international project competence. For him, nobody is likely to be fully prepared for what is to come. It may be a better strategy for organizations to select according to potential, and then provide powerful support mechanisms such as coaching to help the individual navigate the stormy waters of their project. Second, Abhijit is keen to stress the importance of 'post-project' KPIs, thereby addressing the challenge that many project deliverables fail to land properly in organizations, and projects slowly fail once the project ceases as there is no mechanism and no person responsible for driving post-project implementation, a true living of the change. It's the first time I have heard this so explicitly described, and there may be an important lesson in there. Third, Abhijit refers to an important body in the field of project management that few mention, namely the steering committee. Its role, its relation to the sponsor and international project leader is partly an ambiguous one – perhaps projects would benefit if its role were

clearer. Finally, what struck me when talking to Abhijit was his experience and level of understanding of global organization; its dynamics, how his role fitted into this, how anomalies existed but how his job was to provide workarounds. I think that senior management gets all this, but those lower (hierarchically) in organizations often don't, which leads to disenchantment, demotivation, disengagement and lower performance – and in the end, added and unnecessary costs. I believe strongly that those with experience should follow Abhijit's lead and step into coaching and mentoring roles to distribute their organizational and project intelligence. What stops people? Perhaps time is the issue; perhaps a sense that knowledge is power. Perhaps no one asks?
Bob Dignen

Part 4: Reflecting on international project management

Take time to reflect on the following questions to help you reach further insights and take practical actions to improve your own project management practice:

1 What is the role of the steering committee in a project? What expectations will a steering committee likely have of a project leader?

2 How useful and feasible is it for projects to plan for post-project KPIs? Why?

3 Which competencies do you currently lack to lead an international project? How could you develop these competencies?

Part 5: Put it into practice

There are a number of very valid insights and ideas for project management present in this case which the reader can learn from and adopt, customizing for their own projects. Take a few minutes to note down your main learnings from this case, and note down some actions for yourself.

Personal insights, learnings and actions

The Italian Creative Network

DONATO NITTI

Profile

Donato Nitti, JD *magna cum laude* (Università di Firenze, 1994); PhD in private comparative law and EU private law (Università di Macerata, 2009); guest professor of EU intellectual property law, IP Institute, Tongji University, Shanghai, China (2015); Honorary Consul of the Kingdom of the Netherlands in Florence; Avvocato (Italian Bar, 1998, Italian Supreme Courts, 2011); Arbitrator at Shanghai International Economic and Trade Arbitration Commission (2015); Founder and partner of Studio Legale Nitti & Associati, with offices in Florence, Italy and Shanghai, China. In his professional activity, Mr Nitti is particularly focused on intellectual property, international commercial law and networks between enterprises. In the fields of intellectual property law, arbitration law, EU law and international contracts, Mr Nitti is the author of several articles and essays (published by Giuffré, Cedam, Giappichelli, Altalex and Euroconference) and a speaker at conferences and seminars. He is a member of the International Association for the Protection of Intellectual Property, Italian Group.

Foreword

As an international project, this case offers an interesting case study of market entry to a new and very 'foreign' culture, China, from a European perspective. Those working in an international project environment frequently invoke the language of 'culture' to frame and make meaning of their experience. This case is a powerful example of this, and highlights the ways in which culture can operate as an organizing principle for those working in projects.

The project management approach in this Chinese context is very much driven by a focus on building and managing relationships within an environment where the meaning and process of relationship building is not necessarily shared by project counterparts, a common challenge for those operating with high levels of diversity. The case offers insights into how to solve this very typical dilemma for those leading international projects.

Interestingly, the Italian Creative Network case is unlike many of the other projects in *Leading International Projects* insofar as it is a project with a clear vision but without a definite or defined deliverable. There is no building to be constructed, no IT platform to be installed, only relations to be established that lay the foundation for potential commercial opportunity. It is interesting to reflect how the management dynamics of such a 'project for potential' may differ from a 'project for planned outcomes'.

Finally, the case profiles a project at the heart of which is a networked approach to success: institutional networks operating together; local companies networking to support and learn lessons from each other; networks being established across borders. Economically, the case stands as an interesting representative of a future commercial model built on long-term reciprocal support and exchange as opposed to short-term exploitation. The case also raises questions as to which project management skills are paramount to drive such longer-term networked types of projects.

Before reading this case, reflect and make notes on a few questions. Then compare your answers to the ideas in the case itself and the final commentary.

1 What cultural challenges might Italian companies experience when entering China for the first time?

2 How can relationships be built and fostered effectively in such an international project context?

3 Which project leadership challenges might be created by projects that deliver potential benefits (possible commercial opportunity) compared to projects that deliver very tangible financial outcomes?

PART 1: CASE STUDY   The Italian Creative Network

Project organization

The Italian Creative Network (ICN) is a project built on a network of Italian companies that aim to begin or develop their business in China. The members share and benefit from a range of services designed to facilitate their entry and growth in the Chinese market. By being part of ICN, the members share services for market entry, enhance reputation and enlarge their Chinese business network. Additionally, ICN members, being members of a group of SMEs wanting to enter a new market, benefit from the sharing process when, for example, experiencing legal and economic difficulties, and so do not face a deeply different cultural environment alone.

ICN was established in Florence on 16 June 2014 and currently includes 11 enterprises from Italy and an individual enterprise from Germany which operates in Italy. Members of ICN work in different industries and economic sectors. Among the organizations there is a group that manages hotels and restaurants, a company working in training and business consulting, a school of jewellery, a trading company focused in e-commerce, a manufacturer of furniture and interior doors, a school of restoration, a manufacturer of fishing equipment, a consulting company focused on social innovation and strategy, an event organizer focused in the healthcare sector, an organizer of wine events and a manufacturer of high-quality food preserves.

The network is supported by a bank, Chianti Banca, which provides facilitated access to financial services and capital. The initial idea for ICN arose from the relationship between the UNESCO Creative City (Shanghai) Promotion Office, part of the Municipality of Shanghai, and the City of Florence. In 2012, the two cities, both global capitals of the creative industries, began a project that established the 'Shanghai Florence Sino-Italian Design Exchange Centre'. The two parties' common intent was to develop creative industry and promote networking between China and Europe, and to provide opportunities for local companies and stakeholders.

After the establishment of the initial ICN network, The Shanghai City of Design office invited ICN to proactively join the Shanghai Florence Sino-Italian Design Exchange Centre project in Shanghai to allow ICN's membership to become an official presence in the Chinese market.

The project is supported by a network agreement (art. 3 Law Decree 5/2009), which is a contract through which two or more enterprises, either sole traders or companies, join to increase, individually and collectively, their ability to innovate and improve their competitiveness in the marketplace via one or more of the following activities:

1 Cooperation in complex activities that a single company would not be able to execute individually.

2 Exchange of information on industrial, technical or commercial performance.

3 Joint engagement in activities already performed by each enterprise.

Although the network agreement shows, or can show, some of the features of other agreements between businesses (consortium, mandate, company agreement, supply agreement, licence, and so on), it is actually different in kind from the others. It is particular to the Italian experience, an experience the EU Commission considers one of the European best practices for the development of the SMEs (European Commission, 2011). At heart, from a financial point of view, the project is a co-investment by a group of companies to build a transnational platform to support and facilitate business development in China for each member. Each company contributes to the network budget to the value of €13,500 every year. The network budget is managed by the network manager in order to realize services and promotion.

Project activity

Overall, the project has mainly four levels of activity. First, it handles the legal and political issues of designing the construction of such a network, and secures the political and financial support of EU and Italian institutions. It then finds, convinces and integrates member companies. After this, it builds up support and a maintenance organization in Shanghai. Finally, it accompanies and promotes the companies on their way into the Chinese market.

The Italian Creative Network is currently composed of eleven companies and continues to be sponsored by an Italian bank which gives financial support to its members. The network has a strong reputation in Italy and China because of the partnership with the Florence Municipality and the Shanghai Municipality. All members of ICN have the opportunity to use offices with work desks, meeting rooms and event venues at the heart of the French Concession area in Shanghai. This is a great benefit for small enterprises that have joined ICN, as they would have struggled individually to afford the costs and expenses of such a location with similar features. Overall, the project has provided and provides the network's members with a constructive relationship with the Chinese institutions to further promote business projects.

Two directors, one Italian and one Chinese, assisted by three employees speaking Italian and Chinese, manage the ICN office. The ICN has Italian advisors, an accountancy firm and a law firm. The Italian law firm has Chinese associates in Shanghai who give support with domestic legal issues. This is a very important form of support since legal fees in China can be very high for foreigners. The organization's directors are available to support ICN members with the development of organizational, commercial and communication strategies for the Chinese market, in studying how to adapt a company's business model to create a successful approach to the Chinese market, taking into account the cultural dimension.

Initial project results

Since its inception in February 2015, the Italian Creative Network has, in only 10 months, recruited and established competent staff, opened a base in a Shanghai Municipality's building and supported business development in China for many of its members. Five of the members have already signed agreements with local partners to develop their business in China. ICN is also supporting other members to re-assess their entry strategy in China. Some are facing difficulties in terms of cultural understanding of the Chinese market. Overall, the project has been highly successful in its opening phases.

Personal lessons learned

'Made in Italy' products and services are considered excellent all over the world due to their quality, the history of the brands and the strong know-how of workers and entrepreneurs. Potentially, business opportunities between Italy and China are extraordinary. Yet China represents for me the most challenging market in the world. In the last 15 years, collaboration between Italian and Chinese companies has not been very strong. The major challenge, as I see it, was (and is still) to create the right way (at business, cultural and social levels) to build effective relationships between Italian and Chinese business professionals. ICN supports relationship building in two key ways. First, ICN managers and personnel continuously help members to be pro-actively involved, both within and outside the network, in starting new business collaborations. For example, ICN members who decide to invest in the Chinese market are supported in organizing promotional events that spread knowledge of an ICN member's products and services in this new market, and allow individuals to connect to key stakeholders.

A second key relationship support activity of the project is the relationship developed by ICN with one of China's most important universities, the Tongji University. In 2012 Tongji began a project that led it to establish a campus in

Florence, the so-called Tongji University Campus in Florence, which aims, among other things, to manage and promote exchange programmes and training courses for students, teachers and professionals in the fields of art and design, cultural heritage, architecture, innovation, fashion, cinema and media. A memorandum of understanding signed by Tongji University, Municipality of Florence and Region of Tuscany appointed the Tongji University Campus in Florence as a platform for the Tongji University in order to organize and promote training courses and activities of the Shanghai Florence Sino-Italian Design Exchange Centre. Accordingly, members of ICN interested in starting or developing relations with the Chinese academic world can easily contact the University far more easily than if operating alone in China.

Summary

To succeed in China, Italian companies have to master a number of key project challenges including learning to:

- invest in a long-term strategy;

- be present in as much as possible in the Chinese market;

- build a strong reputation and a good trust relationship with their Chinese partners;

- develop institutional partnerships;

- find ways to get to results by utilizing and managing a networked approach.

Overall, managing relationships successfully is the single biggest critical success factor within this international project.

Project outlook

The Italian Creative Network wants to enlarge its memberships and will evaluate its results after the first year in order to improve its operations and organization. It's important to remember that the ICN initiative is unique in Italy and perhaps in Europe. Critically, it is now an experiment that aims to demonstrate that international business in China cannot be only an export-oriented initiative; it cannot only be an exit strategy from the current European economic and financial crisis. In order to realize business in China, it's important to understand that it implies a totally new starting point, driven by a long-term strategy and investment.

Part 2: Interview

Q: You talk a lot about relationships and the importance of relationships, but you also talk about challenges. Can you say a little more about these?

A: Yes, so in terms of lessons learned, I found working in China is difficult; the culture is very different.

Q: **In what ways different?**

A: Well, obviously the language, Chinese, which is more than just language; it defines and influences reasoning and it's all a long way from European. Economically, UK, Germany and Italy all are big economies, all facing transitional difficulties, but China has a long history, a clear future, lots of resources – economic and intellectual, so we're not so needed – and that makes it more difficult to begin relationships. And relationships, you know, are key to business. In China, it was my experience that if you can build relations – Guanxi – then you can work well there.

Q: **What is Guanxi?**

A: You know the meaning of the word, Guanxi, it's a word made of two characters – 'close system' which means difficult to enter but once in, so difficult to exit. And you know the process of building relations is very different to the Italian way; you have to build carefully and take the long and very personal way. For example, I held a speech at a conference about IP law, and near me was a young guy, and we got talking and we discussed; this was October 2014. In January 2015, I invited him to dinner. In March I wrote to him again, dinner, and so on. And after two years and exchanging of presents, I was invited to his event, an exhibition, and he came with his father – I was the first guest to sign the guest book, I had dinner with wife and his mother-in-law in Shanghai, and we began to speak about cooperation. That guy, that boy, is head of a joint venture between Walt Disney and biggest construction company in China; he's one of the most important managers in China.

Q: **So is relationship building something you need to allow to grow? You can't force it?**

A: Things come if you wait. The Chinese always say how surprised they are at my patience. Westerners always want things at the first moment; they're hurried, they want to define everything in the first two meetings.

Q: What about trust?

A: Yes, trust is slower and much more a deeper process in China. And this has a number of consequences. For example, it's important when you think about the technical expertise of people. Some people can work with quite low technical competence if they have a trust network. For example, there was a Chinese lawyer who I worked with, I read some of his contracts; at a technical level he wasn't a great lawyer but he had really big clients because he has very good relations. So, just remember, things are very different to Europe. You simply need to adapt.

Part 3: Commentary

Here are some reflections on Donato's case and interview.

Donato's case is of significant importance, especially for all enterprises that plan to or already have business with China. The case highlights the challenges, and what has to be achieved to be successful. Very often enterprises project their experiences from their homeland, their experiences from other areas, onto a new area to be explored, especially western-oriented enterprises and people who are often less relationship oriented. It is important to be very patient to slowly build up a business and accept the reduced speed – and an environment (or a system) with partly or totally different rules and customs. The enterprise's management, the sponsor and the project manager of a project with or in China should be aware of this. One of the first activities should be to assess people with influence in China with whom a sustainable trust-based relationship is possible, even if this takes time. And to continuously develop these relationships.
Peter Wollmann

Donato's case highlights one of the major challenges that I see when working in and leading international projects, namely, having to cope with higher levels of diversity. Here the challenge Donato and I discussed was attitudes to relationships, of fundamental importance everywhere. I'm sure we could also have explored diverse and challenging differences in perspective on the meaning of leadership, teamwork, decision making, timeliness etc. His message is a very strong one around flexibility and the need to adapt; essentially, it means slowing down. Taking time to get to know someone, taking time to think through a strategy which makes sense for both parties, and taking time with respect to the partnership, which has to be in the longer and not the shorter term. There are no quick and dirty raids here. To succeed, you need to be in it for the long term.

So many of the problems of professional interaction stem from a lack of time; a lack of allocated time to relationship building, and a lack of thoughtful time management which avoids having to push people to deliver when they either aren't in the mood to deliver or don't have the resources. They say patience is a virtue. I would say it's a necessity which makes good business sense.
Bob Dignen

Part 4: Reflecting on international project management

Take time to reflect on the following questions to help you reach further insights and take practical actions to improve your own project management practice.

1 Reflect on your own attitudes to relationship building. What is your style? What is your tempo? How far does it suit those around you?

2 What is your own attitude to time? Are you someone who is impatient and drives for quick results, or more calm, but perhaps takes longer to deliver? How do people around you in projects now or in the future think about time? How might you manage diverse expectations?

3 Several markets are seen as key for the future including China, India, Brazil and Russia. How could you learn more about the business cultures in these countries, and prepare yourself for future projects?

Part 5: Put it into practice

There are a number of very valid insights and ideas for project management present in this case which the reader can learn from and adopt, customizing for their own projects. Take a few minutes to note down your main learnings, and note down some actions for yourself

Personal insights, learnings and actions

Reference

European Commission (2011) Communication from the Commission 'Review of the Small Business Act for Europe', 78 final, *Eur-lex* [online] http://eur-lex.europa.eu/legal-content/EN/TXT/?uri=CELEX:52011DC0078

Financial incentives in international projects: can money buy commitment and drive performance?   03

STEFAN PAP

Profile

Stefan Pap is a management consultant based in Switzerland. He helps clients in financial services, telecommunications, consumer goods and the non-profit sector design and implement business transformation initiatives. Stefan has led change efforts across different continents and is experienced in managing complex multi-stakeholder engagements. He began his career at Deloitte Consulting and later joined McKinsey & Company as a project manager in the firm's corporate finance practice. Stefan holds an executive master's in change management from INSEAD and an MBA from the Kellogg School of Management. In his free time, Stefan enjoys skiing, hiking, sailing and scuba diving. He writes a blog on change management-related topics at www.stefanpap.com.

Foreword

This case embraces project management and change management, and examines the role of financial incentives in driving commitment to participation in projects and change processes. The project context is within the operational site of one of the world's largest airport ground-handling companies, a company present at nearly 200 airports and employing more than 30,000 staff. A project was initiated to identify (through bottom-up consultation) cost-saving opportunities to offset declining revenues, a very typical initiative in many organizations today. The end objective was to put in place more efficient and effective processes – so the need for structured change management was implied by the project very clearly.

Those managing the project decided to integrate financial incentives which would drive commitment to perform in the project, and to engage with and embed change in the organization. Stefan was engaged in the project as a consultant with a deep understanding of change management and associated motivational drivers that lead people to commit to or resist change. He later on conducted a research study to understand the impact of the financial incentives introduced during the project.

The case draws on Stefan's academic background, initially placing the project within the broader context of change management and motivational theory. It offers fascinating insights for those leading projects or change processes, both in general terms of how people are motivated to engage and commit to projects, and more specifically on the potential use of financial incentives to drive performance, with clear indicators as to when this approach might be productive and when counterproductive.

The case begins with some introductory reflections around change management initiatives, and then moves through an examination of theories of 'commitment' and the general role of money in incentivizing commitment, to an examination of the specific airport operations project, and outcomes of that project.

Before reading this case, reflect and make notes on a couple of questions. Then compare your answers to the ideas in the case itself and the final commentary.

1 What can motivate professionals to commit a huge effort to challenging project work?

2 How effective do you think it might be for an organization to set up financial incentives to drive higher levels of performance in a project among team members and the team leader? Why?

PART 1: CASE STUDY   Financial incentives in international projects: can money buy commitment and drive performance?

Introduction

Constant and disruptive change has become normality for many businesses over the last 30 to 40 years. In response, the 1960s and 1970s saw the rise of academic and popular publications on the topic of change management, highlighting the growing importance of this topic. In their original 1979 *Harvard Business Review* article on 'Choosing Strategies for Change', Kotter and Schlesinger (2008) cite an earlier study undertaken by The Conference Board that predicted that 'the ability of organizations to respond to environmental change' would become one of the major themes for business success in the next 20 years.

In hindsight, they could not have been more right. However, more recent developments in the areas of technology and globalization have led to even stronger pressures on businesses to change in the first decades of the new century. Consumer-oriented industries, such as travel, media or finance, are being forced to adapt their business models within a few years to suit new customer interaction channels created by the internet and the social media revolution. Traditional manufacturing industries are also often facing a new marketplace with former low-cost suppliers from emerging countries such as China suddenly turned into head-on competitors with stronger technology and a more favourable cost base, as is happening for example in the lighting industry (McKinsey & Company, 2011).

With all these challenges, knowledge about how to best manage organizational change continues to be of high importance. Yet despite the growing body of research – the vast experience which many managers have collected in the area of change management, and the armies of consultants who are readily available to support their clients – there is still a great deal of doubt regarding the success rate of change initiatives. A recent survey of global companies reported that two-thirds of change initiatives were not considered successful by the organizations' executives (Shin, Taylor and Seo, 2012). When one looks at the reasons behind these failures, it often comes down to individual managers or employees who do not feel in some sense 'committed' to the proposed strategic direction, and who are not willing to adapt to new ways of working. This view has also been taken up in academic research on change management with an increasing focus on the central role of the individual, acknowledging that organizations can only change successfully when individuals alter their behaviour (Choi, 2011).

From a project or programme management point of view, it is often hard to understand why certain managers or employees do not participate in a change effort. One will even see 'blaming' of individuals for being inflexible, too rooted in the status quo, or following their own agenda. On the other hand, if you speak to a manager in a country organization that is at the 'receiving end' of a global project, you will hear reasons such as stress caused by too many initiatives happening in parallel, lack of clarity (what should we do and how?) and leadership (why should we do it?), interpersonal problems with the sponsor of the change effort, and also political fears such as loss of personal influence or anxiety about future career options.

Working through all these issues requires time and resources, and managers tend to look for shortcuts to increase employees' commitment and accelerate behaviour changes. One relatively obvious idea is the use of money to make the change more attractive for the affected staff. 'Managerial common sense' about how people are motivated (Heath, 1999) suggests that paying someone explicitly to adapt a certain behaviour should increase motivation and trigger the targeted change.

Through a quick review of available academic research on 'change commitment' and a concrete case study, I would like to shed more light on this question and help the reader understand when and if the use of financial incentives could be a good idea to drive change, and examine this in the context of international project management.

Theoretical background on 'change commitment'

As mentioned above, organizations as a whole can only change when individuals alter their on-the-job behaviour in appropriate ways (Choi, 2011). For that to happen, people need to feel committed to the organization and to the new direction (Seo *et al*, 2012; Herold, Fedor and Caldwell, 2007; Herscovitch and Meyer, 2002) and have the necessary psychological resources to be able to cope with the change (Taylor and Cooper, 1998; Fugate, Kinicki and Prussia, 2008; Shin, Taylor and Seo, 2012).

But what do we mean by commitment? According to Allen and Meyer (Allen & Meyer, 1992), there are three different types of commitment:

- *Affective* commitment: an employee's desire to remain with the organization out of a positive emotional bond.

- *Continuance* commitment: an employee's wish to remain with an organization due to perceived cost of leaving.

- *Normative* commitment: an employee's sense of obligation to remain with an organization, for example, derived from positive experiences of the organization.

All three types of commitment will lead to compliance with the explicit requirements of a change effort, but only affective and normative commitment will lead to cooperation that goes beyond minimal rule compliance (Herscovitch and Meyer, 2002). This implies that an employee who experiences only continuance commitment, ie feels that the cost of leaving the organization would be too high, might comply with the change, but is unlikely to show discretionary cooperation that goes beyond the minimum.

Affective commitment has the strongest impact on positive employee behaviour (Herscovitch and Meyer, 2002). It typically develops when individuals start to derive part of their identity from associating with an organization or course of action. In general, there is evidence that commitment will be stronger if it is created through positive emotional experience before the start or during the early phase of a change process (Seo *et al*, 2012). This could be done through co-creation, appropriate training, and empowerment of individuals.

The role of money

Traditional economic theory was built on the assumption that all individuals act fully rationally and always try to maximize their expected benefit from a situation. When Frederick Taylor developed his scientific management approach in the early 20th century, he argued that the deal between organizations and their members should emphasize extrinsic factors: 'what workers want most from their employers beyond anything else is high wages' (cited in Heath, 1999). However, during the past decades increasing evidence has become available that this statement is not true – humans are neither rational decision machines nor do they purely look for extrinsic motivation in the workspace. Rather, humans judge options (such as how to react to a new incentive scheme) in emotional and often irrational ways (Gneezy, Meier and Rey-Biel, 2011; Constantinescu, 2010).

What becomes increasingly obvious is that monetary (extrinsic) incentives are not the only motivational factor for employees in the workplace. Next to financial (extrinsic) motivations, Fehr and Falk (2002) identify three intrinsic factors that drive employee motivation:

- the motive to reciprocate;

- the desire for social approval;

- the desire to work on interesting tasks.

If companies manage to cater well to these motivations of their employees, they are likely better off in the long term than if they focus purely on money. Even more, researchers have found that changes to a compensation model can have indirect psychological effects on the intrinsic motivation of an employee. If used in the wrong way, financial incentives can backfire and negatively impact employees' performance.

Ernst Fehr, a professor at the University of Zurich, who is considered to be one of today's most influential economists in Europe, conducted an experiment in 2002 (Fehr and Gächter, 2002) that showed how the introduction of an explicit incentive might reduce employees' voluntary effort. In the experimental set-up, participants were divided into three groups: one without a variable incentive, one group with a positively framed incentive ('bonus') and one with a negatively framed incentive ('fine'). The latter two options resulted in exactly the same pay-out pattern, the only difference being the 'framing' used in the communication to participants. However, what happened then sounds counter-intuitive from a traditional, 'strictly rational' point of view – participants with the negatively framed incentive (the fine) showed lower levels of effort than those who were promised a possible bonus. Even more surprisingly, and in contradiction to what many would expect, *participants who did not receive any kind of incentive showed the highest level of effort of all three groups*. So, what happened was that money somehow changed how people viewed the task at hand.

To be clear, this doesn't mean you don't need to pay employees at all. On the contrary, there is strong evidence that high base salaries motivate employees for higher performance (Akerlof, 1982). It's only when companies start to introduce explicit remuneration for certain outcomes that things become more complex. For example, an explicit financial incentive can lead to a feeling of impaired self-determination when individuals perceive the locus of control to have shifted from inside to outside of the person affected (Frey and Jegen, 2001). Furthermore, an intrinsically motivated person could feel that their intrinsic motivation is rejected by the principal, a fact which debases the motivation's value. As a result, individuals could feel a negative impact on their self-esteem, which would lead them to reduce their effort. A monetary reward could also reduce the social approval an individual receives for carrying out a task (Fehr and Falk, 2002). In some corporate environments, we could expect that an employee's social approval from their peers would reduce if they are perceived to be performing a task purely for the money rather than based on intrinsic motivation or a wish to cooperate.

According to general interest theory (Eisenberger, Pierce and Cameron, 1999), the content of tasks and the context in which they are presented, including reward, can increase motivation when they convey a positive view of the task (eg working on a highly paid task can be perceived as being prestigious). Conversely, financial rewards reduce intrinsic motivation when they communicate that the task is irrelevant or antithetical to the needs, wants, or desires of the agent (eg if the employee perceives the fact that he or she is offered a bonus as an indication that the company considers the task to be contrary to the employee's interests).

However, there is also some evidence that the mentioned psychological effects can be offset by very large incentives, at least in the short run. In an experiment with high-school students collecting donations, Gneezy and Rustichini (2000) found that effort decreased when a small donation was offered to students compared to no financial incentive at all. But, once the amount of the donation was increased substantially, effort started to increase as well.

In conclusion, what this means is that using money to motivate people to follow a certain course of action is likely going to be an expensive effort. And, even then, there is no guarantee of success. In situations where substantial financial rewards are at stake, one can also find evidence for a so-called 'choking' effect where the performance of employees actually deteriorates because they cannot deal with the higher level of stress associated with big reward opportunities (Mobbs, 2009).

Project case study scope

This project was initiated at a large airport operation of one of the world's largest airport ground-handling companies. At the time relevant for the study, the company was present at nearly 200 airports and employed more than 30,000 staff. The airport observed was the largest and economically most important in the company's network, with around 2,500 employees in a non-unionized environment. It offered all sorts of white-collar (eg check-in and gate handling) and blue-collar (eg baggage loading) labour performed at an airport to its customer base, which consisted of national and international airline carriers.

In late 2010, the company was undergoing a major cost reduction programme at the airport. The objective of this programme was to identify cost-savings opportunities, mostly through process or technological changes, to offset revenue declines driven by lower price levels.

The company employed the help of an external consulting company to run this cost-reduction programme. The consulting firm chose to use a 'bottom-up' idea-generation process that involved asking a fairly large number of staff from all departments to come up with possible improvement ideas. Employees would participate in several rounds of idea generation workshops, remain involved in the subsequent detailed assessment of possible improvements, and would eventually also champion the implementation of *their* ideas. As one result of this process, there was fairly widespread involvement of staff throughout the organization. However, the involvement of unit heads (the middle management layer) varied. While some actively participated in the idea-generation process, others were rather reluctant to participate or even openly opposed any changes that would result in a larger deviation from the status quo.

Hence, the company looked for a way to solidify the involvement of those unit heads who already actively participated in the project and to obtain, in addition, the commitment of their more critical peers. Eventually, the decision was taken to implement a new incentive scheme to support the project, making it financially more attractive for unit heads to look for cost-saving opportunities. The new incentive scheme was introduced in April 2011 and remained operational until the end of that year. The initial experiences with the incentive scheme were mixed. While some unit heads reacted positively, there was also critical or cynical feedback. Therefore, the company decided to stop the new scheme after the first cash bonus payments had been made in 2012. There was, however, the understanding that a new reward model would be introduced in 2014 to compensate for the financial loss.

Money offered motivation to some, but not for all

In 2013 I conducted a number of in-depth interviews with managers and staff who were involved in the change project and the following period. The aim of these interviews was to get a better insight into how employees experienced the introduction of a financial incentive scheme on a cognitive and emotional level. Based on academic research, I expected to find two motivational impacts of a newly introduced incentive model (Gneezy, Meier and Rey-Biel, 2011) – a direct positive price effect that would increase employee motivation, and indirect psychological effects that would crowd out some of the employees' intrinsic motivation.

The interviews I conducted showed clear evidence for both effects. Several of my interview partners indicated that they felt motivated to follow the new behaviours and perform at a higher level through the introduction of a new financial incentive. Some of the key comments include:

> 'I tried to achieve a good result so that my wife would also be happy [referring to the additional income available to the family].'

> 'Yes, it was a very attractive bonus–- financially very interesting.'

> 'I really tried to get higher savings wherever I saw an opportunity.'

> 'I found it interesting and welcome! ... It was always at the back of my mind – I was thinking what do I need to do to realize the 2 per cent cost reduction.'

On the other hand, there were also statements that clearly indicated some crowding out of intrinsic motivation in about half of my interviews. These statements included comments such as:

> 'To me this felt like management wanted to turn us into small "hustlers" like the people you find in banks. I'm not into this kind of ego trip.'

'I took the money, but I'm not motivated by it. I'm more concerned about what others think about me... when I read my job spec it says what I should do. I don't need to be paid extra to follow it... when my boss tells me "you have to do this" I will try my best, but when he gives me money to do it, I don't.'

'It's a nice to have, but goes into the wrong direction. Individual performance is a character trait, but nothing that should need additional compensation.'

Interestingly, the responses were relatively 'black and white' with regards to a positive or negative motivational impact. There was only one interview partner who provided explicit evidence of both effects – all the others expressed either a purely positive or negative view of the incentive programme.

When looking at the interview partners in more detail, there is some evidence that interview partners with lower base compensation levels viewed the extra reward more positively and also generally tended to be more likely to change their behaviour. This concerned especially the younger, less tenured managers, some of whom have substantially lower levels of compensation than their more senior peers. Therefore, for a manager with lower base pay, the additional bonus potential would seem more generous in relation to their overall level of compensation and could really have a 'lifestyle impact' that might offset possible negative thoughts.

Another observation is a noticeable difference in how managers in different units reacted to the incentive programme. In the so-called passenger area (eg check-in and gate activities), which covers mostly 'white-collar' tasks, many of the staff are fairly young, a large portion works part time, there is an equal gender split, and many of the employees are not fully dependent on their job with the company. Many don't need to support a family and look more for flexible working hours than high income. The baggage-handling area has quite different characteristics – here, nearly all employees are male, most come from modest educational backgrounds, many have been with the company for a long time, depend on their income to support a family, and frankly do not have too many outside options. The work is physically demanding and dangerous as shown by occasional accidents.

These differences led to the emergence of two distinct cultures, which becomes visible in the way managers view their role and how they interact with their staff. To illustrate this difference, let's see how two managers, one from the passenger side and one from the baggage-handling side, each responded to a question on how they felt when communicating saving measures to their staff:

Passenger services: 'I just said we're going through tough times. I had no problem with it. Staff didn't know about my bonus.'

Baggage-handling services: 'This is the wrong way. I felt like we should push our employees into the "pain zone"... only focused on economics, but not at all on staff... we should push our staff like slaves. It felt irresponsible.'

Role differences affected how managers described the impact of the new incentive programme on their intrinsic motivation. Baggage-handling managers were more likely to make statements that support the crowding out hypothesis.

Money led to increased short-term compliance, but not to long-term commitment

Commitment to change manifests itself in a mindset that 'binds an individual to a course of action deemed necessary for the successful implementation of a change initiative (Herscovitch and Meyer, 2002). If we want to measure commitment, we can look for evidence of this mindset (eg through positive statements about the change or the objectives of the change) and we can also identify concrete evidence for behaviour that is in line with the change. Normative or affective commitment could be demonstrated by specific discretionary behaviour. In our case, this could, for example, include the implementation of savings measures. However, to be clear that such behaviour is the result of change commitment and not a direct price effect linked to the financial incentive, it would need to be accompanied by some form of mindset or long-term attitude change. Ideally, we would like to see the behaviour remain even if the financial incentive is taken away.

Around half of my interview partners provided examples of discretionary behaviour that was in line with the change objective of creating a more entre-preneurial and cost-conscious environment. Examples for concrete courses of actions include:

'Yes, there were several concrete ideas that I helped to implement – for example, we reduced staff in the ticketing office.'

'I took higher risks in staffing [the risk of being understaffed and not meeting service levels], and, for example, I exchanged staff with other departments.'

'I did some small adjustments, eg saving in training hours.'

'Yes, I made a lot of changes in shift plans.'

However, at the same time, there was only one interviewee who felt that the implementation of the new reward scheme had a lasting effect, stating that it 'was a trigger to try new things' and resulted in 'more proactive planning'. None of the others linked their actions to any lasting mindset change, and, as one interview partner pointed out, they might have enacted the same behaviours without an explicit incentive: 'Those who had been proactive before continued being so... there were no lasting savings due to the incentive scheme... most of what we did was not replacing sick people and reducing some of the back-office hours.'

Therefore, it feels safe to conclude, based on the interview results, that the incentive scheme did not result in higher change commitment. Even though we could observe some concrete actions that were in line with the new behaviour, it seems that those were directly linked to the extrinsic motivation provided through extra compensation, but not to an increase in commitment.

Money changed the psychological frame

Introducing the concept of money into any interaction can make people feel more self-efficacious, which makes them less likely to cooperate with others (Zhou, Vohs and Baumeister, 2009; Vohs, Mead and Goode, 2006). Whenever an organization uses financial incentives to change employees' behaviour, it consequently runs the risk of losing some of the benefits from cooperation between staff, with likely negative long-term consequences. Implementing a new reward scheme, such as the performance bonus at my research site, can lead to higher transparency when managers realize that they do not receive the full reward potential and hence earn less than some of their peers. Also, this feeling of being undercompensated has been associated with various detrimental outcomes such as high turnover and lower product quality (Mitchell and Mickel, 1999).

During my interviews, I found some evidence for a deterioration in the level of cooperation between peers. Three of my interview partners hinted at such an effect through statements like:

'It became more competitive as there was a direct monthly comparison. Some of the unit heads were very adamant – they came to me and said, "You have to do this or that because of the financial incentive!" There were also discussions around exchanging staff that we did not have before. As a result, a trainee programme got cancelled because nobody wanted to cover the cost.'

'People became more pedantic and cooperation suffered.'

'There was some mistrust and envy.'

Much stronger was the evidence that nearly all managers who did not receive the full bonus felt treated unfairly compared to their peers, as evidenced by the following assertions:

'It triggered discontent. People were happy with what they got until they saw the direct comparison to what others received.'

'It felt unfair and unproductive, some people were just lucky. Overall, this was more frustrating than motivating. Nobody wanted to admit that they were interested in it, but then everyone spoke about the money.'

'Overall, it felt unfair – especially for those who wanted to achieve the bonus but couldn't, who got very frustrated.'

'I really tried hard to get savings, but others had more without doing much for it.'

With lower cooperation levels and increased dissatisfaction with individual compensation, the company might have incurred some negative psychological side effects through the introduction of the new reward model. I have, however, no clear evidence that there resulted any tangible short-term or long-term consequences. While interviewees claimed that cooperation suffered to some extent, and some mentioned their dissatisfaction due to a perceived unfairness of the system, all also said that today, after the incentive scheme has been discontinued, they did not feel any lasting impacts on their peer relationships.

People relate differently to the concept of money (see Mitchell and Mickel, 1999). While some of my interview partners welcomed the additional challenge and felt motivated by the opportunity to increase their income, others had mostly negative associations and mentioned feelings like being 'bribed' or being controlled. Two interview partners even noted that 'taking money' would have a negative impact on their self-esteem.

This could lead to a conclusion that before deciding on the introduction of incentives as part of a change programme, an organization would need to get a good understanding of how the affected employees relate to money. This was also reflected in the statement from a member of the senior management (who was not a direct recipient of the bonus):

'Some people changed their behaviour, others less. Good performers were sometimes frustrated and the bad performers didn't really improve by that much. People here were used to a bonus of a few per cent; now suddenly they had the opportunity to get a substantial amount. They could not handle this sudden change.'

Removing incentives can be costly

The status quo bias (endowment effect) is a cognitive bias that explains a strong preference for the current state of affairs (Kahneman, Knetsch and Thaler, 1990). People experience any deviation from this current baseline as a loss. For financial incentives, this implies that employees will always look at their current level of compensation as a baseline. If a rise in compensation is granted, the new, higher level of pay will quickly become the new baseline for employees and any deviation back to previous levels will be looked at negatively. In addition, people generally overweigh losses compared to gains and are very reluctant to give up any goods they have already acquired. So, removing an additional compensation once it has been granted could imply that employees will be less satisfied with their pay than they were originally at the same level of compensation. This is shown in the illustration below, which one of my interview partners drew up to express how he felt.

Figure 3.1 Status quo bias

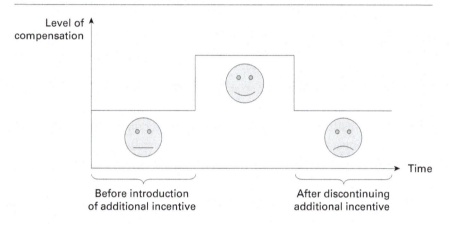

During my interviews, half of the managers made statements indicating some level of discontent with their level of compensation after the performance bonus programme had been discontinued. These included statements such as:

> *'I lost around X thousand in compensation. I would feel very bad if this was not compensated.'*

> *'I would be unhappy if there's no replacement for the bonus. I don't think that I would leave the company, but I surely would be discontented with my level of compensation. The new bonus set off some of the raises we did not get in the last few years.'*

> *'I would be quite unhappy without a replacement for the bonus.'*

Naturally, there was a relatively large overlap between the persons who generally reacted positively to the introduction of the bonus and those who expressed discontent about its discontinuation. However, there were also exceptions, such as a manager who had very much opposed the explicit nature of the bonus scheme (link to cost savings), but also felt strongly that a replacement should be found.

Lessons learned

The incentive scheme integrated as part of a larger transformation project led to a very mixed set of results. Some employees, especially when a possible reward was high compared to their base compensation, focused purely on the monetary gain and ignored potential implications on their intrinsic motivation. For these employee groups, using financial incentives can have a positive short-term implication in terms of seeing the targeted behaviour change.

Other employees, who have a different mental concept of money or have been socialized in a different organizational culture, put substantially more emphasis on intrinsic motivators and can react negatively to an explicit behaviour-linked reward model, even in the short term.

I could not find any evidence that the financial reward increased change commitment. Therefore, the observed positive effects can be predicted to vanish once the reward is taken away, which leaves no long-term positive effect. At the same time, there are critical psychological effects. Increasing financial rewards can have negative effects on cooperation and lead to higher stress levels. Most of these effects mean that the long-term implications of a change-based reward model are likely negative for the organization.

An organization that is undergoing a major behavioural change effort and considers the use of financial incentives to trigger or solidify behavioural changes needs to be very prudent in the design and implementation of such a reward model. The company in my case study eventually decided to withdraw the reward scheme. This was partly driven by discontent and questioning of the programme's fairness by some of the managers, and partly by the limitations the programme placed on senior management's ability to directly interfere with departments' resource-planning decisions. The latter resulted in frequent discussions around bonus eligibility for savings decisions that were mandated and not based on a manager's decision.

The overall project did have a short-term positive impact (in terms of seeing targeted behaviour) on around half of the interviewed managers. However, as discussed before, this impact was not due to an increase in commitment to change, but rather due to a direct motivational effect of the monetary reward that ceased once the reward was taken away.

Conclusion

The sense of adopting financial incentivization as a driver to raise commitment levels in projects will depend on the individual preferences of an organization's employees, on the corporate culture and on the specific needs of the situation as discussed above. There are cases in which it will be appropriate, especially in the short term, but then there are also cases in which such a measure would have a negative impact. The possible options for an organization are summarized in the below figure.

Figure 3.2 Cultural receptiveness profiling

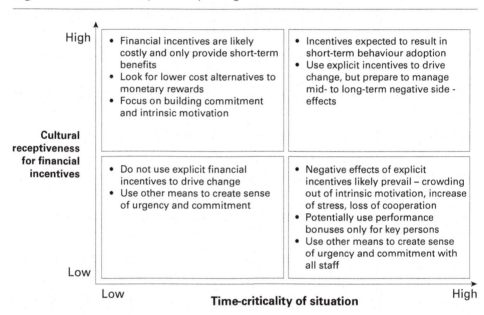

A reward model cannot be seen as a substitute for other activities targeted at increasing commitment (such as offering an opportunity to contribute to the design of a change, role modelling, intense communication, and training), but rather as a supporting measure next to the regular change programme.

Part 2: Interview

The following is the summary of a series of personal conversations between Bob and Stefan.

Q: Just to summarize the whole article very simply, are you saying that the use of financial incentives to drive project engagement with internal and external stakeholders may work, or it may not? It really just depends on the situation.

A: It's a little more complex. Yes, situation is core. It depends fundamentally on the organizational culture and the people involved, of course. But, just to refine your summary a little, in general, theoretical research indicates that financial incentives are an expensive way to trigger short-term behaviour change and tend not to lead to lasting commitment and can even backfire. So they're both very expensive and risky. There may be some who are positive about the measure, but also some who can react negatively. For example, if you want to sell a company, and you need to incentivize some form of improvement just in the short term, to support the sale, it could trigger that impact.

Q: So, it could be appropriate in an environment used to financial incentives?

A: Yes, investment banks for example. Here it can be a very natural way to do things. However, a sudden shift to an explicit financial incentive model can be dangerous. That said, though, at the same time you do need to make sure your existing compensation model does not contradict the behaviour change you want to see happen. So if you want people to act in a more strategic way, for example building new relationships, which takes time, but you only compensate for revenue in the current year, it doesn't make sense. Financial incentives must not contradict what you want people to do.

Q: Were you surprised yourself by your findings?

A: Not really. Research and experience of the last 10 to 15 years supports this position.

Q: How far do you think those leading projects generally under-estimate the complexity underlying change processes and the challenge of getting buy-in?

A: Generally, they under-estimate, yes, how long it takes to implement change according to any plan, and yes, people tend to underestimate the problems of getting buy-in.

Q: In your experience, what engagement/motivational processes are typically and most successfully used? Or is a hopeless task, as so many change initiatives are said to fail?

A: No, it's not a hopeless task. In fact, there are many good models which you can apply for change management. I think, broadly speaking, there are three main elements: people need to have a sense of discomfort with the status quo; then they need a compelling vision of what a better future could look like; and then you need to have a clear process of how to get from A to B. I mean, if you want people to change, then they have to understand why they need to go to something new. And sometimes it is not so obvious, or not enough time is dedicated to making it obvious. And with the process, what is often overlooked is the clear process notion of co-creation: doing things with people, showing basic human respect at an individual level, showing a sense of trust and belief in the individual – all this can be about very personal things at times.

Q: Given the complexity and scales of some changes, is it likely that those leading projects will be able to use any engagement trigger successfully?

A: I think it's about involvement, talking to people, listening to them, taking concerns into account. It is about co-creation, and you need to follow through. If you start something and then people don't hear back, or you don't do anything with the input, it's not good. It needs to be sincere. That will often mean it is difficult to take shortcuts; or, may even mean you need to involve people more than you think is necessary. But under high pressure, both the sponsor and project leader can make a decision to cut the change dimension short, cut it short for time reasons or cost reasons, and they might know that this is not a textbook solution. But these are systemic or organizational pressures which tend to compromise theoretically sound processes. You have the awareness you should do A but you still do B because of external pressures.

Part 3: Commentary

Here are some reflections on Stefan's case and interview.

Stefan's article gives a clear and brilliant message: you cannot buy motivation, support and engagement with money in general. You have to give people a really convincing case, you have to take efforts to finally convince them, you have to 'walk the talk'. Generally speaking, money cannot substitute for real leadership. This is not entirely a new insight, but one easily forgotten under high pressure.

Real leadership depends, among other things, on a personality with empathy and an appreciation for people, on an adequately positive and entrepreneurial mindset, on broad cross-cultural experiences and some key expertise. On the basis of these leadership skills, it is possible to create the right setting for motivation, to realize a high-performing team tailored to the concrete context. Motivation has to be a key topic when setting the project up; one has to reserve enough time for this, and it is crucial to review motivation levels on a regular basis.

Peter Wollmann.

Part 4: Reflecting on international project management

Take time to reflect on the following questions to help you reach further insights and take practical actions to improve your own project management practice.

1 How do you motivate others in your international project role? How much time do you dedicate? How effective is your motivational behaviour?

2 What are the factors that typically undermine motivation in an international project environment? Decide some measures to act on these specific demotivators.

3 In which situations might some form of financial incentive be valid in your international project contexts?

Part 5: Put it into practice

There are a number of very valid insights and ideas for project management present in this case which the reader can learn from and adopt, customizing for their own projects. Take a few minutes to note down your main learnings from this case, and note down some actions for yourself.

Personal insights, learnings and actions

References and further reading

Akerlof, George A (1982) Labor Contracts as Partial Gift Exchange, *Quarterly Journal of Economics*, **97**, pp. 543–69

Allen, N J and Meyer, J P (1996) Affective, continuance and normative commitment to the organisation: an examination of construct validity, *Journal of Vocational Behaviours*, **49**, pp. 252–76

Choi, M (2001) Employees' attitude towards organizational change: a literature review, *Human Resource Management*, **50** (4), pp. 479–500

Constantinescu, M (2010) Neuroeconomics and decision-making process, *Theoretical and Practical Research in Economic Fields*, **1** (2), pp. 209–217

Eisenberger, R, Pierce, W and Cameron, J (1999) Effects of reward on intrinsic motivation – negative, neutral, and positive: Comment on Deci, Koestner, and Ryan (1999) *Psychological Bulletin*, **125** (6), pp. 677–91, doi:10.1037/0033-2909.125.6.677

Eisenkopf, G and Teyssier, S (2013) Envy and loss aversion in tournaments, *Journal of Economic Psychology*, **34**, pp. 240–55, doi:10.1016/j.joep.2012.06.006

Fehr, E and Falk, A (2002) Psychological foundations of incentives, *European Economic Review*, **46** (4/5), pp. 687–724

Fehr, E and Gächter, S (2002) *Do incentive contracts undermine voluntary cooperation?* Institute for Empirical Research in Economics (Zurich University), Working Paper No. 34

Fehr, E and List, J A (2004) The hidden costs and returns of incentives: trust and trustworthiness among CEOs. *Journal of The European Economic Association*, **2** (5), pp. 743–71

Frey, B S and Jegen, R (2001) Motivation crowding theory, *Journal of Economic Surveys*, **15** (5), p. 589

Fugate, M, Kinicki, A J and Prussia, G E (2008) Employee coping with organizational change: an examination of alternative theoretical perspectives and models, *Personnel Psychology*, **61** (1), pp. 1–36, doi:10.1111/j.1744-6570.2008.00104.x

Gneezy, U, Meier, S, and Rey-Biel, P (2011) When and why incentives (don't) work to modify behavior, *Journal Of Economic Perspectives*, **25** (4), pp. 191–210. doi:10.1257/jep.25.4.191

Gneezy, U and Rustichini, A (2000) Pay enough or don't pay at all, *Quarterly Journal of Economics*, **115** (3), pp. 791–810

Heath, C (1999) On the social psychology of agency relationship: lay theories of motivation overemphasize extrinsic incentives, *Organizational Behavior & Human Decision Processes*, **78** (1), pp. 25–62

Herold, D M, Fedor, D B and Caldwell, S D (2007) Beyond change management: a multilevel investigation of contextual and personal influences on employees' commitment to change. *Journal of Applied Psychology*, **92** (4), pp. 942–51

Herscovitch, L and Meyer, J P (2002) Commitment to organizational change: extension of a three-component model, *Journal of Applied Psychology*, **87** (3), pp. 474–87, doi:10.1037//0021-9010.873.3.474

Kahneman, D (2002) *Maps of bounded rationality: a perspective on intuitive judgment and choice*, Nobel Prize Lecture held Dec. 8, 2002 [online] www.nobelprize.org

Kahneman, D (2011) *Thinking, Fast and Slow*, Farrar, Straus and Giroux, New York

Kahneman, D, Knetsch, J L and Thaler, R H (1990) Experimental tests of the endowment effect and the Coase theorem, *Journal of Political Economy*, **98** (6), p. 1352

Kotter, J P and Schlesinger, L A (2008) Choosing strategies for change, *Harvard Business Review*, **86** (7/8), pp. 130–39

McKinsey & Company (2011) Lighting the way: perspectives on the global lighting market, *McKinsey* [online] www.mckinsey.com

Mitchell, T R and Mickel, A E (1999) The meaning of money: an individual-difference perspective, *Academy of Management Review*, **24** (3), pp. 568–78, doi:10.5465/AMR.1999.2202138

Mobbs, D D (2009) Choking on the money: reward-based performance decrements are associated with midbrain activity, *Psychological Science (Wiley-Blackwell)*, **20** (8), pp. 955–62

Seo, M, Taylor, M, Hill, N, Zhang, X, Tesluk, P E and Lorinkova, N M (2012) The role of affect and leadership during organizational change, *Personnel Psychology*, **65** (1), pp. 121–65, Doi:10.1111/J.1744-6570.2011.01240.X

Shin, J, Taylor, M and Seo, M (2012) Resources for change: the relationships of organizational inducements and psychological resilience to employees' attitudes and behaviors toward organizational change, *Academy of Management Journal*, 55 (3), pp. 727–48

Taylor, H and Cooper, C L (1998) Organizational change: threat or challenge? The role of individual differences in the management of stress, *Journal of Organizational Change Management*, 1 (1), p. 68

Tversky, A and Kahneman, D (1992) Advances in prospect theory: cumulative representation of uncertainty, *Journal of Risk & Uncertainty*, 5 (4), pp. 297–323

Vohs, K R (2008) Merely activating the concept of money changes personal and interpersonal behavior, *Current Directions in Psychological Science* (Wiley-Blackwell), 17 (3), pp. 208–12

Vohs, K R, Mead, N L and Goode, M R (2006) The psychological consequences of money, *Science*, 314, pp. 1154–56

Zhou, X, Vohs, K D and Baumeister, R F (2009) The symbolic power of money: reminders of money alter distress and physical pain, *Psychological Science*, 20 (6), pp. 700–706

Distilling experience: a career in international projects

04

JOSÉ MORENO CODINA

Profile

José Moreno Codina is currently president of the consulting firm Applied Viability (AV Group), which is in the process of becoming a full member of The Transformation Alliance (with consultancies in most of Europe and global alliances with a core number of 800 consultants). For the last two years although to a lesser extent at this stage, he has served as an internal consultant for Zurich Insurance Company (General Insurance) for the Latam Region.

From 1999 until April 2014 José was the managing consultant at Towers Watson, in Portugal (until 2010) and Spain (1999–2014). During the first stage of his professional career, he worked for 23 years (1974–1996) in top management positions in the insurance industry in the United States (Boston) and in Europe (London), for six years as the Spanish Chief Financial Officer (1977–1982) and for 15 years (1983–1996) as the Spanish CEO and vice president of the board for Commercial Union (now AVIVA).

José gives frequent presentations and writes articles for the insurance community on motor insurance trends, industry pricing developments, bancassurance distribution and other general management topics. From

1997–2009 he led the insurance section of the CUNEF (Universidad Complutense de Madrid) master's degree in financial management. José has been vice president of the UK Chamber of Commerce in Barcelona, a member of the Advisory Board of the Insurance Intermediaries National Association (2009–2013), President of the International Insurers Club in Spain (2007–2013), and a member of the Spanish Advisers-Managers' Institute IC-A (2010–2014).

Foreword

José's case is less about a specific project than a synthesis of a life's experience of working in international projects in a variety of contexts. Interestingly, José manages to draw a number of important generic lessons from a range of specific project experiences that are often highly individual and governed by a number of unique factors relating to a specific commercial environment, a project type or a particular individual psychology. He also draws the reader very strongly back to the human factor, and the need to engage with and manage relationship building as a priority within one's international project leadership practice.

Before reading on, reflect on a number of key questions addressed in the case. Then compare your experience and answers to the ideas in the case itself and the final commentary.

1 How would you categorize the different types of international projects that are run in large multinationals today?

2 How important is networking for those leading international projects? Why?

3 What could be the value of a mentor to an international project leader?

PART 1: CASE STUDY   Distilling experience: a career in PM

Introduction

I have worked for over 30 years in the field of international project management. The following is a synthesis of this experience, and a bundle of insights and experiences that I believe could be of interest and value to others working in challenging but also highly rewarding environments. There are actually a series of contexts, including the project context or type of project, the organizational culture, the commercial sector (in this case, insurance), and always there is the personal context, the particular preferences and approaches brought by the specific individual. My reflections touch on all of these in some way.

The project context

The projects in which I worked varied quite significantly, from those focusing on single and highly specialized activities to projects that involved some form of integration of several functions and perspectives to produce a far more complex output. I have been involved in many cross-functional projects in international insurance companies which were initiated to ensure that cross-fertilization of best practices and ideas occurred and were really shared and adopted when feasible. Other major projects I have worked on are M&A related, and focused on topics such as value retention, working to a first 100-day integration plan to make sure that value is kept in the newly formed company. These types of projects typically involve functions with actuarial, HR and also PM expertise.

The organizational context

One of the most consistent aspects of my experience of working in international projects has been the need to cope with the presence of significant differences in company strategy and culture. In my experience, the existing organizational culture is one of the most deterministic forces at play in the success or failure of a business project. Yet the obstacles, challenges and difficulties created by company culture is something that is usually grossly underestimated. For example, during my 23 years at Commercial Union, its strong British insurance values and behaviour evolved the company from being the leading P&C risk carrier of the '70s into the specialized international life and savings company of today. Its cultural imprint also had critical effects at a project level, whether in the general or life business or in the functional content of projects, in IT, finance, distribution etc. During my nearly 15 years at Towers Watson, a need to fit the different cultures of the three segments of the business (risk consulting, benefits and talent management) was at the centre of the strategy adapted in each cycle of the company. It will be very interesting to see how this evolves over the next year, with the merger of Towers Watson with Willis.

The insurance context

The insurance industry is now highly internationalized with its basic product, risk protection, well correlated with the cultural bias and 'modus operandi' of specific local markets. There are numerous examples of ways in which insurance is practised differently according to the needs of local market requirements. For example, in post-Soviet Poland, as the banks were not trusted as required, life insurance was sold highly successfully via a direct sales force distribution channel. Effective management of such a sales organization required that one understood well the context of its beliefs and behaviours.

Risk and actuarial consulting, another major piece of the insurance industry, is also, by the nature of its clients, highly internationalized. However, its way of doing businesses in respective markets with diverse regulatory frameworks is differentiated. In the United States, Europe and China, motor insurance price optimization is conducted to very different logics. Some consultancies, it is my belief, are careful to 'package offers' for all markets; in other words, they believe one size fits all. Instead, they should prefer a 'tailor-made' proposition for individual markets.

The human context

I believe that each project (and life) situation is very different and past success does not guarantee future client satisfaction. For me, it is the people, the team, in a particular project that are the key to that success. Their resilience, communication skills, diversity, patience and cultural adaptability are as important as their technical skills and knowledge. But above all of these, ethics, values and behaviours that embody and enable respect and collaboration really make the difference. At the end of the day, as with so many human activities, it is particular individuals (with their ethics, characteristics and qualities) in a given project who are the ones that matter. With globalization there is a danger, paradoxically, of leading corporate players underestimating these important human aspects. In my opinion, the human factors will actually become more and more important because we are facing an almost physical law that people's capacity to change is simply less rapid than the speed of change being driven by leading business players operating globally.

Human beings value respect greatly and need to be treated with understanding. Creating a project and organizational culture with such values is going to be a key to success. We see it now in the way more and more global organizations since the last economic downturn are trying to build and rebuild reputation and a sense they stand for something, with an unprecedented emphasis on values, beliefs and positive behaviours. Whether employees really buy into the claims made, and whether leadership is truly behind such ultimately ethical initiatives, is open to question.

Career lessons learned

Some of the key lessons I have learned in the course of my career are below.

1. Use mentors

One of my personal success factors has been my continuing use of mentors throughout my project management career, people both within and from outside the organizations where I worked. Why have I done this? It's basically because no single person can know everything, so the ability to leverage a network gives you a greater intellectual scope to draw on and to help deal with complex business problems. I can't follow and keep up with all business trends. I can't be an expert in analytics and operations at the same time. But by knowing people expert in a range of areas, I have been to be able to distil this knowledge to a focus point in my role as leader, and to take good decisions. For me, this is also a kind of mindset with flexible boundaries which is needed to drive large and quite amorphous modern companies. There is always an organigram, a formal organization, but that doesn't mean much. Leadership is really about understanding beyond the formal level of an organization, navigating the organization, and driving through the formal organizational chart, using the experience of others rather than starting from scratch every time.

2. Be transparent

I guess the second major principle is what I would term transparency. In one sense it's an ability to share, a kind of generosity. It's not always easy to be transparent, to volunteer information when you think it makes sense, for the company to put to good use. This desire to open up and give information is an effort; it takes an effort to communicate it especially maybe with people you don't like too much. But I think professionalism has to go beyond personal chemistry.

3. Combine relationship expertise with analytical expertise

Of course, relationships are hugely important. But this whole area actually didn't come easily to me. I used to take refuge in my technical expertise, and gain respect from that. But I think relationship management is more important. A close friend helped me understand relationships, mainly coming from the sales side. He asked me to stand up once in front of 33 CEOs to make a toast. I still remember the event; it was a big effort. But it was a kind of breakthrough for me, and I gained confidence in relationships after that. A lot of business is about gaining trust, handling different resistance levels, and being patient with that resistance; after all, maybe it's justified. It's also about building alliances, and asking for opinions of allies trusted by resisters in meetings, so that the ideas come from them and have more weight than just coming from me. Fundamentally, it's being seen to be polite, and being a good listener.

4. Deal with culture

Culture is also important. People are very different. If you are a New Yorker who grew up in Queens, you have to be careful working internationally; you cannot simply go and say what you want, and demand it immediately. As a German controller, you have to be careful not to demand perfection immediately. But it's also important to bring something, to bring your own culture into another culture, so that you bring value, and create a kind of mixture. Semantics and languages are also a key part of all of this. Terminology has very different meanings between different functional groups; 'net result' has one meaning to management, another to underwriting. What is 'large loss'? What is 'average cost'? You have to ask clarification questions like, 'What do you mean?' In some ways, all this terminology is a kind of a mask; people hide behind the terms rather than making the effort to explain things well. Part of this is connected to a fear of being exposed as not knowing. It's also not taking responsibility. You know, big organizations rely a lot on process and procedure, which makes people complacent. But however well designed a process is, all processes have weaknesses. Smaller companies are more person oriented; the management teams take accountability for making sure processes work. Big companies could learn a lot from this.

5. Choose team members wisely

Finally, I guess it comes back to choosing the right people to make a good team. This means you need diversity in the sense of people who are complementary; as a basic attitude people need to be enthusiastic and selling the project as a kind of business partner. You need people who can communicate, who are not over-prescriptive and say it has to be done like this. You need people who can explain, who can describe the benefits and explain what difference the project will make.

Part 2: Interview

The following is a short extract from a series of personal conversations between Bob and José.

Q: As a consultant, do you approach projects in different ways? I mean, do you have a way of analysing which type of project you're dealing with?

A: I think we can analyse projects in different ways, in multiple ways. If you draw a graph, on one axis you have a line, from a more business-as-usual project to one that is more strategic or more transformational.

You can have another axis, from normal to very innovative. You can have national to multinational. There are more. How specialized the project is, or how general it is. You have functional and multi- or cross-functional projects. And the needs and success factors in each type will be different.

Q: And the most challenging ones combine these?

A: Yes, those which are highly innovative, highly technical, highly international, and so on. These are the most demanding, I think. So you need some navigation; you need to know which project you are in.

Q: What is your general perspective on the major project management bodies and the tools and template that they offer? Useful?

A: I always try to focus on what we're trying to achieve and whether that is what the client expects, and go for it in a reasonable way, keep communication open, that's what I focus on. All these templates are without sense for me. If you spend half your days and nights filling in templates, you risk losing focus. I have one project at the moment. I have to deliver a very large turnaround, over 50 million euros. I'm not going to fulfil any template.

Q: As a consultant, I imagine that getting close to customers is very important to you.

A: Yes, you need to build good relationships. You also need to convince a lot.

Q: What is your talent there, with convincing?

A: I deal a lot with pricing projects, looking at pricing models. And we have really global expertise. We know all the software providers. So we bring expertise to the table – the best in the world in this case. We bring a lot of information from the market, so benchmarking.

Q: Is that expertise ever a disadvantage if you don't take stakeholders with you? You are too far from the customer?

A: I see the risk but this is part of our expertise. Convincing is not done in one shot; it is best done during a journey and it's about evolution of a solution. You need to start, do what is feasible in the circumstances, but do something significant in the circumstances. With pricing projects, the journey is to clean up, create a base, make a first profit, keep building it up, add other channels and keep building up the business.

The relationship with the client. It needs to last a long time. It's an extended process.

Q: Just one final question, you mention culture in your piece. What does culture mean for you?

A: It's about the way you do things. It's about not what you say but how you say it. It's about the impressions you make in the first minutes. You don't want to start very wrong.

Q: So, you mean managing the other's perception.

A: Yes, and it also means you create, as a project manager, your own immune system.

Q: What's that?

A: When I was in Barcelona, I often heard the phrase, 'We in the UK do it in this way'. It was sometimes frustrating so you need to create an immune system so it doesn't affect you. You know, people who insist we need to have it on Monday at 09.00. Create an immune system for that too, and for the team against negative parts of the corporate culture which may be toxic for them.

Q: Is that a key leadership behaviour, to build a buffer to the team to protect it, to have a kind of resilience?

A: Yes, it's very important to be resilient.

Part 3: Commentary

Here are some reflections on José's case and interview.

It is a pleasure to read the case of an experienced project manager who used to work on both sides – as an employee/manager of an enterprise and as an external consultant. It is very useful to know both perspectives very well. I couldn't agree more to the five key lessons José worked out.

1 **Use mentors.** *Younger project managers especially, who should be keen to learn, should carefully select the right mentor who can act as a sparring partner with all their expertise and knowledge, but who does not force the mentee in any special way. Conversations should help the mentee to understand the environmental organization and system and how to cope with it. To have open conversations with a great mentor is a significant privilege.*

2 **Be transparent.** *It is always underestimated how strong transparency is as a tool. This is even valid in organizations which tend to be less transparent and which are focused very much on political games. The strong project manager who plays a transparent game in such an environment breaks a* *pattern, which will give him or her an advantage. The only thing to be regarded; you need to able to take a bit of a risk.*

3 Combine relationship expertise with analytical expertise. *It is very evident that people who base themselves solely on their technical and analytical expertise very often fail. A more holistic approach recognizes that people are not machines but human beings and that for really successful projects an emotional component is necessary – and this is covered by good relationships.*

4 Deal with culture. *I think this aspect goes through all the articles in the book. It is absolutely evident and one of the key success factors.*

5 Choose team members wisely. *A strong project manager should always insist on selecting his team without too many political restrictions. And he or she should place a high priority on forming and developing a high-performance team. If you have such a team in place, you will always find a solution, even in critical situations, as everyone will follow the same target without resistance.*

Peter Wollmann

José's insights are many and varied. A couple of things really struck me. First, his deep and sustained use of a network across his career. Many professionals either dismiss networking as a nice-to-have, or see its value but don't invest sufficient time, or simply build too narrow a stakeholder set. José's commitment is strong and related to a simple but powerful logic that he can't know everything, so he has to connect to people with the knowledge he lacks. His thoughtful development of a knowledge network to inform his decision making is unusual, in my experience, and a practice that demands thought from the reader. Second, and it might seem like a small comment, but it's the idea of convincing people in the course of a journey. I often meet frustration in clients as they try to influence others and run up against a wall of resistance. The truth is that they are pushing too hard and too soon. Influencing and engagement clearly have to be calibrated to context and the status of a relationship, and cannot be quickly and dirtily accelerated by dumping the 'right' facts on people.

Bob Dignen

Part 4: Reflecting on international project management

Take time to reflect on the following questions to help you reach further insights and take practical actions to improve your own project management practice.

1 Which person around you in your current organization might be a useful mentor for you? Why? How can you best approach this person to ask them to act as your mentor?

2 Which types of projects are you currently involved in or likely to be involved in going forward into the future? Which network is important for you to be successful?

3 Which negative parts of your organization impact your project? How can you build you own immunity from these influences?

Part 5: Put it into practice

There are a number of very valid insights and ideas for project management present in this case which the reader can learn from and adopt, customizing for their own projects. Take a few minutes to note down your main learnings from this case, and note down some actions for yourself.

Personal insights, learnings and actions

The Nordic Leadership Study Tour to India

RANA SINHA

Profile

Rana Sinha is a consultant with a strong background in planning, organizing and providing human resource development functions in diverse cultural settings with a rich experience of over 30 years. Of Indian and Finnish parentage, he was born in India and has lived in many countries. He currently lives in Finland and runs his own consultancy, which specializes in intercultural business consulting, presentation skills, working and managing in an India context, as well as helping foreigners working with Finnish companies. He is currently doing his PhD in social sciences at the University of Leicester, UK, focusing on how biethnic adults adjust to the workplace. He has an MSc from the University of Leicester, a teacher training certificate from the University of Cambridge, a Bachelor's in Science from the University of Calcutta as well as an MBA from the United States. Rana speaks fluent Finnish, Hindi, Bengali and several other languages.

Foreword

This case outlines a leadership training project which takes leaders from Europe to India to learn first-hand the challenges of leading a short project in a 'foreign' context, all within a year-long management education in Finland. It is an interesting project on a number of levels. For example, the case generates a number of interesting insights and observations shared by

Rana around the nature and practice of leadership by leaders today, particularly on the dangers that can attach to notions of 'expertise' and the diverse manifestation of trust in different cultural settings. The case also highlights the role of emotions in international project life, and the need for those operating in such contexts to develop emotional capability.

Additionally, the project offers an interesting blueprint for the development of international leadership skills in a way that abandons traditional seminar environments and universalist platitudes deriving from Anglo-American leadership traditions. Here we see international project management facilitating deep and challenging learning processes by means of international project management; it's truly experiential.

Before reading this case, reflect on the following questions. Then compare your answers to the ideas in the case itself and the final commentary.

1 What could be the main challenges of leading such an international project as described above? Why?

2 What do you think are likely to be important success factors for the person leading the project? Why?

PART 1: CASE STUDY
The Nordic Leadership Study Tour to India

Introduction

The Nordic Leadership Training Institute (NLTI – *the name is fictitious for reasons of confidentiality*), situated in Finland, is a leading provider of senior leadership training in an international setting. It aims to provide relevant personal development learning processes by identifying and finding access to key areas of international development and market trends that impact international leadership. This is a constant challenge for all institutes in this field of professional learning.

The Nordic Leadership Study Tour to India, developed by NLTI, was a one-year educational project and the key component of an international executive leadership programme. Course participants came from a variety of countries and professional contexts, and were all working as senior leaders in their home countries. The primary project *purpose* was to give participants the opportunity to test their course learning and enhance their own expertise by engaging in activities or personal micro-projects/case studies situated within a real-life international business environment and series of professional networks.

The overall educational project formed part of operative corporate talent and knowledge management processes that aimed to successfully facilitate real learning and create business impact. The objective was to provide world-class learning impact for the students along with excellent networking opportunities at reasonable cost in an unfamiliar business and cultural environment that would move delegates out of their comfort zones.

The learning process in India was primarily experiential, using insights generated via facilitated self and group reflection to stimulate learning from own and others' insights via analysis of experiences, and develop understandings of these experiences and their meanings for international leadership.

The specific *goals* of the project covered four major areas: *learning impact, quality networking opportunities, continuity* and *costs worthiness.* The measurements of the success of achieving these *goals* were carefully defined and involved:

- comparison with figures of previous tours conducted in other destinations;

- delegate feedback at the planning stage as well as during and after the tour;

- feedback from professors in Indian universities involved in supervising learning;

- feedback from business leaders in India directly involved with the delegates in the case studies.

The *stakeholders* of the project, with the relative significance for each stakeholder, were as follows:

- A leadership programme training director (the success of this project would directly affect the overall success of the leadership training programme and reaffirm the programme director's competence and reputation).

- A project manager (the success of this project would be a significant career merit and valuable reference of professional skills).

- Leadership programme participants (the learning impact and synergy from networking would be of great value in their professional careers).

- Training provider project office staff – part of the training programme and project funding came from public body grants requiring extensive documentation and reporting (the overall success of the leadership training programme guaranteed increased funding and reputation for the institute and thus improved job retention for all the office staff in a volatile labour market).

- Senior business leaders in Indian business enterprises, chosen to correspond to sectors which the educational project participants had selected for their cases (the case studies and corporate visits gave the business leaders a valuable opportunity to discuss real-life business challenges with peers coming from a different culture).

- University professors in India (the project was a great opportunity to test how the learning aspects of their intervention would be utilized by foreign trainees coming from unfamiliar cultural settings).

Project process

The project process had four stages:

1. Definition

This stage involved first establishing the overall feasibility of the educational project in India through an evaluation of possible contact points and generation of potentially suitable activity or case-study scenarios for the participants. The project dedicated three months to decide if India would be a viable and worthwhile destination for such a tour and, if found to be a non-destination, for an alternate destination to be identified. The four learning outcomes, and accompanying measuring processes, were used as a baseline for evaluation: *learning* and how to measure it; *case studies* and how to evaluate their worth for the students; individual corporate visits with defining parameters, contact processes, tour logistics and ways to quantify and measure their effectiveness and suitability; and finally, how to measure the success of the project.

Seven specific dimensions formed a KPI dashboard to profile the success of the project, utilized at three pre-defined checkpoints spanning the duration of the entire project:

- budget;

- timing;

- scope;

- quality;

- customer satisfaction;

- project team satisfaction;

- personal and professional development.

Budget and timing were strictly monitored as there was practically no room for straying beyond what was allocated. The relative weightings of the above dimensions were almost equal in importance, and not defined with mathematical precision.

A preliminary stakeholder analysis was very useful at this definition stage and it included four questions, the answers to which were used to support planning:

a Who are the stakeholders?

b What do they want?

c How can they impact or impede success?

d How can they be satisfied? How do they measure success?

2. Planning stage

This stage involved four sub-phases:

a Utilizing the Work Breakdown Structure (WBS) to break the project into smaller, clearly outlined segments to generate clear tasks with explicit who-does-what sections.

b Scheduling or estimating individual task durations and defining the links between tasks using the Critical Path Method to produce a tentative schedule that suited the overall timeline projections of the whole project.

c Defining resource requirements and resource availability. Since this was an international project, this required consideration of many cultural factors of interaction and communication. Clear knowledge of holidays in different locations and logistics constraints was also imperative.

d Establishing the cost baseline or task budget and fitting this to the project expenditure plan, which was given by the training institute and the leadership programme director.

e Milestone mapping was conducted. The project being a multicultural project, milestones had to be clearly marked, communicated to all the stakeholders and repeatedly cross-checked to ensure understanding and commitment. The milestone meetings generated high value for every member as they were opportunities to bounce ideas, apprehensions and insights off the other members.

3. Execution stage

The importance of proper preparation and the rich milestone meetings were constantly appreciated and there were no significant disruptions or challenges in the execution stage.

4. Closing stage

This involved checking if all monetary obligations had been met and all planned events had been checked by the project team as it concluded. Written feedback in the form of anonymous web-based feedback was collected from the participants while oral and direct feedback from the other stakeholders was asked for. Everybody gave feedback, which was extremely important as all the stakeholders except the leadership trainees would participate in the next tour programme and their concerns about improvements had to be considered with suggestions implemented effectively. The formal ending of the project had to be timed to happen before the graduation of the leadership course trainees, as this was a requirement from the institute.

Key challenges

Being cross-cultural and international, the project was complex and four main constraints affecting success were identified:

1. Time constraints on participants

It was vital for each stakeholder to plan time effectively, both in terms of managing their own and giving sufficient allocation of time to their local educational project whilst balancing significant responsibilities at home in the background, which were always pressing. Additionally, building in contingencies to cope with the unexpected – airline strike at short notice, absences of critical people in the local project – proved to be important in planning.

2. Personnel contingency planning

The total duration of the project was one year and the risk that the programme participants might change jobs or otherwise become unavailable was a significant one. Accordingly, substitution or replacement processes (personnel contingency) had to be considered and planned for seriously. In reality, change of personnel happened only a few times and sufficient handover or briefing time for the new person was achieved without damage to any individual or the overall project.

3. Cultural issues

A number of stakeholders needed to acquire cultural skills to manage an international project of this nature and magnitude. Most noticeably, some key stakeholders tended to assume that communication and interaction patterns/ working relationships with people from other contexts and cultures would be exactly the same as in their own cultures. Misunderstandings arose from a lack of understanding of individual contexts, and the relative priorities of topics attached to those contexts.

In the early phases of the project, diverse expectations of hierarchy produced a degree of misunderstanding and conflict during the methodology challenges carried out by Indian academic staff, a process designed as three-pronged. First, staff asked the participants to articulate clearly and precisely what they had learned; second, they played devil's advocate by pointing out theoretical assumptions in their modelling of answers and probed the issues; and third, they prepped junior students to debate core issues with the participants so that the participants needed to justify their choice of methodology and approaches and also why they rejected other approaches. Students from cultures with relatively high power distance were not used to having academic staff and fellow students (some much younger and more junior in hierarchy) challenge their findings or opinions, for example by asking, 'You have used this approach to formulate your opinion, why did you not use the another approach that some writers advocate and on what grounds are you saying that your omission of the other approaches is valid?' It took some time but eventually this highly interactive debating atmosphere became accepted and valued. That was interesting to observe.

4. Financial constraints

Project cost variations due to economic or geopolitical factors had to be considered in advance. For example, rising salary costs could erode project margins; terrorist attacks – real or threatened – could necessitate a location change of project activity. These issues were discussed by management steering the project. Fortunately, little margin erosion actually materialized but it was an important consideration during planning.

Project results

The project delivered on a number of KPI parameters including:

- number of corporate visits arranged;
- quality of corporate visits measured by interest generated and insights gained;
- actual networking generated by the participants;
- punctuality of every event and travel logistics;
- staying within the budget.

The impact on the learning of the leadership programme participants was measured using self-analysis, with everyone asked to fill in anonymous online feedback directly after completion and then having a face-to-face review session three months after the tour completion. The delegates all considered the various learning impacts to be valuable for themselves.

Stakeholder expectation management was rather challenging as some stakeholders' expectations were slightly unrealistic. However, this slight expectation–result mismatch, mostly at the beginning stages, was not a critical issue as people quickly learned to re-evaluate their perspectives and the same stakeholders eagerly participated in a repeat project two years later.

Lessons learned

1 *Drafting of a one-page formal project charter document* proved to be a very good idea. It was created at the planning or defining stage and pasted onto the project folder used by the project manager, his boss and other team members. It served to remind everyone what the original content, objectives and budget of the project were and eliminated confusion about the intended benefits, the source of funding and project sponsors. This helped to ensure that the answer to the question, 'Are we doing what we are supposed to do?' was never forgotten.

2 *Exchanging of feelings* was useful in maintaining morale, surfacing issues and offering opportunities for innovation. Participants regularly discussed the *feel* of how things were between the main stakeholders at the designated milestone checkpoints (mostly between the project manager and his boss, the training director in this case). Being able to freely voice one's feelings – just feelings, like intuition, which cannot be substantiated by facts – created an openness to learn and share from mistakes and bring insights from other projects. These were mostly informal discussions over lunch or coffee. But I also used a more formal practice of encouraging everyone to contribute weekly insights related to the project (see Appendix 3). These observations could also be tangentially related to the project, for example something related to the organization, their experience of cultural differences or even how people reacted and related to the changing and challenging weather of the day. It was an opportunity to identify key issues/concerns, which then could be addressed later with rational arguments or with a plan of action. We did not keep written records of these discussions as that would have been too much work and could perhaps have destroyed the process.

3 *Reaffirming or promising commitment to do individual tasks* by clearly voicing, 'So let me repeat what I have promised to do' or 'Let me repeat what I'll be expecting from you by...' proved very useful. It turned out unexpectedly to create a relaxed and fun-filled atmosphere, as well as clarifying the pragmatics of what would happen; and working with humour was in fact much more effective. The fun aspect came as we did this reaffirming with humour – people joking with each other that they would not fulfil their promises. In the end, everyone got used to this and controlling became fun.

Summary

This project was a fascinating and thoroughly enjoyable cooperation. The stakeholders were all satisfied with the outcomes and expressed so clearly. If I had to redo this project, I'd spend some more effort on fidelity of communication, ensuring no breakdown in communications and trust, especially when management restructuring has created a lot of stress for project funders and the training programme delegates. Sudden policy changes in organizations, irrespective of how well individuals deliver results, impact significantly on motivation and people's ability to learn new things. So keeping things clear, and everyone on track in an uncertain context, whilst managing to be comfortable with a lack of clarity, is really the art of running such projects.

Part 2: Interview

The following is the summary of a series of telephone conversations between Bob and Rana, which ranged across the specifics of this project and project management and international leadership in general.

Q: So how did the leaders cope with learning in a new context such as India? What do you observe?

A: One of the more interesting observations was an attitude among senior leaders of 'I know. We don't need to be told. I am an expert.' There certainly seemed to be a general reluctance to admit weakness, even in a learning environment, as there were some feelings that it was competitive. So there was very little feedback from those participating, and feedback was more about strategic or hard topics than human interaction or soft factors. It's funny, but people didn't say what they had learned. They would just say it was interesting. I think this is partly role driven because outside of the programme, this attitude largely disappeared – people were very nice and open.

Q: Was this ever a real problem, if you know what I mean?

A: Yes, in one case, this produced a real issue. I had briefed people around gift giving, and the importance in India of making it meaningful, not just handing over corporate literature and pens, as this was likely to be seen as insulting in some way. I was very explicit on this and said it twice in long briefings. But one guy insisted on doing it his way – with pens and literature, some sort of anti-bribery statement. And it upset one participating president of a huge company, which meant he lost face in front of subordinates, so much so that in fact this client refused to participate in the programme anymore, so quite an expensive situation. I did debrief with the group afterwards, but getting people to really and truly see things from another's perspective was and is very, very difficult. Understanding the need to be open is easy; doing it is a very complex thing for human beings. In fact, it wasn't the only incident. I had one guy take pictures with a mobile phone in a factory despite being told explicitly not to do it. He did it and he had to return home when it was noticed. It was really messy, that one. It was actually escalated to a government minister and company board member.

Q: But these guys are very smart people?

A: Absolutely. Strategic planning is excellent; numbers and Excel sheets are not an issue. But ask them to go outside their comfort zone, on the people side, that was the weakest point – people skills. We talked about it but only one or two were really actually good at this; some progressed but for most it is simply deeply challenging.

Q: Coming back to your summary of the project, you did mention effective and meaningful communication as a lessons learned for you as project manager. You said you would try to ensure 'fidelity'. What did you mean by this?

A: Yes, I guess, depending on a participant's people skills, I would be much more of a control freak around key information, and when I thought their emotions or values might cloud a decision. I used to think people were CEOs so you can't baby feed them. But you can't assume people will get what you say or act on what you say, unless you get basic and very explicit.

Q: Can you give me an example?

A: Yes, even with e-mails I got into the habit of affirming and reaffirming tasks. 'I am going to do it this afternoon after 15.00. I'll be waiting for your e-mail at the latest by 14.30 before I do this. Is that ok?' I started using this after the project too – the trainees also still use it, by the way. Sometimes I have to find a way to explain a little bit what I am doing, that I am this kind of person, that's why I am saying this, I'm meticulous, I am not saying you are stupid. And this works and makes sure that the critical things get done.

Q: But what about trust? This seems to reduce trust in some way?

A: It's interesting. Trust, which is implicit, in Finland is very strong as a concept, like an oral promise or a gentleman's word. But things have been changing in the last 20 years – the meaning and practice of trust building. And you know, in India, trust is very much like this too; we don't need to write it down. We will both remember the promise; this is based on oral tradition over millennia. But at the end of the day, it's about setting clear expectations. Can you and I, and everyone, perform as expected? Do we both understand what is feasible and worthwhile? Will everyone perform as expected? These expectations have to be articulated.

Q: Why 'realistic'?

A: I think it's important not to just focus on having clear and defined goals, which we all explicitly agree. We need to set the right goals. I see a lot of younger guys, very ambitious, in these international projects; they come in and overperform. They seem to hit all the targets but they create a mess, and ruffle so many feathers, create so much disturbance in the organization, that everything fails in the end when they walk away after the project. I remember one of the greatest managers I ever saw was this gentle 70-year-old guy, a fantastic people operator, and his job was always to come in after projects, after these smart young operators, and smooth things out, get people back on board. So all it's complex. But people skills at the end of the day are critical.

Part 3: Commentary

Here are some reflections on Rana's case and interview.

As I stated in the introduction, I think this case offers interesting insights across a number of levels, not least in the use of such an international project for the development of the international leadership skills much needed by global corporates and internationalizing SMEs. However, I see a number of core learnings emerging from this case around a set of generic international project issues.

The first issue for me is planning. Lack of experience often forces those planning international projects to plan unrealistically, to use timeframes for simple domestic projects to plan complex and highly uncertain international ones. Political forces also conspire to drive over-optimistic planning. For example, tighter scheduling with lower associated cost often gets the project through the approval phase. Three of Rana's key challenges explicitly attempted to plan for the unknown – stakeholders were openly asked to be realistic in planning their own availability, to put in place succession plans in case they had to move, and to consider broad socio-economic and political risks to the numbers in the project business case. That sounds smart from my point of view, yet it is rare. Many of the international projects I meet are compromised even before they get started due to unrealistic time, resource and budget planning.

Second, Rana explicitly addresses the role of assumption. We all know that assumptions are dangerous but we still make them, possibly in the hope that they are true and that life just gets simpler as a result. But when working in international contexts, with unfamiliar people, technologies and environmental forces, we need to beware of false assumptions which can waste time, generate conflict or lead to costly failure. Communicatively, those leading projects cannot fully avoid assumptions. But what they can do is start surfacing them – 'I'm assuming that... am I right?' – or challenging – 'Are we assuming too much if we say that...' Effective international project communicators work explicitly with the language of assumption. Making things visible means things get discussed and not, well, assumed.

Rana also touches on the human tendency to hide behind expertise. This is a common phenomenon between professionals but is highly corrosive to open and honest conversation, reduces the possibility of effective feedback and limits innovation in projects as people fear making mistakes. Those leading projects need to discuss the meaning of expertise in their teams, clarify the meaning, opportunities and boundaries of failure, and agree to be brave with each other when they don't know something.

Finally, there are strong messages around communication here. Miscommunication is by far more the norm than we care to admit, often because we have to imagine the reasoning behind others' words. What does this mean? It means, say what you want to say very explicitly – be clear with the what. But also explain the why, why you are saying it the way you are, in order to ensure mutual understanding and mutual goals. It's a simple adaptation but one likely to drive success when communicating internationally.

Bob Dignen

Part 4: Reflecting on international project management

Take time to reflect on the following questions to help you reach further insights and take practical actions to improve your own project management practice.

1 What could be the advantages and disadvantages of using similar projects to those described by Rana to develop future international leaders?

2 How useful are past experience and expertise for leaders when coping with challenging new contexts and learning processes like this?

3 How can humour be used a constructive leadership tool when leading projects?

Part 5: Putting it into practice

There are a number of very valid insights and ideas for project management present in this case which the reader can learn from and adopt, customizing for their own projects. Take a few minutes to note down your main learnings from this case, and note down some actions for yourself.

Personal insights, learnings and actions

A large global regulatory-driven programme in a large insurance company

06

PETER WOLLMANN

Profile

Peter Wollmann has been the responsible manager of a complex global programme at Zurich Insurance Company since 2013, located at its headquarters. Additionally, he is in charge of strategic change management at the German business unit and additional headquarters projects.

Prior to this, from 2005 he worked within Zurich as the German head of project portfolio management and strategic business development, having worked as head of strategic planning and controlling in Zurich's German business unit from since 1985. Pre-Zurich, Peter built up and later took the lead as senior vice president of strategy in the department of strategy, planning and controlling at Deutscher Herold, later the Insurance Group of Deutsche Bank. This also included the development and implementation of project and project portfolio management in the insurance group, and leading diverse large change programmes.

Peter is author and publisher of many articles and books on strategy, project and project portfolio management

Foreword

This case describes a global programme in one of the world's top five global insurance companies. The programme is both a strategic and an operative transformation; it develops the philosophy of a function, processes, methods, tools and technical infrastructure, and introduces a new way of working with automation, requiring the development of people across the whole involved cross-functional community. The project scope is very broad, vertically and horizontally. Vertically, it is intended to significantly change the role and way of working of an entire critical function of an insurer worldwide, in a standardized and professional way in the enterprise context. Horizontally, the implementation is intended to be done globally, which means in all regions and business units.

A key consequence of this broad scope is that the project's global ambition runs up against diverse regional and local political, cultural and technical environments, which means that an intelligent blend of push based on conviction and global standards, and pull based on recognition of local exceptions/additions negotiated in a joint timeline for finalization and later completion has to be found. Additionally – as in all large enterprises – the programme competes, in general, for rare resources (budgets, capabilities and capacity) and so has to be visible and always aligned with key enterprise strategic and operative ambitions on all levels.

One key insight – which can be safely generalized following cross-company conversations with peers – is that there is *never* enough knowledge or even information or data at the headquarters to schedule a programme like this in the so-called waterfall way. On the contrary, there will be new insights, new facts and issues, and many surprises to be discovered on a regular basis over the full lifecycle of the programme in relation to understanding of roles and responsibilities, methods and tools, technology, and corporate politics.

If you as a reader are reflecting on the case, either as an academic or at a practitioner level, you might ask and answer three key questions at this stage:

1 What are the challenges of running a project without all the knowledge at the beginning needed to plan effectively?

2 What types of resource constraints can impact on the management of large international projects? How can these constraints be handled?

3 How useful is it for projects of this type to have 'quick wins' to build reputation and visibility? What are the problems with aiming for quick wins?

PART 1: CASE STUDY

A global actuarial programme to fix regulatory requirements and bring the actuarial function to the next level

Introduction

This case describes a global programme which is both strategic and mandatory from a regulatory point of view, positioned within ongoing global measures to stabilize the financial industry by, for example, optimization of accounting standards (IFRS), of equity requirements (Basel II, Solvency II) and of control systems (SOX). These initiatives were intensified after recent finance crises, with regulators more focused on surveillance of finance industry enterprises.

In this context, a realistic and sustainable statement relating to the so-called claims reserves in the quarterly and annual balance sheet has overwhelming importance as it is a key indicator – one of the top three – of declared profit. For non-actuaries or insurance specialists, the quarterly P&L (Profit and Loss calculation) and the balance sheet should contain all relevant information with impact on the short- but also mid- and long-term financial situation of the enterprise. The largest loss position in a general insurance company is claims. Not all claims will be finally fixed, that means paid, by the deadline of the quarter end. Some reported and therefore known claims will be still open, which means they are work in progress. Some claims are known to customers but have not been reported so far, and some claims are not transparent either to the customer or to the insurer. The calculation of these claims, which have to be reflected in the quarterly P&L and balance sheet, is difficult, but of immense importance. Non-sustainable reserving for future claims will sooner or later affect the profit of an insurer tremendously.

Reserving is run by reserving actuaries who are in intensive discussion with related functions like claims, underwriting, pricing, finance etc. The statement of the reserves is always a joint effort but it is, ultimately, under the responsibility of the actuarial function.

Zurich decided to address issues arising from past practices to fulfil regulatory requirements and to respond appropriately to fast-developing new equity and accounting standards, but also to gain competitive advantage by developing a high-performing internal actuarial function to an industry-leading position.

Programme overview

This programme is conceived to develop global actuarial guidelines for every possible situation, creating a standardized and sufficiently automated reserving process incorporating standard methods and tools with their usage guidance, and an efficient and high-quality data supply in a standardized technical infrastructure with appropriate data management tools.

The developed concepts, contents, processes etc have to be regionally and locally piloted/tested, optimized and finally implemented in four regions and the 32 business units of the enterprise in a mostly comparable way. Additionally, the actuarial community has to be developed to make the best use of all of this, integrating it into day-to-day business – also with the other related functions. At the end of the day, the actuary has to refocus their role away from the historical one of data hunter and data manager/manipulator to one of process, tool and database engineer, and analytics consultant to top management.

In summary, the specific goals of the programme cover six major areas of organizational development: professional standards content; working processes with applied methods and tools in an adequate structure with clear roles and responsibilities; necessary IT technical infrastructure; data management to secure supply and quality; personal development including new role adoption; and organizational knowledge management and cross-functional cooperation.

Measures of success during this organizational transformation are both qualitative and quantitative:

- Quantitative metrics for the programme management referring to programme delivery completeness, in time, to quality, on budget etc.

- Quantitative metrics for the programme outcome referring to the productivity of the reserving process, its costs and average time needed, and also decreased number of mistakes, rework requirements etc.

- Qualitative factors based for example on outcomes of peer reviews on reserving quality, standards penetration of the organization, use of the developed methods and tools but also reputation of the actuarial function within the whole organization.

- Qualitative factors also based on feedback from top management at all levels.

The key stakeholders of the programme are as follows, situated in the headquarters as well as the regions and countries of the global enterprise:

- Global chief financial officer (CFO), chief executive officer (CEO) of the general insurance segment (GI), global chief operations and technology officer (COTO), chief operating officer (COO) GI, CFO GI, global chief claims officer (CCO), global chief underwriting officer (CUO).

- Regional CEOs, COOs, CFOs, CCOs, CUOs.

- Local CEOs, COOs, CFOs, CCOs, CUWs.

- Group actuarial, regional and local chief actuaries and their actuarial teams (the whole reserving actuarial community).

- Diverse global, regional and local business intelligence (BI) and IT teams.

- Leaders of global and local programmes with interfaces.

- Group communication.

- Regulators in diverse countries.

- Group investor relations.

- HR/HR development.

Programme proceeding

The programme follows the Zurich Project/Programme Management Framework, which is a PMI-derived framework that has been tailored to Zurich requirements. It has the classical phases such as initiation, conceptualization, analysis and design, development, testing, implementation, finalization, post implementation (transfer to business as usual) etc. In the case of the programme, agile approaches integrate in the form of iterative steps which create loops in the standard (waterfall) approach/phases.

1. Concept development in the central team

a The key concepts were/are being developed by the central programme team, involving some regional/local representatives. The results (including standard reserving guidelines, standard reserving processes, standard professional reserving methods and tools, standard regional/local target operating models and organizations for reserving etc) were/are piloted in selected business units in the regions to gain feedback from them to effectively test and calibrate the concepts.

b The technical infrastructural and data management concepts were/are developed by Zurich BI and IT as blueprints to be tested in real business unit environments.

2. Concept piloting and testing in real local environments

a The selected business units ran a comprehensive pilot or test in an environment under absolutely real preconditions. The normal and expected outcomes are issues which have to be categorized in terms of either a generic or more local nature. Another outcome is a recommendation for general implementation worldwide.

b Local inventory had to be calculated to clarify local preconditions for the standard technical infrastructure on which the diverse actuarial tools should run. This process was started with selected business units.

c In the same business units, a local inventory had/has to be achieved to clarify the options to implement data management solutions which could ensure data supply and quality.

3. Feedback from piloting and testing provided to central team

a The selected business units came back to the central team with their findings. Findings might reflect general areas of improvement for the global blueprints (standard reserving guidelines, standard reserving processes, standard professional reserving methods and tools, standard target operating models and organizations for reserving etc) or formulate requests for special local adaptions of the global blueprints. Additionally, important requirements for the local implementation were to be identified, with special obstacles to be regarded.

b Additionally. the options for implementing/integrating the necessary technical infrastructure for the functional tools (eg for enterprise solutions instead of local solutions) and for databases are developed (reflecting which local capabilities and capacities for implementation have to be confirmed in advance). This outcome always has two parts: one part with input and recommendations for the general global roll-out and one individual part concerning how to run the roll-out in the concrete business unit.

c Finally, the analysis of data availability and quality, which includes the status of data extraction from feeder systems and the underlying data catalogue and data model, had to be performed delivering insights and proceedings for development or calibration of the intended global roll-out but also recommending how to run the roll-out in the concrete business unit in detail.

4. Integration of feedback from piloting and integration into a global blueprint

Global blueprints were modified and roll-out plans scheduled in detail. Resources, timelines etc were decided together with the regions and the local business units. It is important that the proceeding ensures that diversity in the parallel local implementations is always secured (so that the regions and the different types of business units are represented to the necessary extent). It is possible that the loop of central blueprint – outcome from piloting/implementation experience – feedback to central team – modification of blueprint etc is continuously repeated as there are always new insights which influence the central blueprint.

5. Global rollout

Parallel implementation according to a roll-out plan to take place with strong feedback and lessons learned components conducted on a regular basis.

Programme management

Programme management is based around an eight-workstream structure, using pragmatic communication, controlling and tracking processes.

a There are three so-called vertical workstreams (actuarial standards, actuarial reserving process with its methods and tools, and actuarial data improvement) with the task of developing the necessary global blueprints. They are called vertical because they develop for their topic standardized global concepts and blueprints with the aim of implementing them for the topic vertically, meaning in all regions. Additionally, there are four horizontal workstreams (for each of the four involved regions) with the task of blueprint piloting/testing, feedback and final implementation. They are called horizontal as they aim to implement the set of global concepts and blueprints after the described feedback loops across functions in the region. There is also one independent communication workstream.

b All eight workstreams have a dedicated team with defined roles and responsibilities for the tasks from the work breakdown structure. Furthermore, there is a detailed delivery plan in place that is documented and summarized in the overall programme plan.

c There are bi-weekly coordination meetings of the vertical workstreams and bi-weekly confcalls/meetings with each of the regional workstreams. A flexible standard agenda is in place with a status evaluation as a focus (RAG-status, which means red-amber-green evaluation, with focus on actions to get or stay green, risk assessment, realized and upcoming deliverables etc). The meetings results are always documented. The philosophy is that these overarching meetings are kept at a management level, whereas operative details are dealt with in the workstream team meetings.

d There are bi-weekly meetings of the project managers with the programme sponsor. Additionally, the programme sponsor participates in vertical workstream coordination and in horizontal workstream update calls on a regular basis. The meetings with the sponsor are, on the one hand, decision and problem-solving oriented. On the other hand, they enable background information provision which supports the management of political issues surrounding the project.

e There are global and local events to calibrate the direction, drive necessary developments and evaluate status and latest outcomes, eg an annual programme workshop and regular regional-level meetings. These meetings always include lessons learned sessions – but also personal development such as tool training, team building and cooperation skills development etc.

f Additionally, there are regular meetings with other global or local programmes and projects with important interfaces.

g The programme manager meets key execs on both an official and an unofficial basis regularly to update, communicate status, prepare decisions etc.

h Those in the enterprise who are responsible communicate programme results to regulators on a regular basis and take their feedback (to be considered in the programme).

i Last but not least, there is a cooperation platform for all programme team members and stakeholders in place with all key documents, plans and results available.

Execution status

The programme is long term in ambition, scheduled in principle for about five to six years, which are certainly required for such a fundamental transformation with such a large data management component.

The programme was started in 2013 and is now mostly finished, with the global blueprints and associated piloting/testing completed, so that the main focus of this year and the next few years is on completion of the roll-out.

Key challenges

It is evident that this large global programme is highly complex.

1. Inherent topic complexity and dynamic

The main topic itself is very challenging. Actuarial reserving is a highly sophisticated area of insurance which needs a rare technical expertise based on a global overview of the insurance industry and its major developments relating to products and associated claims development globally, with diverse customer behaviours in different legal environments. There is intense and fast-developing professional discussion on the topic worldwide, driven partly by a fast-moving regulatory environment, so new perspectives are being created constantly and have to be absorbed in real time.

2. Data management associated challenges

Data management in global companies, which is often not totally optimized, is challenging to standardize in change processes. Data supply mostly comes from 'feeder systems' which are very different across the world. Standardization requires the definition of a joint global data catalogue (with definitions having to be understood in all local languages and mapped to local definitions and local data items in respective feeder systems), a joint data model, and the setting up of global data management tools which can work in diverse local environments in a comparable way. A great deal of expertise and knowledge about these diverse local environments is needed, and the time taken to collect and coordinate this knowledge and information is normally significantly underestimated: it can take much longer than expected. Additionally, it is normal that during piloting and final implementation a bundle of pure surprises will arise, and this needs to be factored into the subsequent blueprint and programme plan.

3. High number of stakeholders and interfaces

A global programme that affects all regions and all business units, and other additional functions and programmes/projects, creates a significant complexity on a number of levels. On a strategic level, it is about alignment with enterprise directions, ambitions, initiatives and senior management support etc. On an operational level, it is about integration in terms of planning processes, budgets, priority lists, processes and availability of human resources. If one calculates only with 10 key stakeholders at a headquarters level, five key stakeholders on a regional level, eight on a local level, and 10 from related projects with interfaces, the programme has to handle over 250 stakeholders globally and locally, with different cultural backgrounds and different cultures (see next topic).

4. Cultural constraints

The cultural differences between headquarters, regional management and local business units are significant in a large global enterprise. Additionally, the differences between continents, countries and regions within countries are remark-able. There is significant diversity across core working areas from communication styles (very direct vs very indirect), to the understanding of hierarchy (formal and implicitly very deeply structured vs informal and flat), to approaches to tasks (neutral, result and deadline oriented vs personal and relationship oriented) etc. A large global programme/project has to manage diverse approaches and build bridges between the cultures.

5. Resource constraints

Large global enterprises tend to have significant competition for senior management commitment, priority, budget and human resources. Problematically, commitment is rarely sustainable for a longer period, as an enterprise constantly has to cope with new environmental influences, events etc. This creates pressure for fast results, short payback periods and quick wins. In turn, this prevents the necessary intensive planning phases at the beginning of a global programme/ project, which naturally reduces productive progress during the early lifecycle of a project. One of the most important human constraints/success factors is the programme sponsor. His ability to trust in the programme managers and their team, and to build a management style based on trust is vital for maintaining commitment even when the programme is challenged by the inevitable bad times and failures that always arise.

Project results so far

The project has realized a large number of deliverables (selection below):

- new actuarial standard guidelines globally implemented and already updated once;

- standard reserving process globally implemented;

- most key actuarial standard tools significantly updated and globally implemented;

- other key actuarial standard tools developed to a first blueprint draft to be piloted shortly;

- large data improvement pilot successfully realized in one business unit;

- significant tactical data fixes in implementation;

- technical infrastructure for key actuarial tools in development and partly implemented;

- programme very well-known and visible over the whole enterprise;

- regulator signals that they are content with the development.

Lessons learned

1 **Formal processes need to balance with informal ones.** There are a lot of helpful frameworks, methods, tools, templates etc for large programmes and projects. However, it is vital to realize that each programme and project is at least partly unique and needs in part an individual solution. As already mentioned in the Introduction to the book, the high levels of detailing, structuring and formalizing associated with classical project and programme management will be viewed differently by people involved, and will have a limited problem-solving impact. Therefore, totally trusting in formal mechanisms is not possible. A programme manager also has to be able to diagnose and handle less formal aspects of the organizational environment, including political factors, informal and unstated beliefs etc.

2 **There is a need to allow enough time for the initial phases of a large global programme.** Time is necessary to develop a full needs analysis, information collection process and establishment of necessary networks. Normally there is high pressure at the beginning to start immediately and work on tangible deliverables. It is advisable to start with on-boarding an initial core team with a critical mass, to develop this core team as a team, to run with the core team a broad preparation phase which includes collecting information and knowledge already available, to start discussion on possible programme/project approaches, to extend the core team step by step to include representatives of all affected parts of the enterprise, and to involve the sponsor on a regular basis to calibrate the programme according to his ambitions, as these ambitions fundamentally drive the programme.

3 **It is crucial to build up sustainable relationships globally and locally.** The performance of a diverse, well-functioning team in an overall environment based on the right level of trust can be high. But this will only develop if enough time is invested in building trusting relationships, in developing a team, in spending time on joint events etc. This so-called soft factor should be a high priority and needs be handled expertly. Within this, it is important for headquarters people to travel to the local business units and to take some time to fully understand these contexts. Overall, the degree of personal interaction and discussion, the effort for communication and alignment in the programme described, were significantly higher than was previously assumed – as was the level of local diversity.

4 **It is necessary that the programme manager has 'political intelligence'; that the person knows the organization, has strong leadership capabilities and a broad experience, and that they are 'culturally and situationally sensitive'.**

In an increasingly complex world that cannot be 'solved' just with formal means and automated solutions, selection of effective leaders is crucial for programme success. Unfortunately, this is an underestimated dimension, and in global companies there is at least 10 times more discussion on budget details than on the selection of the right people for a crucial project, and so more value is potentially destroyed by poor selection than by going over budget. However, this a broader systemic issue of large enterprises, which is not directly under the control of the programme or project.

Part 2: Interview

The following is the summary of a series of personal conversations between Bob and Peter, which ranged across the specifics of this programme and programme management, and international leadership in general.

Q: **Which are the success factors for a global programme like yours, Peter?**

A: Oh, my programme is no exception to what you can read everywhere in the literature; there are two categories, one with the hard and one with the soft facts. The hard facts criteria, for example, ask the programme manager to apply diverse methods, tools and proceedings (which is easy), but also to prepare carefully a programme with an intensive conceptualization and initiation phase and an adequate team. This is very often not fully possible due to several enterprise constraints, and the arising issues have to be fixed in a creative way, which normally leads to the soft facts category. Here we have, for example, a powerful, committed and trustworthy sponsor, adequate change management integrated in the programme plan, and good and respectful interaction with stakeholders. It's nothing new, often the same, but always different in parts in individual situations.

Q: **How important is the selection and the learning curve of a global programme manager?**

A: I'm not an HR expert but I would stress firstly that there is a special type of personality that fits for project and programme management. If you need too much certainty, structure, guidance, then you had better not apply for a leadership role. You may be perfect as a subject matter expert giving professional input.

Q: So what is the profile for an international project manager?

A: If you like uncertainty, maybe because you see the design options and the opportunities in it, if you like and understand politics in large organizations and can cope with the long persuasion processes of upper management and experts, if you see it as a partly sporting challenge, then you are at the right place in my perception. Then you should start getting experiences, be always open to understanding that there will be new situations that ask for things you have not learned so far. You have to stay flexible and take over more and more responsibility, and to check to which degree you can cope with stress and also failure. And you have to love other cultures with other rules as a challenging but enriching experience.

Q: **Can I ask you about the classical global–local issue, and how global ambition runs up against diverse local contexts in international projects? Can these opposing needs ever be reconciled or is there always a loser, and the loser is probably local, at least from a local perspective?**

A: I think that the picture of winners and losers doesn't work in this context. If you have a global blueprint that doesn't fit local, and you push it through, then it will not work – and then you have two losers. It is very normal in a diverse world that standardized blueprints very often do not work locally without adaptions. If you can work to create a cooperative situation between global and local to jointly create the right interpretation of the standardized blueprint in the local environment, you produce two winners. The winner–loser schema never applies.

Q: **You talk about the problems of planning and the fact that significant 'surprises' are inevitable. Two questions: is this sufficiently recognized among the PM community, particularly those who advocate classical IPMA or PMI approaches? With your experience, can you anticipate which surprises might surprise you?**

A: Yes, the professional PM community does reflect this. This is, besides the need for more speed in projects, one of the reasons to proceed in projects in an agile way. Normally the key problem in companies is that classical financial planning, and especially budgeting, requires certainties which can often not be delivered by projects. In the described programme, surprises were identified and anticipated, and changes in the plans were communicated to make them official.

Q: Another planning question. The pressure for quick wins often competes with proper planning. Should those leading projects refuse to deliver quick wins? What is your advice?

A: It depends on the project character. If you build up a large plant in another country, you do not need quick wins. In large transformations, you normally have to offer something, which is, by the way, not bad, as you get early proof points if your concept works. Additionally, quick wins convince your stakeholders, so it makes sense to think of striving for some. How much is possible will depend on the project.

Q: If I turn to communication, one thing you refer to is 'building bridges between the cultures'. In terms of advice for those starting on such programmes, what practical tips do you have for this?

A: I would propose to have an intensive inventory of the relevant cultures to be regarded, which might be built up by a mixture of personal visits, which builds up trust, and frequent interaction and communication in calls and videoconferences. If you are sensitive to culture, you will easily get to a point of understanding.

Q: With internal communication in big projects, with sponsors, in terms of managing a sponsor, what do you see as the top three challenges, and what are the solutions to these challenges?

A: I think it is difficult to answer this question in general, as the three challenges are always connected to the character of the organization and the personality of the sponsor. This question needs its own book.

Q: OK, but more generally, you mention 'political intelligence' as a key leadership quality. What is that?

A: You should understand that each organization has its official and unofficial (hidden) rules. And you should be able to accept that in large organizations with a lot of important players there are different perceptions and interests that have to be reconciled, and that there is no absolute (theoretically) right answer, but an answer which fits best. Technocrats often believe in one truth, which is not very helpful.

Q: If there are no right answers, it might mean that some things may not be totally manageable. And this fits into your final comments, that the 'broader systemic issue of large enterprises... is... not directly under the control of the programme or project'. Does this mean large projects, to some extent, are not wholly manageable?

A: Yes, you also need a bit of luck, which means you need a kind of constellation in which the project can be successful.

Part 3: Commentary

Here are some reflections on Peter's case and interview.

Peter's general approach is striking for me in a number of ways. Firstly, he shows high sensitivity to the organizational contexts of projects, and suggests that it is vital for those leading large projects to understand the constraints and opportunities presented by the 'system' of their own organization, a kind of animal with its own logic driven by current technologies, management KPIs, political agendas and diverse beliefs of senior management, which may not be aligned. I share this perspective of organizations and see, although I train people for a living, the limits of developing personal competence in the face of unfavourable systemic circumstances.

Peter also stresses the importance of cultural mapping, creating an 'inventory' as he puts it. This reminds me very much of the work of Martha Maznevsky at IMD, who has researched diverse international teamwork, and recommends a process of Mapping, Bridging and Integrating, where the last stage is around exploiting synergies offered by diverse perspectives. Finally, and where Peter and I also agree, is the need to remain open, to avoid the tips and tricks approach to management of complex environments, with the realization that while we need vision and a sense of purpose, our conviction needs to be moderated with a degree of doubt and humility. Surprises will happen, good ideas will occur, new elements with pop up – so those operating in these international contexts need to stay agile and in learning mode at all times.

Bob Dignen

Part 4: Reflecting on international project management

Take time to reflect on the following questions to help you reach further insights and take practical actions to improve your own project management practice.

1 What is your own approach to planning? Is your general preference to structure and set deadlines? How far do you like to stay open and agile? What are the expectations of those around you? What approach will work best in your projects?

2 In which ways is 'data management' a part of your own project challenge? What can you do to handle this challenge?

3 How far might luck play a part in your projects? How can you optimize your chances of being lucky?

Part 5: Put it into practice

There are a number of very valid insights and ideas for project management present in this case which the reader can learn from and adopt, customizing for their own projects. Take a few minutes to note down your main learnings from this case, and note down some actions for yourself.

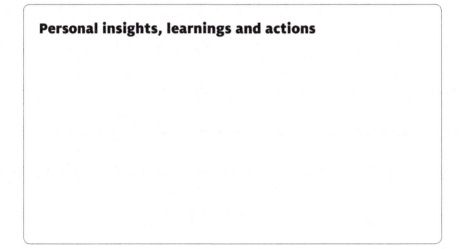

Personal insights, learnings and actions

An iterative evaluation of an online class to increase inclusion of international learners in an online forum

07

DR SHARON LALLA

Profile

Sharon Lalla has managed large- and small-scale projects in both industry and academia for 15 years. In industry, her project management experience led her to understand the importance of leadership, effective communication, and effective teambuilding. After earning a doctorate in education technologies from Pepperdine University, she took a leadership role in administration of education technologies at New Mexico State University (NMSU). At NMSU, she led efforts to transition from WebCT to Blackboard, which included the implementation plan and just-in-time training for faculty across the university system. Her current focus is on improving the quality of online teaching grounded by measurable assessment, instructional design, and pedagogy.

Sharon is also college assistant professor in the education department. Her expertise includes accessibility and universal design for learning in online teaching. Published papers and titles include the following: Practising low-context communication strategies in online course design for international students studying in the US (2015), *9th International e-learning*

Conference Proceedings, Las Palmas Canaria, Spain; Assessing the impact of quality in online courses (2014) *Quality Matters Higher Education News;* Klein, S and Lalla, S. A (2011) Digital ecologies: observations of intercultural interactions in learning management systems, in *Culture, Communication, & Cyberspace: Rethinking technical communication for international online environments,* ed Kirk St. Amant and Filipp Sapienza, Baywood, Amityville, NY; *Values Guiding Hispanics to Enroll and Depart from College: A narrative inquiry* (2007) Pepperdine University, Proquest: UMI 3282289.

Foreword

Sharon's case provides interesting insights for those leading and working in international projects on a number of levels. First, her challenge to manage students working in an online international educational context has many parallels to those leading virtual international project teams, not least in terms of inspiring and building collaboration, and improving critical thinking in diverse group contexts. One of the central preoccupations of Sharon's case also happens to be a major life pre-occupation of Bob Dignen,[1] one of the contributing editors, namely, how to create an inclusive environment in international teams which are often unfairly weighted towards native English language speakers owing to their linguistic advantage over non-native English speakers, when using English as a lingua franca. It is a phenomenon which creates serious inefficiency and relationship strain in the corporate world, and Sharon's case provides concrete proposals on how to handle the issue. Finally, the case examines the community of next-generation international project leaders, smart young graduates who will bring their experiences of successful online collaboration at university to the corporate world, and use this to inform their conduct of projects. It is timely to become aware of these expectations and norms now rather than later.

Before reading on, reflect on some key questions addressed in the case. Then compare your experience and answers to the ideas in the case itself and the final commentary.

1 In what ways might an online collaborative environment be made more inclusive for non-native English speakers? And in parallel, how can designing specifically for non-native English speakers make an online collaborative environment more inclusive for all participants?

2 How does more participant choice over *how* to collaborate within an online environment impact on participants' buy-in and inclusive group practices?

3 In which ways do online learning communities in today's tertiary education institutions mirror the experiences of those working in virtual international project teams?

PART 1: CASE STUDY   An iterative evaluation of an online class to increase inclusion of international learners in an online forum

Introduction

This small-scale project was conducted at New Mexico State University to increase inclusion of international learners in online discussion forums. It was designed to improve instructional and learning processes for international students in a 16-week online course at the University using an iterative process – applying insights gained during the teaching of three iterations of the same online course.

The composition of the students in a given class could include local, in-state, national, and international learners, with international learners consistently identified as the 'minority'. This course was 100 per cent online with no synchronous requirement. As online courses and learning managements systems offer very little to connect learners to each other and to the instructor, the online discussion forum can play an important role in the online environment.

The online discussion forum was typically identified by the term bulletin board, which was basically a threaded group discussion (Wood and Smith, 2001); it is an asynchronous, text-based tool that presents a multitude of opportunities for social engagement, collaboration, and cooperation. In this class, this forum was used to support collaborative and cooperative learning experiences. Collaborative learning is a method of teaching and learning, where instructors create an environment for the communication activities and then learners and sometimes instructors enter into discussions to explore ideas, make meaning for themselves, come to mutual understandings, and solve problems collaboratively (Cecez-Kecmanovic and Webb, 2000). Cooperative learning extends collaboration by involving teamwork (Chickering and Gamson, 1991) on common tasks such as creating group reports and participating in group projects.

For over 15 years this instructor has taught in higher education using the online delivery mode. During that time, she has continuously modified the design of the online discussion to more effectively meet learner needs. Consequently, she felt confident of the success of the online class discussions. Experience had shown that while some learners did not initially like the discussions, they began to really enjoy them by the end of the semester. However, the key to good teaching is continuous modification and adjustment (Bender, 2003). As a result, observations over time identified some common behaviours in a group of learners not considered mainstream students – the international students. In this case study, which spanned three iterations of this course, Chickering and Gamson's (1987) principles of effective teaching and the SWOT analysis, which is more commonly known in the business environment as a lens to determine strengths and weaknesses, were used to guide this evaluation.

The purpose of the evaluation was to examine my own practice and subsequently improve the learning experience for international learners. Data used in the evaluation included one-on-one conversations and feedback through e-mail and discussion boards from international learners, periodic learner satisfaction surveys from all students, and literature reviews.

Project overview

The composite of the class varies each time this course begins. As a result, at the start of each semester, learners are asked to complete a learner profile survey which seeks demographics such as gender, nationality, and physical location. Upon review of the results of the survey, it is determined that there are usually as many learners who are on campus as those who are not on campus, although this is a class that is 100 per cent online. The number of international students in each class ranged from 5 per cent to 25 per cent, which puts them in the minority.

In the class, students learn how to contribute to the text-based online discussions by applying critical thinking strategies, finding evidence to support their ideas, collaborating to form new ideas and perspectives about a particular topic or concept, and working on group projects. Initially, learners are less than favourable about the text-based online forums, but with regular feedback and accountability, they begin to enjoy the learner-to-learner interaction. A question or scenario is offered each week and learners are prompted to respond with a unique reply supported by evidence from their instructional materials. They are also expected to reply to others throughout the seven-day window. When learners have questions, they usually e-mail the instructor using the learning management system. Each week, there is a different topic in the weekly discussion forum. Contributions to the discussion forum count toward 40 per cent of the grade.

The instructor takes on the role of a facilitator in discussions. The role of the facilitator is to guide discussions but not lead them. The facilitator does not typically respond in the discussion forum unless she adds relevant questions or resources to the conversation. Instead, each week the facilitator provides private individual text-based responses using an open comment field and a rubric evaluating quantity of responses, quality of responses, and critical thinking. The facilitator tends to provide more substantive comments during the beginning of the semester and gradually responds less as learners progress. Generally, the ratings are lower at the beginning of the semester, but they improve each time learners practice. This is a scaffolding approach to ensure that the comments are substantive, thought provoking, and demonstrate critical thinking.

Later in the semester, the facilitator adds the cooperative activities which focus on group work. Small groups of two to four learners form to collect data and present team projects. Shared documents are used and additional knowledge of technology is required at this point.

At the end of the semester, learners are anonymously surveyed to evaluate the effectiveness of the discussion assignments. Findings indicate that over 90 per cent of the respondents enjoy the discussions and do not feel the need to have more presence by their facilitator in the discussions themselves.

The key stakeholders of this project include this teacher, international students taking the online experience, and future teachers and learners in online forums.

The problem

Although using online discussion forums to collaborate and cooperate has been successful over the years, it was observed that learners in the United States seemed to adapt to the virtual online environment more easily than the international learners. International learners had more questions, appeared to be non-responsive, or asked questions in the forum which appeared as though they were not reading the course material. While the solutions offered by the design of this course seemed to be welcomed by all learners as indicated by my end-of-semester surveys, the instructor began to explore the reasons for the observed differences in behaviour. This evaluation continued with a few iterations of this course as observations, small redesigns, and more feedback from international learners were obtained; it was iterative with a goal to be more inclusive of international students.

One common observation made was that US learners seemed to favour e-mail as the preferred form of communication while international learners sought to communicate with their facilitator in person, either through a Skype meeting, web conference meeting, or in the instructor's office, depending on the learner's physical location. The most common behaviour was the international students' concern for their grades in the class and their confusion about assignments. During individual meetings, it was determined that these learners were truly concerned about doing well. Most conversations revolved around issues with the user interface in the learning management system, assignment clarity, and course navigation. After meeting with learners, the instructor observed an increase in the quantity and quality of contributions to online discussions and cooperative work.

Throughout the process of course iterations, the instructor also began to search the literature to learn more about the needs of international learners. The inclusion of international learners introduces a number of complex cultural issues, but some similarities were more easily determined. For example, international learners typically speak English as a second language. This led the instructor to research English as a second language. In addition, articles were also read about the experiences of international learners (Allen, 2010; Bista and Foster, 2011; Bevis, 2002; Chen and Bennett, 2012; Lee and Rice, 2007; Martirosyan, Hwang and Wanjohi, 2015; Yeboah, 2011; Zhang and Kennedy, 2010), various topics on intercultural communication (Hampden-Turner and Trompenaars, 2000; Hall, 1976; Hofstede, 1980) and topics about culturally responsive classrooms (Cartledge and Kourea, 2008).

The intervention

Good teaching is continuous and adjusts to the needs of the individuals in the online classroom (Bender, 2003). Using the seminal work of Chickering and Gamson (1987) as a lens for measuring current strengths and weaknesses regarding my effective teaching practices, the following SWOT analysis was conducted on the online discussion design in its current state. The following seven principles of effective teaching were evaluated based on learner surveys, grade results, and my own personal experience in the classroom:

1 learner–faculty contact;

2 cooperation among learners;

3 active learning;

4 prompt feedback;

5 time on task;

6 high expectations;

7 respect for diverse talents and ways of learning.

As a result, the following Strengths, Weaknesses, Opportunities and Threats were identified and related to the seven principles of effective teaching.

Table 7.1 SWOT analysis of the seven principles of effective teaching

Strengths	Weaknesses
• Learners' satisfaction at the end of the semester with online discussions (3, 5) • Learners' ability to use evidence to support ideas (3) • Learners' ability to bridge ideas, connect opinions, work in groups (3) • Learners' respect for one another (2) • Minimal need for instructor to intervene in discussions and group work. Can be a facilitator (1, 6) • Learners get one-on-one feedback from instructor (4)	• Need for support (1) (2) (4) • Need for connection and inclusion (7) • Limited intercultural communication (2) (7)

Opportunities	Threats
• Learners feel more connected • Learners feel safe to communicate • Increase collaborative learning • Increase cooperative learning	• Learner isolation • Reduced learning • Instructor indifference • Lack of inclusive practice • Learner retention

Findings

Based on the SWOT analysis, attention was paid to the student needs identified in the weakness category: teacher/learner support, connection and inclusive practices, and intercultural communication.

Need for teacher and learner support (1) (2) (4) (cooperation, faculty-student, prompt feedback)

During individual meetings, it was determined that international learners were truly concerned about doing well but had some difficulties with clarity in a number of areas. The English text-based technologies which largely comprise the learning management system often caused confusion. As a result, most conversations revolved around issues with the user interface in the learning management system, terminology, assignment clarity, and course navigation.

Barriers found included:

- text-based instructions describing how to use learning management features;

- unclear clock times to indicate assignment deadlines;

- unrecognizable words such as 'module' or 'assignment box' commonly used to identify LMS features;

- varying navigation practices through the virtual environment which resulted in missed information such as unit overviews.

In addition, it was evident that international learners had a common need for some aspect of physical connection with their facilitator which is generally lacking in online communication activities. Synchronous experiences using synchronous tools such as Skype, web conferencing, telephone, or traditional physical meetings were sought.

Redesign modifications

As a result of barriers found in the curriculum, a number of design elements were revised in the course to address the needs of international students.

Design elements to improve teacher and learner support

The following design elements were added or modified to be more explicit with the home language and to offer additional ways to vary text explanation. Other considerations included providing guidance regarding prerequisite competencies such as minimum technology skills. Further exploration indicated that a few adjustments to the structure of the virtual environment also needed to be made in order to make it more inclusive:

- Add time zone for all support services, including tech support. Add links to everytimezone.com.

- Contact relevant support areas to include their time zones for support availability.

- Identify technology prerequisite skills and resources to self-evaluate and/or improve technical skills.

- Provide description of minimal computer, internet, browser, and technology required.

- Point to translator applications for browser, learning management system, and other content when possible.

- Add visual instructions for using various technologies that supplement text format options, such as closed-captioned videos.

- Provide set-up tests for using technologies prior to requiring use of the technology, such as shared GoogleDoc files.

- Provide more images to visually represent workflow, learning objectives, etc.

- Provide a glossary of terms for terminology used in this course such as 'learning module', 'discussion forum' and include discipline-specific language.

- Redesign to improve navigation and add a video depicting how to navigate through the course.

- Provide assignment schedule with clearly identifiable date/time format.

- Provide expected instructor response times to learner communications and to assignments.

- Provide synchronous options to communicate with the facilitator such as Skype, web conference, Viber, and telephone.

- Offer synchronous opportunities to meet with the facilitator and record sessions for those who cannot attend.

Need for connection and inclusion (7) (diverse talents and ways of learning)

An observation made during the conversations was that international learners felt uncomfortable about asking questions in the forums for a number of reasons, including fear of being called out or as a form of respect to others.

Redesign modifications

Inclusion is an intentional action which offers full integration of all learners in the virtual environment. Redesign ensued to create a personalized learning environment not only for international students but for mainstream students as well. In order to provide a more personalized learning environment, seeking more student feedback is essential.

Design elements to improve connection and inclusion

The following strategies were included to create a more personalized environment in which to interact.

More student voice activities:

- Solicit at least one ground rule from each learner about a communication protocol for the netiquette pledge (see end of article).

- Ask learners to define personal work preferences regarding synchronous and asynchronous delivery modes, group experiences, skill sets etc (see end of article).

- Ask learners to self-assess and share their leadership styles.

- Ask groups to work collaboratively to create their own group communication protocols (when to meet synchronously versus asynchronously, expectations of group members etc).

- Require learners to participate in peer evaluations.

- Prompt learners to complete a mid-term anonymous check-in survey.

- Offer opportunities for ongoing learner suggestions (ie suggestion box).

- Prompt learners to complete a final student satisfaction survey.

More real-time teaching preparation.
The facilitator used student feedback to personalize the virtual environment. Since the information gathered is only a snapshot of learner needs, personalization is expected each time a new group of learners convenes. Opportunities for listening to learner needs was also made more strategic and relevant through improved learner satisfaction surveys and feedback solicitations. The following strategies were implemented:

- Begin personalization by letting students get to know you (the facilitator).

- Encourage learner responses to peer introductions and allow more time for such responses.

- Provide multiple ways for learners to contribute their work but provide a clearly stated rubric.

- Share survey results and/or adjustments made as a result of survey data or student feedback.

- Form groups based on preferred work preferences (synchronous, asynchronous, leadership style etc).

- Use final survey for subsequent review and modification of next course iteration.

Need to address barriers in communication (2) (7) (cooperation, diverse talents)

Discussion board responses seemed to have different meanings for international students. Agreement was often their responses to others' opinions to encourage a collaborative environment. This was limiting our perspective of these learners.

Redesign modifications

Simply stated, intercultural communication is a study of how different cultures communicate and perceive the world. The international students in this case study indicated that they didn't feel comfortable disagreeing with others. Initial efforts to improve intercultural communication are only a seed for future redesign.

Design and teaching elements to improve intercultural communications

More work will be required in subsequent iterations of this course, but the following modifications have been made:

- Facilitator models by using name of student in each communication.

- Facilitator models by ending communications with a kind salutation or emoticon.

- Revised rubric includes points for respectfully challenging and/or bridging ideas.

- Return students periodically to expectations of rubric and negotiated rules about communication.

- Display link to class-defined netiquette pledge in all discussion forums.

Project/intervention course till now

The redesign was iterative based on this instructor's experience in the course and regularly solicited learner feedback for a period of three course iterations. The result was a more inclusive environment for international learners as well as all other learners in the virtual class. Responses to the modifications indicate that these changes have increased overall satisfaction of online discussions and have reduced isolation for all students in the class.

Strategies included modifying design components to be more explicit about supportive resources and assignments, and a more personalized environment was created to increase motivation and buy-in from learners. Pedagogical strategies are now more adaptive based on the needs of each individual class. Finally, more attention was placed on teacher-to-student and student-to-student communications.

Implications

This small-scale case study offers future potential to international project management teams. Since travel budgets are continuing to drop significantly, it will be more important to recognize the opportunities afforded by online communication and internet technologies. Communication has always been a major concern when participating in any collaborative and cooperative work. When adding the virtual environment to the mix, the complexity increases exponentially. In online forums, there is little in terms of visual cues typically present in face-to-face communication to ameliorate some of the potential negative effects of communication.

In addition, with the advent of online education in the late '90s, growth of distance education serves a larger more global population. As a result, the quality of the educational experience is continually being explored. Universal design for learning is a framework that optimizes a teaching and learning environment for all learners. By paying attention to learners in the margins, we disrupt mainstream teaching to the benefit of all.

Personalization also has positive effects on personal motivation. By listening to the needs of the teams who will be using the virtual environment, project managers may benefit from increased productivity.

Finally, the virtual environment is relatively new and we are learning that it can be an effective way to communicate, cooperate, and produce valuable products. The same attention given to the design of collaborative physical spaces must continue to be invested in the design of collaborative virtual spaces. New competencies could be required by project managers regarding online facilitation, core virtual design elements, and available and emergent communication strategies and tools.

Part 2: Interview

Q: A lot of your work with groups is motivated by the notion of inclusiveness or something you told me, Universal Design Learning. What is this exactly?

A: Universal design for learning is a framework used to address the needs of those students who are typically marginalized – usually the minority in a given group. There could be a single student with a learning difficulty, students with low socioeconomic status, a physical disability. The belief is that if you address the learners at the margins, you increase the learning opportunity for all. And international students were to an extent marginalized. The course design and structure had not been designed for them. This project was an attempt to address that.

Q: So this project was about improving the environment, the online environment, so it worked for international students?

A: Yes. The virtual classroom has to be strategically created. In the same way that a physical classroom is inviting, a virtual environment also has to be welcoming so students can enter and feel safe to communicate. Part of this strategy starts with the behaviour of the facilitator and the other students, but just modelling as a person with power is not enough. It's more effective if you let participants contribute to the creation of their environment; research indicates this. Let them contribute to the creation of their virtual world.

Q: To make the course more inclusive towards the international students, on the language side of things, what strategies did you give students?

A: I think it's more complex than just a few strategies. I separated the issues thinking in terms of low- and high-context communication. Low-context communication strategies involve addressing explicit language issues. So one of the first things we did was look at the LMS interface, which is very text based. It wasn't enough to offer text-based instructions. Videos with captions to demonstrate visually how to use the LMS tools were also added. We created glossaries to explain potentially unclear terminology. We provided information about translation tools. We even created a graphic syllabus, basically, a visual way to view the same content. High-context communication strategies, on the other hand, are much more complex and I am currently evaluating that in more detail.

Q: So you really tried to create clarity in the environment?

A: Absolutely. Clarity is very important, especially in an online environment. In face-to-face conversations, we constantly restate, repeat and can look at people's reactions to ensure that a message is coming across. Online, it's much more difficult because there are no visual cues. So much is tacit and implicit online. We now work with a tool here to increase our attention to clarity. Quality Matters offers a rubric which picks out eight major design components of an online environment. It is learner-centred and clarity is its major lens.

Q: But don't modern learning management systems handle this now?

A: It's naïve to think that technology will just do the job. The biggest problem is the fact that people assume things are clear, even teachers with years of experience.

Q: So, you said that even experienced teachers make false assumptions.

A: Absolutely. You know, what is clear to you is not automatically clear to someone else. We do peer reviews where we review a course from a student perspective. It's surprising how much is unclear. This review process really gives teachers a real understanding of learner needs.

Q: Was the fact that much of the interaction was asynchronous and text based, did that make it clearer to the students that they had to work harder to communicate clearly?

A: In some ways, yes. The need to negotiate meaning is more obvious because you don't have visual cues, such as voice tone; the communication is faceless. To increase the potential for a safe and collaborative environment we worked with common protocols, a netiquette.

Q: That sounds a little bit like the notion of norming in professional teams. Can you say a little about this?

A: Yes, so for group work, individuals are asked a number of questions about how they like to learn, their preferred team style and leadership style, whether they prefer to work synchronously or asynchronously. You can see the kinds of questions in handout 1 [see Appendix 2]. We wanted to create groups according to their preferences. For collaborative work, we also set up very clear protocols in terms of communication behaviour. We began with facilitator-stated norms. But it was also important to make the students responsible for this, so we asked them to tell us their most important protocol. So everyone would make a statement about what was important for them, and then they would commit to following it.

Q: So, like they were defining their own communication culture?

A: Yes. Exactly. And this setting of behaviours, or rules, and following of rules, done by the group for the group, has a big impact.

Q: Can I ask a little about the content of the course, because there are two dimensions here. The content of your online course actually has an objective collaboration, the development of collaboration skills and critical thinking skills. Can you say a little about this?

A: In discussion forums, we focus on three main areas. The quantity of communication – how active are they in the discussion. I also look at quality: do people say substantive things for the discussion? And then on critical thinking skills, it's a question of asking if the students came up with new ideas, profound reflections, and if they were able to bridge between and link the ideas in the group to create new insights. This is what I mean by critical thinking skills.

Q: And do students take on these collaboration ideas?

A: Yes, they're motivated to do it this way. There is also intrinsic motivation, as people see themselves getting progressively better, and it helps the group to collaborate.

Q: Is this like training?

A: No, it's more of a facilitated approach. Within the online discussions, the facilitator is not highly active in giving input during the discussion; the facilitator might contribute additional questions to stimulate the discussion but generally, we give private and individual feedback that is positive to encourage individual contributions. You have to be careful. We don't want to 'call someone out' in front of others. This prevents people from communicating naturally, which can be counterproductive. So you have to be careful how you facilitate and manage feedback.

Q: In general, how long does it take for students to work with these ideas, and to communicate the right amount with good quality and a good interactive or collaborative process?

A: About half-way through the semester, maybe seven weeks, so not too long.

Q: Overall, how far do you feel your work relates to project management?

A: I think it does on many levels. You know, today's students will be tomorrow's workforce. This means that they will bring their learning experience to the table. They'll remember the tools that worked well and will share that knowledge in the workforce. In fact, their expectations will probably be higher having experienced successful collaborative and cooperative online forums such as the one we offer.

Part 3: Commentary

Here are some reflections on Sharon's case and interview.

Interestingly, many of the solutions Sharon comes up with to enrich her facilitation practice are directly applicable to the world of international project management, and leadership of virtual teams. I have seen many corporate project teams decide on the development of a glossary of terms to overcome the problem that the same English terms mean different things in different places. The need to go multimedia, using a blend of e-mail, one-to-one calls, conference calls and face-to- face meetings, avoiding the easy reliance on text, is also commonly recognized. Really importantly, the idea of groups or virtual teams setting explicit rules of interaction and collaboration, and ensuring that each individual has the right to include their own rules, is something I have seen applied actually in a network of over 2,500 people with one client. The feedback message is powerful – rule setting and regular reviews of rule setting drive performance in diverse virtual teams. Probably what I miss is training for native English speakers to speak a better English to non-native counterparts. Native speakers believe they slow down and speak simply. But this is a complex competence which requires intensive training over an extended period.

Bob Dignen

Part 4: Reflecting on international project management

Take time to reflect on the following questions to help you reach further insights and take practical actions to improve your own project management practice.

1 How useful do you believe training for native English speakers might be which trains them how to communicate effectively – slowing their delivery, speaking less complex language – with their non-native speaker colleagues? Why?

2 How effective do you feel the joint setting of communication rules might be for virtual project teams who want to create an inclusive and effective collaboration culture? Why?

3 Which communication rules do you think would help your project teams to communicate effectively, either face to face or virtually? List down five rules and discuss them with your project colleagues.

Part 5: Put it into practice

There are a number of very valid insights and ideas for project management present in this case which the reader can learn from and adopt, customizing for their own projects. Take a few minutes to note down your main learnings from this case, and note down some actions for yourself.

Personal insights, learnings and actions

Note

1 Bob Dignen has authored an e-learning for native English speakers entitled 'Speaking better English internationally', the only e-learning of its type to date as far as is known, and which has been rolled out globally by one of his major clients.

References

Allen, T (2010) Perceived barriers to English language learning among international school learners, Dissertation, UMI Number: 3433012.

Bender, T (2003) *Discussion-based Online Teaching to Enhance Learner Learning: Theory, practice, and assessment*, Stylus Publishing, Sterling, Va

Bevis, T B (2002) At a glance: international learners in the United States, *International Educator*, **11** (3), pp. 12–17

Bista, K and Foster, C (October 2011) Issues of international learner retention in American higher education, *The International Journal of Research and Review*, **7** (2), pp. 1–10

Cartledge, G and Kourea, L (2008) Culturally responsive classrooms for culturally diverse learners with and at risk for disabilities, *Council for Exceptional Children*, **74** (3), pp. 351–71

Cecez-Kecmanovic, D and Webb, C (2000) Towards a communicative model of collaborative web-mediated learning, *Australian Journal of Educational Technology*, **16** (1), pp. 73–85

Chen, R T and Bennett, S (2012) When Chinese learners meet constructivist pedagogy online, *Higher Education*, **64**, pp. 677–91

Chickering, A and Gamson, Z (1997) Seven principles for good practice in undergraduate education [online] http://teaching.uncc.edu/learning-resources/articles-books/best-practice/education-philosophy/seven-principles

Chickering, A and Gamson, Z, eds (1991) *Applying the Seven Principles for Good Practice in Undergraduate Education*, 47th edn, Jossey-Bass, San Francisco

Christensen, C M, Raynor, M E and McDonald, R (Dec 2015) What is disruptive innovation? *Harvard Business Review* [online] https://hbr.org/2015/12/what-is-disruptive-innovation

Hampden-Turner, C M and Trompenaars, F (2000) *Building Cross-Cultural Competence: How to create wealth from conflicting values*, Yale University Press, New Haven, CT

Hall, E T (1976) *Beyond Culture*, Doubleday, New York.

Hofstede, G H (1980) *Culture's Consequences: International differences in work-related values*, Sage, Newbury Park, CA

Lee, J J and Rice, C (2007) Welcome to America? International learner perceptions of discrimination, *Higher Education*, **53**, pp. 381–409, DOI 10.1007/s10734-005-4508-3

Martirosyan, N M, Hwang, E and Wanjohi, R (2015) Impact of English proficiency on academic performance of international learners, *Journal of International Learners*, **5** (1), pp. 60–71

Wood, Andrew F and Smith, Matthew J (2001) *Online Communication: Linking technology, identity and culture*, Lawrence Earlbaum Associates, Mahwah, New Jersey

Yeboah, A K (2011) Factors that promote transformative learning experiences of international graduate-level learners, Dissertation UMI Number: 3505134

Zhang, Z and Kennedy, R F (March 2010) Learning in an online distance education course: experiences of three international learners, *International Review of Research in Open and Distributed Learning*, **11** (1) [online] http://www.irrodl.org/index.php/irrodl/article/view/775/1481

Implementation of a global performance management system 08

VOLKER HISCHE

Profile

Since 2004 Volker Hische has been managing director of the academy of CSC, one of the largest global IT companies. The CSC Academy has the mission to develop and educate clients of CSC on special topics in human capital management for (global) IT organizations as a precondition for being profitable. Additionally, Volker has a strong background in HR management. He was previously Human Resources Development Director and Chief Learning Officer at a global enterprise with operations in Europe, Middle East and Africa (EMEA), managing a number of major projects connected to global performance management, succession planning, talent management and the concept of global career framework. He is an Associate Professor for the Human Capital Management MBA at Lake Constance Business School, and a Certified International Project Manager, International Project Management Association and Certified International Project Management Trainer (IPMA).

Foreword

Volker's case is based on his and his many colleagues' international project experience in the same industry over the last twenty years. This article summarizes these experiences in a very real and at the same time fictional project in an enterprise we will call 'Acme'. The project that is described represents efforts to bring global standards to a diverse and relatively fragmented set of local organizations, in this case HR. There have been numerous similar projects with related targets in a large number of companies over the past 20 years. In this context the project lead, Tom, had the challenge of driving the project with close linkages to Acme's 'one global organization' strategy. Tom's special challenge was to 'bridge global imperatives with local needs', gaining acceptance and deep buy-in along the way. His other challenges were many, not least the fact that he was operating very much in the so-called Wave One of globalization in one of his organizations, which was relatively immature in terms of international governance and processes, so that Tom had to create his own rules of project implementation as he went along.

Naturally, such a change process required a lot of effort in project communication. Volker is bold when suggesting that almost 80 per cent of Tom's job consisted of managing communications. His range of engagement and control strategies is broad, and eventually brought him success.

Working virtually also presented itself as a potential major obstacle. Volker indicates that Tom's project team had no collective physical meeting for the first 18 months of the project. His 'planes, trains and automobiles' solution is admirable, if exhausting, and his blending of one-to-one meetings and group virtual telephone calls offers an interesting model of virtual leadership.

Before reading this case, reflect and make notes on a couple of questions. Then compare your answers to the ideas in the case itself and the final commentary.

1 How can project leaders 'make the case for global' when leading transformation projects that restructure and reduce local operations in favour of global steering?

2 What's the best way to integrate one-to-one and virtual group meetings when leading an international project team?

3 What are the pros and cons of showing too much flexibility during local roll-out of a global solution?

PART 1: CASE STUDY   Implementation of a global
performance management system

Company context

Acme is one of the world's leading next-generation technology providers in the IT industry, encompassing roughly 70,000 employees. It has the aspiration to lead clients on their digital transformation journey. The company provides innovative, next-generation technology services and solutions that leverage deep industry expertise, global scale, technology independence and an extensive partner community. The enterprise serves leading commercial and international public sector organizations throughout the world.

Project scope

In the early 2000s, Acme decided to become one global enterprise organization for two main reasons:

1 Acme's growth was fuelled by external acquisitions. Thus, aside from a harmonized global controlling process, a lot of diverse local operational processes and systems were in place, including procurement, marketing, HR, travel management as well as many other internal processes. This had a number of impacts for the company, such as high operational costs and efforts.

2 Acme closed large outsourcing deals with global clients. Client workforces had to be transformed to the company on a global scale. Thus, Acme had not only to demonstrate to its clients the capability to deliver outsourcing services on a global scale but also the capability to operate its own internal processes, particularly such as HR, on global scale.

To become 'one enterprise' was a huge challenge for Acme since, up to that point, most of the business had been successfully managed on a local scale. The management philosophy was predominantly local: as long as local business units delivered their numbers, everything was fine. As a result, local business units maintained a strong local culture with their own practices, habits and patterns. In fact, each local unit had something approximating its own business model. However, due to factors mentioned above, the whole organization had to transform to one global business model.

Thus, the company decided to conduct a large transformation process, implementing a global operating model in order to meet clients' needs. As a result, global business units were established with the need to harmonize, first of all, local HR processes and systems. A programme was set up to implement global

HR processes and procedures including global roles, performance management and career models. Tom was in charge of developing and implementing the programme in EMEA (Europe and Middle East) for 25 countries covering approximately 25,000 employees.

Project categorization

The project was an organizational change project as it not only focused on the implementation of HR processes and standards but simultaneously aimed to change the culture of the company from a diversified organization to an operating model which used global standards and practices. Although the senior management recognized the cultural diversity of a global company, there were no specific cultural change activities in scope. This was left to the regional representatives managing organizational change in the regions. As CSC had at this period of time only a little experience of managing projects on a global scale there was, aside from a committed end date, no global implementation strategy in place, nor did there exist an agreed global implementation plan.

Project profile

- **Purpose:** Strengthen Acme's capabilities to act as a global company by implementing global HR processes.

- **Goals:** Implement an intraweb-based performance management system for EMEA following a two-phase approach. Phase 1 – implement a work flow-based document based on Word. Phase 2 – implement the intraweb solutions which supported the new process.

- **Scope:** All European countries where Acme was operating excluding Eastern European Countries and South Africa. A sequence was defined.

- **Schedule:** A two-year approach following defined milestones (Analyse and Design, Build, Implement). The timing was mainly defined by IT considerations, namely the solution cycle of the intraweb solution.

- **Approach:** Implementation needed to be done as a Big Bang because large parts of the business act across cultures. Employees belong either to a region (for example, UK), a horizontal structure (for example, Global Infrastructure Solutions) or a vertical organization (for example, Financial Services). This was challenging for the project approach as new processes and systems needed to be implemented simultaneously. Global Infrastructure Solutions (GIS) had employees in all countries. Thus, for GIS it was a 'must' to implement the new performance management system simultaneously in all countries, while for the UK business it was a local decision when to implement for the employees there. Later on, this structural conflict became very important when addressing an appropriate implementation strategy.

- **Global stakeholders:** Corporate HR, Corporate HRD, Corporate Application Services, EMEA HR vice president, HR directors, EMEA presidents.

- **Constellation:** The project was set up in a relatively non-project-oriented environment. For example, HR management assumed that special tasks (like projects) should be managed by the individual accountable in addition to his/her day-to-day business. Thus, the level of project management competence depended on the individual's experience and skills.

- **Organization:** Acme as a whole is a matrix organization, and project organization could be characterized as project management by influence. There were no dedicated resources allocated to projects. Project members had to do project work in addition to their day-to-day business. Governance was not formalized. It was up to the accountable project manager to set up a governance structure. The appointment of project managers was usually executed by a senior manager.

- **Own role/roles:** Programme manager. In addition to Tom's accountability as project manager for the implementation of the performance management process in EMEA, I also managed the implementation of a leadership development programme, long-time succession planning, role-based qualification programmes and the career development framework. As all these projects followed a common purpose (implement a one HR organization in Acme) Tom acted as the accountable programme manager.

Project intervention

The project was one of the first real global projects in the history of Acme, and was set up as a top-down initiative. Senior management was informed at the annual management conference that the board had decided to implement a new HR operating model on a global scale sponsored by the HR vice president corporate. Consequently, HR corporate defined and designed the new processes and procedures of the HR operating model. Interactions between global functions and local functions were limited due to the complexity of the organization. However, there was a clear commitment and expectation from the corporate HR VP that all business units had to implement the new performance system.

The main challenge for Tom was to get EMEA perspectives aligned with overall corporate interest to implement global and harmonized HR processes. The following proved to be significant components of the challenge:

1 The regions with their local management were strong players in the arena. Although the regional heads in EMEA were informed at Acme's annual management conference by the Corporate HR vice president that Acme was striving for a new global HR operating model which included a new performance

management process, EMEA's regional heads were not supportive of having their local HR organizations changed. This was particularly the case as they were under the influence of their respective HR directors. Reduced authority, lower quality, data protection issues and language limitations were the main fears. Furthermore, the new process was initially perceived as a very US-driven initiative. Europe, in its diverse cultural dimensions, was not seen as being taken into consideration at all. Indeed, the new performance management process had been designed by HR Corporate alone, without any participation from other local/regional organizations.

2   The HR organizations in EMEA were used to operating independently. Local legislation, local data protection laws, local labour representatives and local needs were primary drivers to have local HR organizations in place with strong local HR processes and systems. Although there was an experienced HR vice president EMEA in charge, there was a strong culture of self-accountability among HR directors in the countries. For them, it was a complete shift of mindset to become part of one global HR organization.

3   HR as a process-driven organization had almost no experience of setting up, managing and steering projects. A quarterly HR leadership conference at EMEA level existed where HR issues were discussed. However, there was no institutionalized governance process for HR projects established.

Project success factors

In general, it was extremely challenging to bridge global imperatives with local needs and acceptance. Accordingly, the following factors became imperatives for successful implementation of the new performance management system, as one cornerstone of a new global HR operating model:

1   Form an effective project team consisting of local HR representatives in charge of implementing the new process in their respective region.

2   Support and coach local HR representatives during implementation in case of resistance, concerns or blockades by key stakeholders such as local management, data protection officers and/or labour representatives.

3   Have all relevant stakeholders identified and managed. For example, UK HR had implemented HR Business Partner roles which I missed during my initial stakeholder analysis. Those colleagues turned out to be key at a later stage of the project as advocates when selling the new performance management process into the business.

4   Make the EMEA HR leadership team accountable for steering the project in terms of progress, issues, priorities and budget. As local HR directors were rather reluctant in implementing the new process, it was necessary to make

any different view, any serious concern and/or any relevant quality issue officially transparent and visible by having the project steered ultimately by the HR leadership team. This was the institutionalized platform for the project to address and solve project issues.

5 Have clear guidance and strong leadership by the Corporate HR vice president in terms of implementation rules. For example, no exemption of implementation or delay of implementation due to specific local needs would be accepted. One Acme organization tried to avoid implementation by suggesting that the new global process did not cover an important local need (an individual development plan for each employee). Although it was well understood that this feature was not yet provided by the new process, it was clearly communicated to the respective HR director to adopt and adapt to the new process.

6 Accept that a global company needs to act globally by running global processes regardless of cultural differences. Although it became obvious that Swedish culture does not emphasize performance differences in the same way as other countries, it was very clear that the organization in Sweden had to follow the same rules of the new performance system as the other countries.

7 Understand and work with cultural differences when dealing with the local HR representatives during implementation of the new process. For example, in France it was key to first talk to the French general manager and then talk to HR representatives. In Germany, decisions had to be made in official meetings. In Italy, decisions were often made in informal meetings when having dinner in the evening.

8 Ensure continuous and regular communication between the project manager and implementation team. Although it seems to be a 'no brainer', it was key to have progress in the countries shared with the whole implementation team so that everybody understood that success was feasible. For example, the UK was the first mover in starting the implementation. When it turned out and became transparent to the whole implementation team that the implementation of the new process in UK had gone very well, the other regions followed.

Project results

The project achieved its goals. Every employee in Acme follows the same performance appraisal procedures. To date, employees' results are clearly linked to the incentive system. A metric for successful implementation of the performance management system was defined by how many employees had completed the annual appraisal process based on the new system. HR Corporate made the figures transparent on an annual basis. Across EMEA, more than 90 per cent of all employees completed the new appraisal process annually

Lessons learned to date

1   A project like this needs clear leadership from its global sponsor on the one hand, with as much involvement and engagement as possible from local representatives on the other hand. It is essential to develop some feeling on how to balance these apparently contradictory elements.

   • Although the project team needs clear direction from the global sponsor with regard to fixed project objectives, it is important to have the flexibility to change or extend the project scope to meet local specifics which are not contrary to the overall global objectives. During the project, it turned out that a few European countries (Italy, France, Spain, Portugal, Germany) needed a multilingual solution, so Tom extended the project scope from one language (English) to nine European languages.

   • Although the project team needs to be very strict about implementation rules, it needs to accept that local representatives might not be empowered enough to manage implementation of a new concept or process on their own. In the northern region of Europe, the local representative in charge of managing implementation for the whole region (Denmark, Sweden, Norway) did not feel empowered or authorized to drive implementation in Sweden as the Swedish organization in Acme had historically managed its HR operations independently. So Tom had to coach and support her to manage the implementation in Sweden.

   • Although there is pain caused by globalization, the project team had to ensure that the organization follows the global roadmap. Project leadership requires the use of a clear escalation process that makes it transparent to all players that some things are non-negotiable. Of course, it is good to try to solve issues with a local team first, but be willing to escalate them to the global sponsor if the local HR management has proved willing to find a common solution.

   • Although the global sponsor of the project has to send clear messages in the kick-off to the local HR representatives on what is expected from them as regards the project, it is also important for the sponsor to ask each team member afterwards about their specific concerns and try to help to overcome them.

2   With regard to cultural differences, in order to implement such global processes in regional EMEA, it is important to adapt one's leadership style to the respective country needs/culture. It is essential to clearly differentiate the implementation approach and mode per country/region.

   The following table shows a summary of various leadership techniques applied by Tom which turned out to be very useful in dealing with the diverse cultures of the countries involved. It is important to understand, though, that this is a very personal view which should neither be generalized nor taken as a recipe. It is based on personal experience with a set of specific individuals that Tom had to deal with during implementation phase. It helped him a lot, though, to accept and adapt to cultural and personality differences.

Table 8.1 Leadership techniques across countries/cultures

Country	Main features	Leadership technique
UK	Pragmatic, clear direction, self-confident	Leadership by control
France	Egocentric, polite, indirect	Leadership by diplomacy
Germany	Formal, reliable, fact-driven	Leadership by arguments
Sweden	Institutionalized, formal, harmony-based	Leadership by negotiation
Denmark	Pragmatic, direct, open	Leadership by collaboration
Norway	Pragmatic, reliable, fair	Leadership by collaboration
Italy	Friendly, informal, unpredictable, less reliable	Leadership by commitment
Spain	Pragmatic, formal, helpful	Leadership by collaboration
Portugal	Pragmatic, formal, polite	Leadership by collaboration
Netherlands	Informal, friendly, self-confident	Leadership by commitment
Switzerland	Friendly, correct, reliable	Leadership by collaboration
USA	Demanding, informal, helpful	Leadership by authority

3 Although this was an HR initiative, it was critical to ensure the engagement and approval of the broader business community in the organization. Acme's business is a people business. Acme earns its money from its knowledge of its people. Thus, most business leaders are highly sensitive with respect to HR initiatives, as they consider HR's main purpose to be supporting the business with appropriate people development processes. Therefore, it was very important to inform and convince CSC senior management of the benefits of the new performance management system. Consequently, Tom organized time slots with each regional head in CSC to discuss any issues or concerns he or she might have regarding the project. The most challenging exercise was to convince the assistants that it was worthwhile for their respective senior managers to spend this time with him. Interestingly enough, after those meetings the

regional business heads were very supportive and helped open doors to further key players, for example within their respective management teams.

4 Stakeholder engagement, including communication, was a key task, and covered 80 per cent of project management activities. It is very obvious that organizational change projects such as these which implement a new global performance management process are underpinned by stakeholder management, particularly if the process has a global reach and is expected to replace all local processes. A variety of stakeholders such as HR managers, business managers, data protection officers, work councils and labour representatives all have a 'stake' in these kinds of projects. The main purpose of stakeholder management is to handle the expectations of relevant stakeholders in order to get their appropriate level of engagement. In theory, you raise stakeholders' engagement by making them at first *aware* of the project with simple information. Secondly, you help them to *understand* the 'why' and 'how' of the new system. Third, you get their *acceptance* by letting them test the new process ('look and feel'). Finally, you make them *own* the new system by incentivizing the desired behaviour. In fact, if you apply this theory in practice, it really helps to increase the desired level of engagement. Consequently, Tom analysed per stakeholder group the current and desired level of engagement, and carried out appropriate measures to help people increase their level of engagement by conducting presentations, one-to-one meetings, workshops, negotiations, trainings, escalation techniques, success stories etc, which took most of Tom's time as project manager.

5 The setting of institutionalized decision-making processes was key as well. In order to get the right decisions at the right time for projects with a global reach, it is absolutely necessary to have an effective decision-making process established, particularly when the involved HR decision makers are not used to making decisions as a team at EMEA level. Thus, Tom agreed with his sponsor to have a time slot with the key decision makers together once a month at EMEA level. Again, this is so obvious that many might think it is not worth a mention. However, Tom had to learn to use these meetings as real decision-making meetings. At first, the opportunity was missed. Initially, when he started, he failed to get clear commitment at the meeting from the leadership team on how to go forward. After some feedback from his sponsor to make better use of these meetings, Tom used those time slots as explicit decision-making meetings with a clear structure: first, describe the issue; second, propose two or three solutions; finally, make a single recommendation before, and significantly, forcing participants to make a decision. It is really essential to confront tough decisions head on. One critical situation in the project was the simple question of which

HR organization should *lead* the implementation: the regional (local) HR organization or the global HR organization? This was obviously a sensitive issue and could only be solved by preparing a decision table with decision criteria, options, evaluations, a recommendation and, finally, a decision. In the end, the local HR organizations took the lead for all organizations in EMEA to implement the new performance management system. In retrospect, it is fascinating to realize that it was up to the project itself to decide how to organize the implementation of global processes within the matrix organization, as there was no clear guidance a priori on which dimension (local, horizontal, vertical) should lead implementation of such a global initiative. In fact, this was the first time in the HR that one dimension of the matrix was clearly in the lead position.

Situation and outlook

Today, the global performance process in Acme is 'business as usual'. Every employee receives an annual performance appraisal. In addition, an Individual Development Plan has been established to ensure sustainable personal development. The process has become an integral part of employee development. It is striking to see now how commonplace it has become to implement global processes at Acme. Due to market pressure and client expectation, CSC's maturity as a global organization has increased dramatically. Managing in the matrix is based on a global operating model with clear roles and accountabilities, imperative guidance as to which organization takes the lead in cross-matrix initiatives, and global change control processes with respect to further developing global processes.

Summary

On reflection, leadership in such a process is critical. And leadership has to demonstrate a balance. It is nice to have all people involved in the process, but it must also be made crystal clear that the programme or project manager is in charge and is accountable in case of failure. Thus, self-authorization and a willingness and courage to really drive forward such a complex implementation process, without being too rude (or let's say too Germanic) becomes a key competence. This implies, sometimes, forcing engagement from key stakeholders when conflicts arise. Importantly, conflict is seldom about the overall goal, and much more about *how* to achieve the objective, which often triggers different views and perspectives. As programme manager, it is vital to authorize yourself to take decisions because it can be very costly in many senses to wait until everybody has agreed to a common strategy.

Part 2: Interview

The following is the summary of a series of personal conversations between Bob and Volker.

Q: It always surprises me that organizations manage projects by adding project tasks to the normal day job. You mentioned this. What are your thoughts on this? Does it still happen in Acme, and with what impact?

A: Yes, it still happens. It's driven partly by need, so people are engaged as an add-on. You know, you can't just have a dedicated workforce hanging around waiting for a project to pop up. So here, we do extra load jobs, but that is rewarded. And in the enterprises I know project management is in the DNA; people are used to it and they can step in and out.

Q: To what degree did organizational immaturity ever threaten the success of the project?

A: Well, for this real and at the same time fictional project, it was mission critical at times. You know the model of organizational maturity and we needed a hero to drive the project, as we had no real processes at that time. So, and it's just my view, it depended a lot on the project lead as an individual.

Q: Did Tom enjoy being the hero?

A: Yes, he liked the pressure. And the project really made sense to him, so he always felt he was doing the right thing.

Q: I think you mentioned escalation in your case. A lot of middle management shy away from escalation for a number of reasons. Tom used it. Was it easy?

A: Seldom and not really directly. But Tom made it clear to one local director who was resisting that if they were not willing to implement in their region, they would have to call the vice president personally and explain directly. There was no call. And actually a lot of people thanked him for that because if one had refused, they would have to explain why they had not refused too.

Q: Interestingly, you mention a diverse and sometimes contradictory set of skills for an international PM. Sometimes it's around flexibility, and sometimes more of a ruthless assertiveness. How realistic is it for companies to either find or train this demanding mix?

A: Training is possible for some areas: learning how to escalate, problem solving, giving and getting feedback and so on. But having empathy and being willing to listen, that's more an attitude that is very difficult to teach. You can give insights and get people to think about it, but it's up to them; you learn to listen by experience. If someone is arrogant, life will teach them, probably with a painful experience. The key success factor – Tom's in this case – was to be accepted by all the teams in the countries. Tom was clear and assertive and oppressive at times, but he always appreciated their local circumstances. And the story of the Swedish lady who didn't feel empowered – Tom helped her. He realized that he had to help her and he did.

Q: What tips and tricks would you give regarding stakeholder management and communication?

A: I work with the four classic communication stages: first, build up awareness, then create understanding, generate acceptance and get them to own the change, and I use communication techniques linked to these four processes. For awareness, give information. For understanding, show how things have to be done and clarify the benefits. For acceptance, get people to look and feel and try it and participate. For owning, you switch from presenting on your own to letting them present the stuff in their own terms. Once they tell you that they want to present it, they've owned it.

Q: And just one final question, you mention meetings and decision making. Did you work with virtual meetings? If so, how far did these present additional challenges?

A: Yes, we used remote working, mainly because of travel restrictions in the company, so we didn't meet for the first 18 months, we just did it virtually. It worked out though. I was in touch with them individually. I just took my car and night trains to Paris or wherever, and it somehow worked out. To manage a team virtually, it needs more clarity, goal orientation and structure or people will lose motivation. So you need to give feedback on progress so people can know directly where they are and where they need to go. You need to manage people even more strictly than when you are face to face.

Q: So more telling and not asking.

A: No, it's not directive in terms of telling, but more in terms of orientation, clear feedback cycles and transparent routines. For example, on a conference call, you ask people very directly what are the concerns and issues in your region when implementing. But I wouldn't discuss it in the conference call. I would just collect it and then solve it offline, but in the next meeting share the solutions of who solved what in which country to share best practice. So it's blending group and one-to-one calls in a particular way.

Part 3: Commentary

Here are some reflections on Volker's case and interview.

> *Volker's case is the story of an enterprise moving to become a real mature global player. It illustrates what a demanding task a frontrunner has to perform, how important the performance of the first global project is, but what success can be achieved. If a PM ever has to run such a crucial frontrunner project, they should very carefully explore the surrounding organization in all dimensions. How mature is it, how ripe is it for global organization? What are the official and unofficial rules that might enable and disable the project? Solid analysis is important for deciding on the right leadership style, which has to fit to many different requirements. On the one hand, you have to push the project to success, but on the other hand, you have to take the people impacted by the project with you on the journey. This is a well-known dilemma without standard solutions, but it needs a sponsor, a core stakeholder group, and a confident and sovereign project director and inner team who are ready to decide and discuss, who are able to reflect and be open to new insights and recalibration of project proceedings.*

Peter Wollmann

> *One of the most interesting comments Volker made to me during the telephone interview concerned listening. The ability to listen, to understand, to empathize, to then calibrate one's own message to the needs of the other, is recognized by many contributors to the book as vital. Interestingly, Volker suggests that the skill is not trainable, rather you just learn to listen through the pain of life experience. It's an interesting insight and may go part of the way to explain why behavioural training of things such as active listening often does little more than build awareness. It often has little impact on behaviour, despite the importance of such behaviours, because the underlying attitude, a humility, a deep curiosity for the other, is simply not there.*

Bob Dignen

Part 4: Reflecting on international project management

Take time to reflect on the following questions to help you reach further insights and take practical actions to improve your own project management practice.

1 How mature is your organization as an international entity? What steps does it need to take to become a more mature global player?

2 How often do you ask for feedback on the way you communicate by e-mail and in telephone calls? What could be the value of asking for feedback more regularly on your virtual communication style?

3 How effectively do you listen? How could you become a better listener?

Part 5: Putting it into practice

There are a number of very valid insights and ideas for project management present in this case which the reader can learn from and adopt, customizing for their own projects. Take a few minutes to note down your main learnings from this case, and note down some actions for yourself.

Personal insights, learnings and actions

Global offensive: project management within 150 days

09

FRANK KÜHN

Profile

Frank Kühn studied mechanical engineering, focused on work science and obtained his doctorate in ergonomics. He has leadership experience in research institutes and the electrical industry. From 1991 he worked as consultant and partner with HLP in Frankfurt. In 2008 Frank co-founded ICG Integrated Consulting Group Germany. He is currently a Business Partner of ICG, and is networked with a wider circle of management consultancies and expert communities.

Frank supports executives, management teams and change teams in strategic projects, change processes and excellence programmes. Progressive Project Management is a focal point. He is a sought-after partner in discussions on future challenges such as how to develop cooperation and organization, change and performance in volatile environments and future industries. He is a writer and public speaker with a multitude of publications and lectures on project management.

Foreword

This case describes a leading global chemical group that wanted to develop and implement a new shared, pragmatic and international PM (project management) standard. The objectives were twofold: first, to deliver more effective project management, and second, to facilitate organizational change readiness. It was envisaged that this new standard would shift the interlinkage of the organization's cultures and motivations, talents and experiences in order to promote the future fitness of the group.

The PM standard was to include the terminology and role definitions, principles and procedures, and methodology and tools required to plan, execute and communicate projects. The initiative, termed Global Offensive, was set up as a train-the-trainer programme, and was to involve practitioners from the organization's worldwide staff as trainers. All locations worldwide participated in terms of developing the standard further, training project staff and providing the offensive with training locations on site.

An external consultant facilitated the offensive, with multiple roles: bringing in project management expertise and material, supporting the core team, preparing and moderating the train-the-trainer workshop, coaching the initiators of the programme, and supervising the trainers.

The case offers an opportunity to reflect on the current practices and positioning of project management as a capability within organizations today, and is a model for organizations looking to revitalize their internal project management culture, which is owned by internal stakeholders. It demonstrates an organization strategically developing project management capability in order to drive higher levels of cross-border collaboration required to support its international operating model. The case also illustrates a successful partnership model, with an external project management consultant working alongside an organization looking, ultimately, to avoid dependence on external agency support, but rather to develop independent project management capability.

Before reading on, reflect on some key questions addressed in the case. Then compare your experience and answers to the ideas in the case itself and the final commentary.

1 What is the value of setting and following standards for the conduct of projects in organizations? Are there any downsides to this? If so, what?

2 What are the challenges and opportunities for using an external consulting company to 'revitalise' its internal project management practices?

3 How feasible do you feel it is to use experienced staff members (instead of pre-qualified PM trainers) to run train-the-trainer sessions to roll out new internal project management standards in an organization, while being coached by external consultants? Why?

PART 1: CASE STUDY
Global Offensive: project management within 150 days

Introduction

Organizational structures today are increasingly short-lived in a globalized economy characterized by volatile cycles of change. Projects are strategically used by organizations to navigate change cycles. Yet projects frequently fail to deliver on their targets, leaving organizations to chase reality, overheating their teams and people as they go.

For many, project management is failing despite being a relatively mature construct that has existed for decades. It is seen by many to have developed into an over-administrated construct. It is increasingly dominated by international institutions that offer frameworks, qualifications and certifications. It often appears that project teams have to focus more on serving frameworks, procedure models and templates, instead of delivering results that impact positively on their organization.

Yet, historically, project management was viewed far more optimistically and positively, as an opportunity to involve expertise and creativity across divisions and departments, to solve new tasks and to deliver innovation. The Global Offensive project was based upon the view that project management still offers potential, that it can offer an excellent opportunity to engage people from different cultures, to support their collaboration and networking in ways that support the international operating model of global organizations, and increases change readiness in times of high volatility.

Global Offensive was initiated by a traditional industrial company, founded in Germany more than 100 years ago. During the previous 20 years it had expanded worldwide, and faced further dynamic development. It was facing various technical and organizational changes and innovations that had to be implemented quickly, cost-efficiently and effectively. This required a proficient and harmonized set of techniques and processes, including project management. Project management, as a newly enhanced practice in the organization, was seen to offer the platform to network the various locations and divisions, to enhance cross-border cooperation, and so benefit more from its diversity of motivations, talents, competencies and experiences. A strategic aim was to be a truly 'global group', not simply on paper, but in the real experience of all its employees. The CEO and the executive team had the explicit desire to promote this offensive.

The following steps were planned across six months:

1 Project management principles defined and documented together with a core team staffed with key players from the executive team.

2 International train-the-trainer-workshop.

3 Pilot training workshops at international sites, delivered by internal trainer team.

4 Application to urgent projects.

5 Evaluation with the executive team.

6 Roll-out to the wider organization.

7 Embedding into the global leadership development programme.

8 Learning and development workshops with the trainer team.

A rapid offensive began

From the beginning of the Global Offensive (see Appendix 1 for full project schedule), the external consultant, recommended by a member of the executive team, was involved. The development of the standard (version 1) took eight weeks. Then, a three-day train-the-trainer workshop took place with trainer candidates from four manufacturing sites meeting, discussing the standard and developing a training concept. This workshop was a real starting point for a cooperative momentum and high commitment spreading in the following months and years.

The subsequent three-day training workshops – delivered by the *internal trainers* – continued to include participants from various locations. An explicit intention was not only to convey the 'defined' new internal standards but also to continue learning from the diverse views, interests and skills.

In addition, the executive team plus the upper management participated in three one-day workshops to become familiar with their roles, bringing in their ideas and concerns, and committing to the Offensive.

Overall, all participants' feedback was extremely positive due to the joint learning experience, the open workshop atmosphere and the fruitful exchange of questions, expectations, concerns and ideas, which was felt to really contribute to a new project management culture. This joint learning culture was further supported during the whole programme.

In the course of the training workshops, the internal trainers established themselves as a team that vigorously promoted the continuous improvement of the project management standard and culture.

Important new projects applied the new project management, raising the planning quality and management efficiency significantly. The comments changed from 'time-consuming procedure' to 'useful for a quick and systematic working progress'.

In the following year, project management became part of the global leadership development programme. The managers participating applied it to their strategic projects and action learning process.

Project results

The project was experienced as a success by all stakeholders. The following were acknowledged as outcomes:

- high general commitment to cooperate and engage with change;

- committed executive team with powerful support from the CEO;

- high engagement and performance of the internal trainer team;

- successful application of new standards to key projects;

- greater capability to engage with change faster (change readiness).

Success factors – why did it all work so well?

An evaluation of the project identified 14 success factors that had determined the success of the offensive.

1. Clear and urgent ideas driving the executive team's demand

A fast and significant boost in project management skills was the clear request from the most senior sponsors. There were clearly formulated ideas about the implementation process and timing: rapid installation of internal staff as the trainer team, then training a larger number of project managers and members, internal communication to a wider audience, and finally the integration into the new leadership development programmes.

The executive team explicitly declared its desire to be involved, to support and have clarity on progress: 'We do not just want to see projects put on green ('everything seems okay'), but also the projects put on amber ('need for increased attention and support') and on red ('need for fundamental decisions'). We want to understand what is happening, to intervene and to help.'

The external consultant's view:

I haven't experienced too often that the company management has involved itself in such a clear, constructive and culture-forming way. I know a lot of companies where the top management doesn't accept any indicators but green ones. Thus, they fail in understanding what is really happening in the company although they think that they lead.

2. Integration of change management within project management

The CEO made a very clear statement:

We are doing this in order to cope with the change challenges we have to face. Project management and change management cannot be discussed separately. Each project has to do with change, and how to take the people on the journey.

A key part of the train-the-trainer workshops was to discuss not only the technical challenges of a project, but also the change aspects affecting people and processes. It was clearly recognized that if a new technical system is to become reality, processes and workflows have to be adapted and people need to be qualified and supported in their motivation to work with the new system.

3 Competence, commitment and presence of a 'core team' of top management

From the beginning, a team of three dedicated members of the executive team promoted the programme actively. Initially, they simply understood themselves as background drivers of the programme. The consultant proposed that they take a more explicit role and, in this way, give a good example of how to take accountability for successful project management. They quickly accepted the proposal and established themselves as the 'core team'. They also accepted the role definition suggested by the consultant: (1) leading the initiative; (2) making decisions on project management content and the development process; (3) reporting to the CEO.

The external consultant's view:

The newly defined core team immediately accepted my proposal. This totally unpretentious pragmatism and openness was overwhelming. From my point of view, this is a cultural factor of the company that is a huge competitive advantage.

Another important factor was the competence and sensitivity of the core team and the upper management concerning the implementation process. They didn't consider project management as rocket science and focused on quick implementation and involvement of people. Therefore, the decision to dispense with initial analysis and interviews, and to focus more on working with the expertise of the core team and the internal trainers, proved to be quick and effective. The outcome was then consolidated during the training and management workshops. They trusted in people and this iterative process. They were proved right as it worked very well.

This also seemed a competitive advantage that enabled speed: a deep and shared understanding of the corporate culture, based upon many years of cooperation.

4. Iterative implementation strategy which facilitated engagement and learning

A confidence in the employees involved and their ability to cooperate, as well as the desire for quick implementation, led to a strategy that renounced perfection in the beginning in favour of a successive 'consolidation process' with repeated loops of learning across all levels of people involved in the project. This loop also kept all participants involved and drew benefit from their experiences and creativity, and any mistakes made. The iterative approach made it possible to involve and connect very quickly the motivations, ideas and concerns at all levels and drive higher quality.

5. Trust in people involved

A key success factor was top management's confidence in the people involved, in their professional and communicative competence, and their learning potential and risk appetite. The strong trust placed in the internal trainers by the core team was vital as the internal trainers had to leave their 'comfort zone' as they took on a new responsibility by rolling out the programme. This confidence inspired the train-the-trainer workshops and created a sense of 'joint endeavour' that in turn created a basis to shift and heighten collaboration across structures and cultures across the broader organization.

> In these workshops, the culture was extremely productive, and the initiative of joint endeavour began to be felt across the company. You could really feel collaboration and empathy grow in the train-the-trainer workshop.

Confidence was also shown in the external consultant who brought in his know-how and helped to navigate both the core team and the trainers across uncertain terrain. Although confidence was initially based upon a personal recommendation, shared experience and good chemistry between the individuals in the workshops built a basis of trust which allowed the workshops to succeed.

6. Early planning with challenging timelines to create a momentum for activity

Timelines for key events were fixed very early, for example the dates and venues of the train-the-trainer workshop and the three pilot training workshops, before there was any clarity in terms of messages, content and participants. This was based on a joint commitment and total mutual trust: 'We don't know what "it" will be, but if we do it together, it will be excellent'.

This way of planning a strategic programme seemed strange. It was so operative! But it worked very well. The events took hold in everyone's mind's eye, each one concentrated on making them a success. This stimulated us very much, and we were very enthusiastic to make it happen.

7. Strict realization of sponsorship, ownership and accountability

Project sponsorship and accountability became an explicit part of the new standard, in the training workshops and in a review session together with the executive team. It was explicitly committed that (1) the project sponsor is accountable for the project goals and for the project outcome (because they have to take key decisions), and (2) the project manager is responsible for leading the project team and the project process successfully.

This created a strong sense of reality and fairness, which inspired commitment. Everyone knew that in failed projects sponsors don't do their job and will ask the project managers to manage everything.

The result of this focus was a shared understanding of responsibility and accountability, and a belief that role conflicts could be addressed immediately, enabling faster and more sustainable decision making for projects.

Table 9.1 Role definitions of project sponsor und project manager

Project sponsor	Project manager
• Accountable for project charter and project outcome	• Responsible for planning, controlling and executing the project, in terms of quality, time and cost
• Nominate project manager and steering committee (option)	
• Make capacities available	• Develop and lead the project team, including external suppliers and providers
• Support project manager	
• Make decisions on stage gates/ milestones on the way, if necessary	• Coordinate project communication and involvement of stakeholders
	• Report to project sponsor, communicate with stakeholders and inform project management office

8. Pragmatic communication and decision-making culture

In combination with early and demanding planning, the project adopted an implementation strategy which required at every step a check to determine if the right decisions had been taken, what improvements were already observed as a result of the project, what needed to change etc. Such iterative feedback strategies only succeed with open, direct and rapid communication. The culture was marked significantly by an uncomplicated communication and cooperative attitude that easily compensated for weaknesses in the planning phase.

> In one case, the question came up of how to involve a very experienced superior. The concern proved to be unnecessary – the superior had been kept informed by the trainer nominated in his division. That was absolutely fine for him.

The external consultant quickly tuned into this communication culture, and supported an approach where disputes were focused on facts, and were never attacks on people.

9 Internal trainers brought quickly onto the stage and up to speed

Initially, as part of the train-the-trainer process, two pilot training workshops were planned for each internal trainer supported by the external consultant as co-trainer. A few weeks later, this pilot support was reduced in workshops with the result that the internal trainers had to deliver the final training workshops earlier than planned and completely by themselves, with the consultant simply as supervisor, not as co-trainer.

> This early handover to internal trainers seemed to me – from my experience with other companies – quite risky, especially concerning the intercultural challenge of delivering international workshops. So we had to discuss the new PM handbook and the training process in detail. And we created a design for the training workshop which provided a lot of activation for the participants, practical exercises, also team exercises, so that facilitation would run easily. In the end, however, it was the enthusiasm of the internal trainers that convinced me that it would work. And it worked, the feedback was overwhelming. The most important factor was the attitude of internal trainers. A teacher-to-student attitude would have made it very difficult, especially as the participants were 'old hands'. So we opted for an unpretentious 'information attitude'. The trainers simply informed about the new project management standard, proposed exercises and relied on good interaction with the participants.

10. Keeping two views of the elephant

Project management is used to cope with the complexity of a new task. It's about making a task manageable by differentiation and subdivision. Examples are role definitions, the milestones and activities on the timeline, the work breakdown structure with the individual work packages, the stakeholder map with their concerns and requirements etc.

Sometimes, people compare the challenge of delivering a project to eating an elephant. On the one hand, project management methodology tells you to cut the elephant into digestible pieces, eg work packages as a way to get the project done. But this is only one aspect of a project. The other side is to keep the big picture and context of the project in mind, which means keeping the entire elephant in view; its social context, the purpose of its existence, its life and impact. In terms of the project, it means keeping in mind the broader project mission, its relevance in the corporate project portfolio, and its contribution to the company's success.

Effective project leadership has to segment tasks but also keep a holistic view. Therefore, the project charter is not only to describe the technical and organizational project scope but also the entrepreneurial context and the linkages to other projects, processes and functions in the company.

11. Pragmatic approach to definitions, standards and documentation

The training participants often asked for absolute and total clarity, eg what exactly is the definition of a 'project' in our company? What kind of tasks will we define to be a 'project'? Are there quantitative criteria? The CEO answered these questions as follows: 'We will call it a project if this seems reasonable due to the size and complexity of a task; if necessary, the executive team will make the decision.' There was an explicit intention of the management to adopt a flexible approach, as far as possible.

In many companies, I have experienced heated debates about the methods, tools, spreadsheets and forms that have to be used to drive a project. Everyone has their favourites that they have honed and promoted over the years.

In this project, we saw flexibility and not rigid obedience to tools. Two key high-level documents were developed: the Project Charter and the Weekly Snapshot, a one-page report. They were discussed and communicated as a standard but many colleagues, especially those from the United States, insisted on viewing these simply as useful templates, as a general instead of formal requirement. It was also agreed to have these templates be valid for one year. Proposals for improvement were to be collected during the year and then implemented if useful. This was again pragmatic and easily agreed. Additionally, there was a clear statement that any single standard was not the answer to every question.

There are many kinds of procedure models: sequential, spiral, agile, experimental ones. Of course, you are free to rely on the concepts and certificates promoted by institutions such as PMI, IPMA or PRINCE2. Most important is that it fits your company and your ambitions. The concept has to serve the company, not vice versa. In our case, the core team defined what should part of the standard (or not) and developed the first draft, and left it open to be developed in the future.

It was clear in the discussions that cultural attitudes to rules and standards were quite different. Some expected definitions and guidelines which would be binding. But a culture of flexibility was promoted.

It was discussed that decisions are not meant to last forever; they are made from today's point of view, to the best of the decision makers' knowledge and conscience! And if new insights come up, the point of view can change. The clear response to this from management was, 'No problem. Your staff know that nobody can see into the future. But they also want you as manager to be honest and clear. If you need to change, then change. But communicate why.'

12. Quick application of standard to key projects – prove the principle

The opportunity soon arose to apply the new standard to a key project. New production equipment had to be installed in order to ensure delivery capability for the next few years, involving the shutting down of an obsolete plant. It took just two and a half days to set up the project. Three workshops were facilitated by the external consultant, involving the project manager and experts from production and controlling. The working mode followed was: 'Plan as deeply as necessary and as quickly as possible, and make use of our new and useful standards.' The experts involved were sceptical about project management and the new standards in the beginning, but they experienced quick progress and sound results. They managed to prepare a project contract (Project Charter), define market and production requirements, set up an opportunity and risk analysis (SWOT), map the stakeholder situation, clarify a work breakdown structure and the project organization, and prepare the next meetings with the project sponsor.

We didn't discuss the pros and cons of project management but just did it – and delivered more outcome than had been expected.

13. Measured improvement

Experience shows that it is difficult to measure the success of project management. There is little opportunity to start a 'control group' and run two projects on the same subject, one project trying the new approach, the other one working 'as always'. Nevertheless, we implemented simple indicators that enabled people to track easily how far a project was on track.

Fulfilment of goals = goals achieved: goals committed

There shouldn't be goals that have been achieved but not committed (lack of focusing, communication and agreement) or goals that have been committed but not achieved (lack of project steering or change request management).

Resource quality = Resources available: Resources needed

There shouldn't be resources available that are not needed now or in the future (lack of resource management) or resources needed but not available (lack of prioritization and commitment on priorities).

Resource allocation = staff involved in projects: staff trained in project management

There shouldn't be staff involved in projects who are not trained (lack of project efficiency) or staff trained who are not involved in projects (lack of training impact).

Investment management = investments realized: investments planned

There shouldn't be more investments realized than planned (lack of planning quality) or fewer investments realized than planned (lack of project results and finance management).

14. Positive management of ambiguity and conflict

One key success factor of the Global Offensive was the positive handling of ambiguities and even conflicting aspects:

- clear guidelines vs. true confidence in the staff;

- quick realization vs. reflective discussion;

- external support vs. internal engagement;

- sound experience vs. openness to new ideas;

- desire for a clear framework vs. development of flexibility;

- global standard vs. intercultural richness.

- certainty wanted vs. iterative process.

This balancing act has largely succeeded. There were 'overshoots' in one direction or another, but they were transparent and well managed. For example, on 'external contribution vs. internal engagement', it was discussed to what extent to involve the external facilitator. This question was solved by breaking it down to concrete actions that should be supported by the consultant and smaller decisions to make this possible. Or the question of framework and flexibility: the team didn't discuss this in principle but what it meant in daily work and made pragmatic decisions – what templates seemed helpful, for which purpose?

The managers and experts involved were open to and tolerant of ambiguity and preferred AND discussions instead of OR (exclusive or) conflicts. They listened to different perspectives and tried to understand the individual interests behind them. They didn't fight for any positions, but found joint solutions, with respect for the other people and their opinions. They succeeded in keeping the right level, avoiding both fundamental debates and getting lost in details.

Conclusions and recommendations

To close, we would like to outline some practical recommendations to those leading or working in international projects:

- Ensure clear communication of the purpose, urgency, and entrepreneurial background of the project. Why is it needed, here and now? How do we want to proceed? What are our true expectations?

- Establish a clear operative timeline. When will each event (meeting, workshop, training) take place? Create a shared mental picture of what is expected to happen during the shared journey.

- Adopt a train-the-trainer approach that will lead to waves of involvement and enthusiasm. Consider who to involve, in which sequence, when, which cultural profile of trainer, and the right participants.

- Start quickly. Create success stories and constructive feedback. project management needs good experiences of courage, enthusiasm and confirmation.

- Use an iterative procedure. Create and evaluate first interim results and consider how to integrate new influences and insights, and how to use the potential of the situation, the current energies.

- Develop a communication culture which is direct, open and quick, and which respects intercultural diversity. Bear in mind that communication is more important than any technical schedule. Be a role model.

- Build quick and immediate understanding of what is happening, where challenges are and ideas on how to keep the project course on track, how to respond quickly to resistance, and how to build credibility with stakeholders.

- Demonstrate active project sponsorship, ownership and accountability. The key players make the project culture.

Part 2: Interview

The following is the summary of a series of personal conversations between Bob and Frank.

Q: You talk early in the case about the need to increase 'interlinkage' in the organization. Was there a need to connect something that was disconnected?

A: I think there was linkage but what they wanted to improve was emotional linkage. So, there were plants and units connected but there was a deeply felt gap in efficiency and communication, and no stability with a big change ahead. The CEO was in doubt if there was enough stability in the organization and in the relationships to handle the change. So one objective was to create a real sense of belonging.

Q: In terms of project outcomes, was a new standard developed and then used by those inside the company?

A: Yes, there was a standard PM handbook developed. But the term standard was a little bit special for the CEO. It meant, kind of, to have a look at if you wanted to start a project, and not that you have to follow the handbook 109 per cent. It was more like, here's something, it's useful, it was developed by experts, you don't need to stick to it so closely, but be prepared to answer if you don't use it, why not.

Q: You mention the project delivered greater capability to engage with change faster. How was this measured or was it just felt? Or both?

A: Well, firstly, the participants said that they experienced a higher level of procedural clarity, and that the project helped them to cope with challenges and hurdles much faster.

Q: That's, of course, a qualitative measure.

A: Yes, it is. We discussed quantitative measurability but the board stated that this was not the purpose of the exercise. Remember, a key part of the purpose was in terms of collaboration and culture building. In the end, what impressed people most was seeing their colleagues in front of them speaking about project management, having the courage to do this, and also experiencing the interaction between them and us who had started to deal with it three or four months ago.

Q: **The process itself symbolizes the outcomes?**

A: Yes, exactly what you say. The process was designed to make it together. And this process and experience of this process inspired the outcome in the wider organization.

Q: **Why do you think so many project managers still underestimate the change dimensions of projects? It's been recognized for 20 years as something to be managed.**

A: I don't think they are given time to do it, time or resources. Communication, resistance and conflicts are not planned for properly in projects. People are provided with time to solve technical problems. And you have the issue of the illusion of power; some senior people believe that if they say do it, then it must happen. And they are so overloaded they can't prioritize their thought. They don't have time to doubt their thoughts, and people on the shop floor, without the experience of change management, they overestimate what they can achieve and underestimate the time needed to achieve change.

Q: **You mentioned that the planning came strangely early. What did you mean? Isn't early planning good?**

A: Normally you plan in a way that you have content in a training course that you have to convey. You have to find trainers to train them etc. What we did here, in the beginning, we didn't know the content or the trainers or the difficulties of recruiting, but we set up a precise timeline, naming dates for training sessions in Europe and, a month later, overseas. And I said, but we don't have the trainers. And they just said that we'd have them. And then I pointed out that we didn't have the content, and they simply answered that there was no problem; they were sure that if we did it together and were motivated, that we would manage it. It was unusual and highly motivational as it demonstrated a lot of trust up front in us. And this was a key success factor in the whole project – the trust of CEO in staff and vice versa.

Q: Can you say something about accountability in the project? It's a word used in many other organizations but without much effect.

A: In many organizations accountability is very big, and very open. Here the term was in smaller pieces. Even their thinking was in smaller pieces; it was all about where to make a quick decision, quick breakthroughs in the longer journey. If thinking is too big, people are afraid to take a decision and to take accountability. Here, what they would say is that accountability is for doing the first step, to start exploration, to contribute a proposal by the end of next month. They made accountability possible.

Q: It's interesting when you talk about dilemmas, and shifting to and from detail to the big picture. Why is this so important?

A: It's again an attitude. Taylorism says that the upper-level managers have to think in terms of strategy and management, while the shop-floor staff have to think in more operative terms. But people work better if they understand the purpose of what they are doing, of what they contribute to in terms of the success and future fitness of the company, of how their part is interconnected with other activities. I think senior management often forgets this.

Q: Handling dilemmas requires a great deal of situational awareness. Is this just experience in the end?

A: I think the key ability is to remain open to different perspectives, which also needs the capability not to get stuck in the dilemma but to be able to explore and question it, to engage with it and push on from it. Look, you can say that a dilemma is a dead end or you can say, let's have a look at what's in it, and perhaps we can learn from it to use it as a starting point for something. It's about creativity. Just to give you an example, in a different company, we had a problem with some team members who didn't walk the talk, who had an expectation of what others should do but who didn't deliver themselves. So we asked the colleagues of these people how they handled it. They told us that they simply bypassed these people if they needed to get stuff done, which didn't solve the problem. So we came up with a new idea; maybe we make them our project managers and give them a role where they are visible and stand in front of a development. And it worked, problem solved. So creative thinking is useful.

Q: A lot of this book is about communication: communication channels, messages, lots of communication. What's the key to communication for you?

A: You need to get access to people. You need a deep activation, not only by telling a story. It's also the ability to listen, to communicate with questions to build awareness in the other person. You need to find a way to involve them in your enthusiasm, your passion. Sometimes it has to be about more than the project; it needs to be about a bigger cause – social, morality. You need a wow effect.

Part 3: Commentary

Here are some reflections on Frank's case and interview.

There are three aspects of Frank's case which are particularly interesting. First, he talks about a very rapid but committed planning process, before resources and knowledge were even in place. In fact, it was a planning process driven primarily by trust in the client organization towards him and the project team, a trust which then inspired delivery on this ambitious planning. For me, it stimulates a lot of thinking into the relative values of leading by soft factors such as trust as opposed to managing by data and key performance indicators. Perhaps connected are Frank's comments on the impact that the internal training team had on its own colleagues, who were impressed by the level of skill and commitment demonstrated by the team in facilitating the programme roll-out. It is an example of project process and content merging. It was the inspirational impact and respect generated by the project process of using internal trainers which contributed significantly to the project's objectives, namely to inspire greater internal emotional identification and collaboration. It seems very smart. Finally, the advocated responses to dilemmas, to use them as an opportunity for creative breakthrough rather than as a time to complain and remain paralysed, is very important. Dilemma and paradox permeate modern international corporate life, and a positive and creative response to such challenges is a must in projects.
Bob Dignen

Part 4: Reflecting on international project management

Take time to reflect on the following questions to help you reach further insights and take practical actions to improve your own project management practice.

1 How important are the internal project standards of your own organization in informing your international project practice? What other benchmarks can or could you refer to?

2 How effectively do you integrate change management into your project management practice?

3 Which dilemmas do you face in your work environment? How can you best tackle these?

Part 5: Putting it into practice

There are a number of very valid insights and ideas for project management present in this case which the reader can learn from and adopt, customizing for their own projects. Take a few minutes to note down your main learnings from this case, and note down some actions for yourself.

Personal insights, learnings and actions

A tale of David and Goliath: storytelling in projects

10

BOB DIGNEN

Profile

Bob Dignen is a director of York Associates. He specializes in supporting international leaders, international teams and networks to become high performing, delivering a broad range of training programmes worldwide that drive international collaboration. He specializes in international project management, coaching those leading complex project environments, facilitating international project (kick-off) meetings and team-building sessions. Bob also coaches professionals in senior leadership positions, supporting the transition to a global or international C-level role. He is available as a keynote motivational speaker for leadership events/professional conferences.

As an author, he recently developed an e-learning, 'English for the native speaker', which aims to enable native English speakers use an English that is effective when communicating with non-native English speakers – a global first! Other titles include *Communication for International Business* (Harper Collins), *Effective International Business* (Harper Collins), *Communicating Across Cultures* (CUP), *Managing Projects* (Delta Publishing), *Communicating Internationally in English* (York Associates), *50 Ways to Improve your International Presentation Skills* and *50 Ways to Improve your Intercultural Skills* published by Summertown, and is co-author of *Developing People Internationally*, a multimedia international team training resource.

He is an accredited facilitator of Fierce Conversations™, a licensed coach for The International Profiler (an intercultural profiling tool), and an advanced practitioner of TMP (Team Management Profile), an international team development tool.

Foreword

Storytelling has long been an important activity for humans, since the very first moments that we learned to communicate to one another our feelings and experiences. As a species we seem born to tell, to recount meaningful stories that represent our values and beliefs, which are confirmed through re-telling.

Although international project management seems to inhabit a strongly empirical world defined by measurement and analytics, it's also a world where stories emerge and play a dynamic role in the fabric of project life. Projects are places where diverse and powerful felt experiences and perspectives live. What happens in projects is often captured in stories, which become living anchors of experience, and justify powerful and often opposing individual and group perspectives.

This case involves multiple and competing stories, and recounts my own experience as an intercultural coach working with a hugely diverse international project team where levels of suspicion and distrust were so high that project efficacy was compromised. My encounter with the team was itself a process of storytelling, with different narratives told to me which competed, clashed and, curiously, slowly revealed themselves as fragments of a larger, more complex story that no-one had yet told. Culture figured prominently within the first story as a device to explain others.

The case offers, I believe, some key insights into human interaction and international project management. At one important level for me, it was a salutary lesson in the dangers of believing the story of culture; human behaviour in projects cannot be understood mechanistically as a product of national culture. It's more complex than that. At a more fundamental level, if we begin to understand the messages of others as stories, containing powerful personal meanings and needs which demand a hearing, then we listen, not to hear somehow a truth, but simply to hear the person and to respect their story. This is the role of coach, and it can be a powerful one. Additionally, as we understand our own messages simply as stories too, we become potentially happier to accept disagreement or rejection of what we say. After all, who can really understand our story? Only we were there.

Before reading this case, I invite you to reflect and make notes on a couple of questions. Then compare your answers to the ideas in the case itself and the final commentary.

1 How important do you feel national culture is in determining professionals' behaviours in an international project context? Which experiences justify your view?

2 How important do you feel storytelling is within international projects? Why?

PART 1: CASE STUDY
A tale of David and Goliath: storytelling in projects

Introduction

So the case begins with my own story, in a cold Nordic country, in a land full of legend and myth, and me on stage telling a tale of culture to a gathered audience. I was actually giving a presentation. The topic of the presentation was, strangely enough, working in international projects and the associated challenges of cultural diversity in project teams. I was delivering a guest lecture at a Nordic university where I was also working as a coach to master's students. They were studying, believe it or not, project management. It seems a far-fetched story at the outset.

After my presentation, which went well I am happy to say, I was approached by a number of individuals with questions. One individual announced himself as the CFO of a major local engineering company; I call it ABC. He said his organization had recently embarked on a huge international project, but that the project was experiencing huge difficulties – could I help? It seemed like an opportunity too good to miss so I gratefully accepted the challenge, and we set up a meeting for the next day.

Chapter 1: The story of Goliath

Having made my way to the meeting, I found myself opposite three individuals: the CEO, CFO and head of the PMO. Clearly this was an important project and topic of conversation to the organization. The first story I was told, which was consistent between the three individuals, laid things out very clearly in white (who was good) and black (who was bad). The story was epic and moral in its dimensions. I heard how a project had been initiated to modernize an aged industrial aluminium plant, a key industry in the country where there was high expertise. At that point, I had little familiarity with aluminium as a global industry, but it was clearly globalized, with smelting plants located all over the world. The size of the project was significant, involving hundreds of millions of USD.

As one of the biggest projects in the country's history, a global multinational partner had been brought on board to drive the project in some form of partnership with the local entity. However, all was not well. Relationships were not working. The project was struggling to deliver, and had fallen dangerously behind schedule. Intervention was needed to get things back on track. Here are some of the kinds of comments I heard; the first of many stories.

- *The multinational is driving the project in a brutal and inhuman manner. Military leadership style (South African, Australian and Canadian) is not working. Moreover, it's incompetent – unrealistic goals and workloads are being set creating pressure, conflict and stress.*

- *This is proven by a survey already conducted by a local consulting company of our staff working in the engineering company. The levels of stress are off the scale.*

- *Come and help. Intercultural issues are derailing the project. These outsiders don't understand how to work here. Their leadership is archaic leadership and failing.*

Forty-five minutes into the two-hour meeting, it was becoming clear to me that this story met my own needs immediately. I was being offered the role of hero and saviour in the face of a monstrous global Goliath. My intercultural knowledge and skills were validated and purchased. I was tasked with creating a training and coaching intervention; I could define my own project. I was to travel to the country to run a series of cultural awareness-raising sessions with local staff at the engineering plant, and to pass on tools to handle (and possibly slay) the Goliath. It was even agreed that I would meet the Goliath. There was much confidence I could tackle the giant head on. I left that meeting feeling pretty good about myself. I had a mission. I had a project to deliver. I was engaging meaningfully with the world of international project management.

Chapter 2

Returning to the country some weeks later, my project started well. I ran a series of small workshops with technical and management staff across the local engineering organization. We talked about culture and cultural diversity. We discussed cultural competence. People listened and were interested. More than anything, they were happy to be listened to. It was semi-confessional. A picture was confirmed of a global multinational transgressing the rules and ethics of the local environment. Even family lives had been affected by the long working hours demanded and high levels of stress generated. Story upon story of harsh and directive leadership emerged. As the stories flowed, I tried to visualize key elements in order to capture key dynamics. One main picture that emerged was the following:

Figure 10.1 Diverse models of teamwork

Project team: Multinational Goliath   Project team: Nordic local

The graphic captured two very different approaches to the project team: Goliath on the left, my Nordic organization on the right. Goliath believes in defining rigid roles and structures. It's hierarchical. It's non-collaborative. There is no trust at all; project deliverables are specified, and micro-managed with sanctions for non-delivery. On the right is the modern and more democratic approach. People are empowered; people enjoy cooperation in overlapping circles of connectivity; the formal leader has disappeared in favour of informal co-leadership; we are talking self-directing and highly competent teams who can be left alone to deliver successfully. The story made perfect sense. I began to get very curious about what it would be like to meet the Goliath. I soon found out.

Chapter 3

My first meeting with Goliath was scheduled one early and very dark morning. There wasn't much light in the Nordics on that November day. As I entered the front offices of Goliath's castle, I could hear the sound of voices. I walked down the corridor to witness two guys in ferocious and very loud verbal combat. It didn't sound pleasant or likely to stop, so I retreated to the corridor and waited. Others arrived and things calmed. Eventually, I was invited to meet a small management team from the global Goliath, including the two angry men. Then I heard my next and very different story.

On first introductions, it was clear that I was working with very smart operators. These guys were focused and clear communicators; the round of introductions revealed that they came with a wealth of international experience of doing tough jobs in very tough places. They were also working for a very successful global organization, one of the biggest on the planet in terms of revenue and profitability. They knew business and they meant business. Yes, there was a touch of machismo. There was actually experience of working in the military. But there was also a very strong focus on care; caring for safety, caring for people, caring to protect lives in dangerous working environments. Care sometimes came across as discipline. One of my favourite stories from my visit was the experience of being disciplined. I was actually told to use the handrail as I walked down a flight of stairs because... walking and not holding, that's how accidents happen.

Care and professionalism? It wasn't exactly what I had expected. So I moved to the project and asked for Goliath's experiences. Was there another story? And I heard very different things to anything I had heard before.

- *We came here with the best intentions in the world. We wanted to transfer all our international know-how, but these local guys are not up to the job! They lack experience and competence. They don't know how to do a project.*

- *They are slow. They don't accept responsibility for their tasks. They make promises and then fail to deliver – repeatedly. They can't even do basic safety right on site. We can't trust these guys.*

- *The only way to make this project work is to exert firm leadership. So we have increased the role of the consulting company in the joint venture in order to push things through and keep quality up.*

- *We have the experience. We know what is needed to make this kind of project hit its time, quality and costs targets. We are providing the leadership required. We have targets to hit and we will hit them. That's what it means to be professional.*

I quickly found myself in a strange position because I believed the story. It seemed compelling. There was story after story about the local engineering company's failure to deliver. There was story after story of safety breaches. There was complaint after complaint about a lack of project management expertise. It seemed real, and some of it matched my own experience. I had worked in the country for over five years; there was a clear acknowledgement among locals that most companies in this Nordic context lacked project management expertise.

I remembered the graphics I had developed with 'the other side' (Figure 10.1) and decided to get a second opinion. The shapes were recognized but they meant something entirely different. The 'Goliath' was, of course, a more box-shaped structure, but then it had to be as a mature and organized project management operation. People knew what they had to do and delivered. Things were measured because that's how to run projects. It produces transparency and accountability. The right-handed set of circles was simply chaotic, no one responsible for anything, but everyone believing they could do something. And when non-delivery happened, fuzzy roles meant that no one accepted responsibility. In one word, it was unprofessional.

What was curious in this story was mention of a new protagonist, a joint venture partner. Who exactly was this, I wondered? They hadn't been mentioned before. So I asked, and slowly a new and more complex landscape emerged, with an increased number of stakeholder groups.

Figure 10.2 Many more protagonists than thought

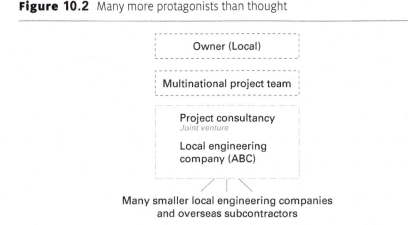

In the background, there was the previously invisible project owner, also Nordic and also local. Itself a large organization, it owned the aluminium plant and had commissioned the multinational team to run the project on its behalf. The multinational team had contracted the local engineering company simply for engineering expertise. However, suspecting a gap in competence, an international project consulting company had also been contracted into an uneasy joint (more like competitive) venture with my local organization. In addition, there were tens of additional small local engineering and overseas expert companies on site in the project, all with very different competence and performance levels.

As I walked the corridors of all the stakeholders' offices, I realized that everyone had different stories. The more I listened, the more it became obvious that there was no common story about the project. How could it be that so many stories existed about a single project? How could it be that everyone blamed everyone else for failure to deliver? This phenomenon couldn't be explained by diversity of national cultures. I began to doubt my own discourse. I began to doubt my own purpose. My own project no longer seemed to hold. It was all far more complex than that.

Chapter 4

I stayed in the Nordic environment for almost two weeks. I spent 10 days, 10 full days, meeting people involved in the project, hearing their stories, making sense of their stories, sharing the stories of others, until I had composed a final and complete story of the project. I wrote a report and I created a PowerPoint slide deck which captured this 'whole' story, a story that had never been told before in the lifetime of the project. Of course, it was not wholly complete – after all, it was just another story. But it was the most complete narrative that had ever been told, and it had buy-in from just about everybody. There was balance and consent, finally.

However, what was striking about my final story was not the level of agreement it eventually generated, it was its complexity and multi-layered-ness, which had initially been invisible to everyone. People could still see their own stories of the project in my story, but there was a bigger and more complex picture now available; the underlying dynamics were visible. The story now became one not of project management, but of project mismanagement.

The full story

As is evident from the big picture, the 'final' number of players or stakeholders involved has increased, with many invisible interests exposed.

Figure 10.3 The big picture

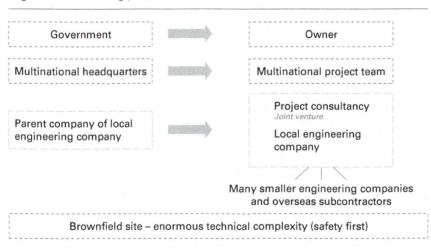

The owner story

The owner had actually not commissioned the project with free will. Commissioning had taken place under considerable pressure from its own national government to run such a project. Why? It was necessary to generate employment and a feel-good factor following the worst economic crisis in living memory, which had shaken the country to the core. Political pressures compromised proper preparation for the project and undermined commitment to lead the project effectively. Things really hadn't started well.

The multinational story

Things were also complicated for the global multinational. It was facing a tough time in its aluminium division, which competed internally with other divisions such as copper, all of which were performing better. There had even been talk of spinning off the aluminium business. This had led to anxiety among those leading the aluminium division, and a decision (partly covert) was taken to get a large project started; it would give visibility and activity, and act against any sell-off decision.

When approaching the Nordic owner to negotiate the project contract, the sales team of the aluminium division had decided to make an offer the Nordic owner could not refuse. Of course, over-selling the project meant that the deliverables and budgets promised were unrealistic. This rapidly became apparent during project execution, which was the responsibility of the multinational team I had met (not the sales people who sold the project).

Notwithstanding this, the multinational project team committed hard to run an effective project, and to do it in the right way. The company had a strong and mature PM framework with strict requirements on quality, accountability and transparency in reporting. This somewhat 'heavy' project culture was about to land in a country in which there was and had never been anything resembling a project management culture. Conflict was inevitable.

There was also extremely high technical complexity. The project had experienced problems from the outset. The technical (electrical) dangers of the site under development had surprised everyone, including engineers on both sides. Renovating and upgrading it safely proved hazardous and time-consuming. The strong safety cultures present in both companies united to slow down the project, producing unforeseen and critical delays. But safety had to come first.

The international project consultancy story (in the joint venture)

This consultancy was global in operations, and used fly-in experts; people jumping in and out of the project for periods of two to four weeks. They didn't live in the local country and had little interest in it. They arrived, worked 18 hours a day for the duration of their 'shift' and then flew home to family for a week. They were highly competent but extremely task oriented. They had little time to dedicate to relationship building so focused on pushing for results. They were paid on a bonus system and if they failed to deliver, they lost significant money. No wonder they were pushy. As the project progressed, they realized the lack of expertise in the local engineering company and pushed for more responsibility to drive the project. This undermined the joint venture concept. But what else could they do? The dynamic of external consultant and home-grown engineer was a generally unproductive one.

The local engineering company story

The local engineering company was actually part of a large local entity with many local companies. Relations between the parent company of this group and the local engineering company subsidiary, my client, were not great. The parent didn't believe in the international ambitions of its subsidiary, and was sceptical of this large project commitment. As a result, it viewed requests for more resources from the group unsympathetically, leaving the local engineering company under-resourced for the duration of the project. Additionally, the lack of deep project management experience, combined with local preferences for collaborative and agile ways of working simply didn't meet the requirements of the multinational's concept of professionalism. In the end, the local engineering company employees' reluctance to move from their own belief system, seen as rooted in collectivism, equality and democracy, proved highly problematic.

Chapter 5

The story has an ending. Eventually, it was clear to everyone that the project was failing, and risked total failure. The range of interests and beliefs had simply been too high to converge. Technical issues alone had almost derailed the project; inadequate resourcing and poor scoping on set-up was claimed by many to have compromised the project before it started. Only a formal restart of the project was seen as a way forward. It was discussed and scheduled. It was actually planned for me to be present, as I had gained a reasonably high level of trust through my many conversations with all members of the project. I was going to be given a role in the creation of a new story, with relationships built upon common ground and mutual respect.

Unfortunately, the event never materialized. Senior leadership in the parent company of the multinational pulled out their head of the project in the local country, restructured the joint venture, and scoped the project deliverable down to a more manageable level. This made it possible for the project to report some level of success in the end, a necessary requirement for the most senior management in front of their shareholders. A happy ending was manufactured, and a final story of project success began to circulate.

The denouement

The experience of this project was for me one of the most fascinating in my professional career. The individuals I met, without exception, were committed and expert professionals looking to deliver value within the project. Unfortunately, the environment proved to be corrupted from the beginning. Different and defensive narratives grew out of this context, as pressure, diversity and technical adversity mounted. Human beings took a position and decided on a story. Victims defined themselves, ogres were named; stories became anchors of this stalemate.

The story is about one project, yet I wonder how many projects it could apply to. Are the best practices of IPMA and PMI simply myths and legends, which fail to appear in the real stories of actual projects? It's complex. Perhaps that's another story altogether.

(*The story, all names, characters, and incidents portrayed in this production are fictitious. No identification with actual persons, places, buildings, and products is intended or should be inferred.*)

Part 2: Interview

The following is an excerpt from a conversation between Bob and Peter.

Q: You mention your early role was as some kind of intercultural expert. You gave a presentation about cultural diversity, you were contracted to solve cultural issues. Yet this proves false in some way. Do you mean to be self-critical?

A: Yes, I do. I think this project experience was a major learning for me not to trust my own beliefs about what I thought to be problems in projects. The challenges people face in these complex undertakings are often highly multi-layered, and involve a lot of factors which are not visible. It's easy to blame national culture as a driver of the problems of team interaction or performance; it's generally far more complex.

Q: So how do you respond now when people use national culture as a way to explain project issues? Do you challenge it?

A: Yes and no. On the one hand, you have to respect people's experiences, their stories. If someone tells you something and provides an explanation, I don't want to be a conversation partner who tries to correct.

It's arrogant and likely to be mistaken at some level because I simply don't know. However, and this is evident in some research I supervised at the University of Reykjavik, I think it's important to challenge over-simplified analysis of complex problems if we want to create better understanding.

Q: Your case is very much about stories. If projects are composed of people telling very different stories, does that mean there is no truth, just stories? How can you lead in such a situation?

A: OK, these are two questions. Without getting too philosophical about the nature of truth, it's clearly difficult sometimes to separate reality from opinion. What was so striking in this experience was that people's versions of reality were so different, and held with such conviction. I hadn't seen this before in this way. Leading in this specific situation became, therefore, problematic. But in the end, the leadership challenge is always around creating alignment between different perspectives, getting agreement about which way to go and how to go there. So leadership was not and is not impossible. But it is never easy.

Q: The graphic in the story showing different attitudes to the project team was very interesting. It seems important for any team anywhere to clarify what it looks like. Do you agree?

A: This is one of my favourite graphics and I use it a lot in training to expose and explore assumptions about core aspects of working in projects, in this case the concept of 'team'. I think different notions of team are often in play in projects, but this is not realized, and a lot of unnecessary friction and misunderstanding is generated. I have used the graphics in team building as a way of getting people to surface the preferences in the team, and then getting the team to draw, to visualize their own notion of team necessary for the specific project. At the very least, it surfaces beliefs and values which might remain hidden, and helps people understand each other.

Q: At one point, you talk about the fly-in and fly-out consultant. Is this dynamic of external consultant versus project staff member commonly problematic in your experience?

A: The role and acceptance of external consultants are always down to the specifics of each individual case. However, I have seen on several occasions that highly expert consultants present in project teams can irritate the organization's staff. They do tend to have specialist expertise; not that it's always the right expertise as the internal staff member in a project often has better knowledge of the reality of their own organization. They often work longer hours, and that creates a disconnect. It's a dynamic that needs to be carefully managed by the project team and leader.

Q: **Finally, you mention project management as a myth towards the end of the case. You don't mean that, do you?**

A: Talking to many professionals working in large complex projects for this book, a consistent theme is the idea that the theory of project management is rarely the same as actual practice. So, there are best practices, guidelines, theories, but in so many organizations today, projects have to be run in a less-than-perfect way, because that's all that is possible. I guess that's the same with many professional disciplines. I just wonder if the gap between how project management is taught, and how it is lived in big projects, is just too wide.

Part 3: Commentary

Here are some reflections on Bob's case and interview.

This case shows a key insight for complex projects involving multiple stakeholders: there is not one truth, there are many. Bob's use of storytelling is used to make this transparent. In my perspective, an overkill from sophisticated methods and tools that we partly experience in project management might conceal this fact. Projects are not a mathematical task (even in mathematics, different ways might successfully lead to a solution). Projects are taking place in a legal, social, political, economic and cultural system (system meant in the sociological definition) with people acting as they are socialized, according to their experienced world and their strong convictions. It is fascinating, but not always in a positive way, how differently an initial situation for a project will be described by different stakeholder groups from inside and outside the enterprise. This is one of the reasons to have an intensive project initiation phase with a comprehensive kick-off meeting to 'check the terroir'.

One has to accept that some 'terroirs' or constellations are so difficult that projects will fail with a very high probability. If the different perspectives, represented by stakeholder groups, do not interact with each other to a minimal reasonable level, there is probably no chance. If they do, and keep a certain level of cooperation, and try to understand the others' positions (without necessarily sharing them), there is a chance of success. The better the interaction and the building up of some respect towards the other position, the higher the probability of success.

It is highly recommended to take time for exploration of all perspectives and stories at the beginning of a project, and to continue this on a regular basis, as the success of the project will depend on it.
Peter Wollmann

Part 4: Reflecting on international project management

Take time to reflect on the following questions to help you reach further insights and take practical actions to improve your own project management practice.

1 Which differences of perspective can be expected in multi-organizational projects? How can these differences be aligned?

2 What are the advantages of using external consultants in large international projects? What are some of the challenges? In which ways can the challenges be managed effectively?

3 How useful is the theory of project management if the practice can be so very different? Why?

Part 5: Putting it into practice

There are a number of very valid insights and ideas for project management present in this case which the reader can learn from and adopt, customizing for their own projects. Take a few minutes to note down your main learnings from this case, and note down some actions for yourself.

Personal insights, learnings and actions

Setting up an RTGS (Real Time Gross Settlement) system in a Latin American Context

11

ALBERTO CASAGRANDE

Profile

Dr Alberto Casagrande is a strategic, economic, and ICT adviser. As founding partner, Dr Casagrande has been an active managing director of The Core Inc., a boutique firm devoted to strategic, ICT and economic advisery, for the last 15 years. During this period, Dr Casagrande has advised both the World Bank and several central banks across the world on financial infrastructural reforms and SME finance. He was senior adviser for several banking sector restructuring projects across the world, and has advised several global players in the insurance sector on strategic issues, also supporting various countries' economic ministries on growth strategies and debt management. Project locations include North and Latin America, Europe, the Middle East and North Africa. Dr Casagrande was previously project manager at McKinsey in Italy, and before that an analyst at the Central Bank of Italy.

Dr Casagrande holds a PhD in economics from New York University, and has held several adjunct professor appointments both at Luiss University, Rome and at New York University. Dr Casagrande is currently senior adviser at the Center for Monetary and Financial Studies in Rome, Italy. He has had several publications in academic journals of global repute, such as *Journal of Behavioral and Experimental Economics, European Journal of Law and Economics,* and *Environmental Economics.* Dr Casagrande is an active angel investor in startups in Europe and the United States.

Foreword

Alberto's case is fascinating on a number of levels. First, it is probably the most detailed case in the book, and really drills down to a granular level on many aspects of a highly complex and sensitive project with enormous strategic impact. It highlights for me the significant technical challenges that face those who lead international projects, here with financial services and tools. Secondly, communication figures heavily in Alberto's thinking and practice, and his approaches should offer insights to those within or about to enter such project environments. Finally, the need for emotional resilience is underlined by Alberto's experience, during which he faced several demanding setbacks and challenges, all of which he eventually overcame.

Before reading on, reflect on a number of key questions addressed in the case. Then compare your experience and answers to the ideas in the case itself and the final commentary.

1 As a project leader, how important and useful is it to escalate issues early during a project to senior stakeholders? Why?

2 For project leaders who need to deliver results quickly, which is better – to be brave and act, or to be cautious and proceed slowly? Why?

3 How significant can a client's negative experiences in the past with previous consultants be for newer consultants entering a project? What can be done to win people over who have negative preconceptions about external consultants?

PART 1: CASE STUDY   Setting up an RTGS (Real Time Gross Settlement) system in a Latin American context

Introduction

This case study is about a country-level payment systems implementation, specifically the implementation of a Real Time Gross Settlement system (RTGS) in a Latin American country which took place for eight months during 2005.

The case is organized as follows. First, there is an introduction to payments systems in general and a short overview of this project. Second, information is provided about the context, initially at country level and then in terms of the country's financial sector. Third, details of the project are provided followed by a snapshot of the project's results and its longer-term impact. Fourth, I give some reflections and insights on the dynamics of the project by looking at various key moments. Finally, the case closes with a project review which examines its specificities as an international project, key lessons learned, and what I would do if I had to do it all over again.

Payment systems

A payment system is any system used to settle financial transactions through the transfer of monetary value, and includes the institutions, instruments, people, rules, procedures, standards, and technologies that make such an exchange possible.

Different payment systems are usually adopted in different countries, partly according to the demands of local users. The systems most known are those in retail, dealing with credit cards, debit cards, and cheques. There is another very sensitive payment system that is very much under the surveillance of countries' central banks, namely that which involves large payments between central bank, commercial banks, and other financial sector providers. This is what is known as a Large Value Payment System. It is very relevant because any failure to settle in such a system, given the high value of the payments, has the potential to cause large-scale systemic inability to settle, therefore, potentially creating large-scale systemic/economic negative impacts.

Accordingly, in order to minimize financial risk across countries, international multilateral organizations (namely, the Bank for International Settlements, the IMF, and the World Bank) have, together with regional organizations and central banks, issued recommendations to operate Real Time Gross Settlements (RTGS) systems, ie to settle transactions in real time on a gross basis, as opposed to the global practice until the '80s of settling on a net basis at end of day.

The project I am describing in this chapter deals with the implementation of such RTGS recommendations in a Latin American country.

Project overview

The project was financed by the World Bank and implemented specifically by the central bank of the country. Following many other countries across the world and the recommendation of major international reference institutions in payments and securities settlement systems (The Committee of Payments and Market Infrastructures (CPMI, until 2005 known as The Committee of Payments and

Securities Settlements, or CPSS) at Bank of International Settlements, the IMF and World Bank) the country's central bank decided to modernize the country's payments and securities settlement system by introducing a real-time gross payment highway between the central bank and the banking system (focused initially on commercial banks).

The central bank initially designed the strategy and then started with the implementation after completing a bidding process for a software provider. Following a visit and consultation with senior representatives of the World Bank, the central bank concluded that an international expert in payments systems was required to support an implementation that was compliant with international standards. So the central bank used a loan from the World Bank and opened a bidding process for international advisers which I won. I advised the central bank for about eight months until the official go-live of the RTGS system. I travelled three times to the country during the period of the project and spent about 100 days on site in total.

Overall, the project was a great success for the central bank and the general financial sector of the country, with sustainability established for the future. As of now, the country's payments and securities settlement systems are based upon the RTGS infrastructure that was created at this time. This infrastructure has been, and continues to be, the basis for further improvements that were implemented more recently, namely in mechanisms allowing Delivery Versus Payments for settlement systems, and in strengthening oversight over payments and securities settlement systems.

Beyond the successful implementation, it was a very enriching experience for me, both professionally and personally. From a professional point of view, I learned key lessons on governance, organization, and implementation techniques. I had the good fortune of meeting an outstanding group of professionals who contributed to the project fantastically, both on the business and the IT sides. From a personal standpoint, the experience allowed me to discover wonderful people, to create long-lasting friendships, and to boost my interest for more international experiences across the world. It was definitely a key milestone both in my professional and in my personal life.

Project context

The country in question is a relatively small economy in Latin America, with fewer than 20 million inhabitants, and a large indigenous population. Its recent past has been characterized by a prolonged and violent civil war, involving repeated injustices against mostly indigenous groups. During such periods, civil rights were often violated and the governing authorities were strongly sanctioned by the international community.

During my stay, violence was still very high. Micro-criminality was widespread, so much so that walking in the streets at night was strongly discouraged. Potentially related to this, from my (limited) point of view, all private events and celebrations I was invited to, such as weddings and graduation ceremonies, took place either over lunchtime or at breakfast.

The country's financial sector is characterized by a preponderance of relatively small banks, not very well capitalized; so much so that several major bank crises had occurred over the past decade. Indeed, a major crisis occurred immediately after I left the country.

Payment systems were apparently well developed for the final user by mid-2000. However, large payments were still settled on a net basis, creating the basis for liquidity domino effects (systemic risk) in the event of the insolvency of any big payer during settlement time. From this context – supported strongly in the early 2000s by both the IMF and World Bank reports on the country's financial sector – it was decided to undertake a major effort to move settlement of large payments from a net to a gross basis, and in real time versus end of day.

The central bank was, and still is, a very highly respected institution in the country, governed by a monetary board composed of the president of the central bank, various economic ministries, and selected members of relevant trade associations which decide on all issues concerning monetary policy and payments systems. A separate bank supervision authority oversees banks' stability and in cooperation with the central bank works to supervise the entire country's financial sector.

Project aspects

When I joined the project, my effort was structured in three phases:

Phase 1: A diagnostic on the current status of the implementation which lasted about a month, and produced a report including a plan of activities on how to move the rest of the project forward.

Phase 2: A hands-on approach supporting the implementation with different project challenges; this included working with suggested and approved corrections identified in Phase 1, and lasted about three months.

Phase 3: A follow-up phase across the implementation lasting about four months, including wrapping up all the activities in Phase 2 in a structured report and advising on key challenges moving forward.

Key aspects of my intervention were the following:

- payments systems' overall architecture;
- governance of the payments systems in country;
- monetary policy and payments systems;

- RTGS system rules and regulation;

- project implementation;

- project communication.

My activities and findings for each area are listed below.

Payments systems' overall architecture

Several observations/issues were posed directly to the central bank, mostly in line with the World Bank and IMF analysis of 2004 to improve the payments systems' architecture. The two major and serious issues identified were: the ongoing situation of high numbers of large payments settled on a net basis through a clearing house; and the lack of Delivery Versus Payments (DVP) in settlement systems. Despite the list of observations being brought to the attention of the central bank, it was quickly evident that it would be beneficial to have more attention on the topic from senior levels in the financial sector to drive decision making. After several meetings with various directors at the central bank, I was eventually introduced to its managing director, who in turn invited me to present to the monetary board, the top financial institutions of the country, and the steering board of the central bank and the whole financial sector. My presentation covered all the strategic issues related to the RTGS system implementation, including governance and monetary policy implications.

Governance of the payments systems in the country

Three issues were brought to the attention of the central bank. First, I raised the issue of a lack of an Executive Payments Systems Board in the country, involving all major financial institutions including of course the central bank, which could foster modernization of payments systems in the country and support related initiatives, including ongoing RTGS system implementation. Second, there was a lack of a dedicated oversight authority within the central bank, usually present in all major western economies, and necessary to oversee payments systems' activities and risks and modernization projects. Third, there was no dedicated structured organization within the central bank to cope with RTGS system implementation.

On the first two points, I intervened exactly as I did with the architecture question, with constant meetings in order to explain and clarify the issue, in particular with both the managing director of the central bank and with the monetary board. In terms of actual organization of the project team in the central bank and project activity, I led the effort of transformation by first designing the desired future organization, and advising on the assignment of initial existing resources to it.

Monetary policy and payments systems

Monetary policy implications and the potential of an RTGS system implementation are usually not clear for local officers involved in monetary policy operations, either at junior or more senior levels. This is primarily due to the highly technical nature of the project. However, there are very important aspects that needed to be emphasized, particularly in terms of the central bank's ability to extract information and insights from RTGS systems, both on a daily basis and in a mid-term perspective.

My approach, as with the governance and the payments systems' architecture issues, was to confront very directly the issue and clarify the situation and my perspective. When I presented this topic to the monetary board, it was the topic about which I received more questions and feedback than any other. Unfortunately, one thing that did not happen and could have helped was the organization of a seminar with the operational team of monetary policy analysts, something that had been extremely beneficial in other similar projects I had undertaken in similar contexts. There were a few reasons for this:

1 Such a seminar was not under the scope of the Request for Proposal (already filled with activities for the designated period) made by the central bank, nor in my specific proposal.

2 The monetary board presentation came too late during my stay for me to be able to organize such a seminar.

3 I was unaware (not sufficiently experienced) that there could be potential misalignment between the project (operational team) and monetary department.

RTGS system rules and regulations

An RTGS system is a very complex and delicate system. It is complex because it involves the interaction of several stakeholders (a system provider, the manager of the RTGS system, system overseer, and system participants). It is delicate because its failure can lead to a whole set of economically very serious implications at country level (so-called systemic effects). Because of such features, international institutions and experts have designed a strict set of principles to be followed in order to be compliant and to manage the systemic risk involved. Such principles, in turn, need to be translated into a set of functioning rules for the RTGS system that are tailored to the country features and are to be approved at country level.

Based upon an initial review of the set of rules already produced, I identified several improvement areas. Such improvements were throughout all areas, with major improvements suggested in the area of facility management, internal control and business continuity. For example, I recommended the creation of a facility system that would support debtors who had difficulties in settling their payments across the day. This issue was reviewed and later implemented.

We then formalized the new rules and procedures in the following formal documents: an RTGS system regulation booklet for system participants, with separate sections for all of the above-mentioned topics, excluding internal control processes for the central bank as a system provider; an RTGS system document for the central bank internal control processes, for exclusive use by the central bank as both a system provider and system overseer; and a plan of informational security and business continuity for the central bank as system provider.

Project implementation

The project was ongoing when I arrived, and my objective was to 'make things happen', ie to get to the end of the implementation process, with the delivery of training, associated materials and achievement of go-live. This implied a revision of the overall implementation plan which, as is typical, had two main and related components: a business component and an IT component.

To cope with the components, an interdisciplinary team was formed at the central bank, with experts from accounting and payments systems from the business side, and the central bank IT department on the other side, plus extra support from other departments to tackle the HR and organizational changes implied. A project leader from the business side reporting to the project director was in charge of the whole operation. Another key contributor was the RTGS system software provider, an international American external organization already in place when I arrived.

The first major implementation challenge was to harmonize the existing rather-too-high-level project plan to the reality of a focused implementation that needed to go live in six months, with all the changes/revisions that I had suggested. This required from my side that I get involved strongly in project planning, which took agreement of the existing owner, an experienced local project manager who reported to the overall project leader. Once we did this, and assigned resources to all tasks, the activities were split into groups with responsible personnel assigned who were very well organized and disciplined. We also established groups for business operations (functioning rules and procedures, manuals, accounting integration), IT (development and testing), training, communication, organization and HR. It was a challenge to align and integrate the different planning methods with the local project plan owner and the project leader. For example, they were not used to having a two-step planning process that involved splitting the plan into very detailed activities for the following six to eight weeks, with less detailed activities coming later, which is a particularly useful method if you need to implement under tight deadlines. However, we sat together, discussed and applied the technique, and it was eventually accepted.

The IT component of the project was soon to be finished, but needed adjustments in order to incorporate agreed revisions. With the testing phase about to get started, I supported the test planning and participated in some of the testing and subsequent revision processes. Key training for external stakeholders had to be prepared when I arrived. This took three months, involved various financial institutions, and covered the business fundamentals of the modernization as well as the IT technicalities of the RTGS system.

Overall, implementation went extremely well, mostly because the central bank implementation team was very good:

1 The project leader was very experienced and decisive. He supervised all activities regularly, at least on a weekly basis. There was one weekly meeting, for example, where all development areas were reviewed. Work was split in a structured way between the various team members. All team members believed in the importance of the project, so motivation was high. There was very fair treatment of everybody in the team, and no major miscommunication/ disagreement took place. Importantly, the general level of skills was very good across the board, including the IT personnel.

2 Collaboration and mutual commitment between both IT and the business areas was very proactive. People were able to anticipate activities needed to realize a task even before having discussed them in detail. We would openly discuss the demand for one activity or another, of taking one direction or another, and would agree collectively on a general strategy on how to move forward. Overall, the application of strict project management discipline and the harmonious coordination between IT and business counterparts at the central bank made it possible to respect the milestones in the plan and to go live only slightly (one month) after our initially planned deadline.

During meetings I leveraged both benchmarks (international recommendations, past experiences) and strict logic in order to convince where necessary. After this, the team would take over and sort out details with high intensity and perseverance. In my experience, such behaviour on the client side is quite extraordinary, because in general either it is difficult to find internal staff so skilled and motivated, or it is difficult to find action-oriented people (oftentimes internal staff can be very skilled, but unable to move activities in a timely and effective manner).

There were numerous examples of good collaboration. Two particularly stand out. First, once, an extra piece of hardware was needed in order to better manage potential disruption to business continuity. After I had convinced the IT directors that this was the case, it took extraordinarily little time for them to complete all required tasks, from negotiation with the vendor to final implementation. As a second example, when we reviewed the material provided by the software provider to help us navigate through the RTGS system and to build the booklets, we found it difficult to understand and use. After some talks with the vendors, we realized that, given the level of improvement required from the vendor and the risks of delays, the best thing would be to rewrite the support materials and produce both a manual for participants and the internal control regulation document. One officer from the central bank took ownership of this and was dedicated to it for just six weeks, very little time. The end product was excellent and helped to allow the central bank to take ownership much more effectively than through the passive reception of documentation from the software provider.

Project communication

Communications were handled very well in a number of areas and contributed strongly to the success of the project.

During my early participation in the project, I noted that the importance of this project was not fully recognized in the country, either within the central bank or amongst key stakeholders in the financial sector. Therefore, I worked very hard to raise the profile and relevance of the project with key stakeholders.

1. Regular communication with the general manager of the central bank

This was a key factor driving the success of my project. It started with a simple lunch and continued through updates that would become at least monthly. Communication updates were always short (half an hour maximum), not written, but always very effective, allowing the general manager to get a full picture of the project and its importance. These conversations convinced the general manager to set up my presentation to the monetary board (see below), another major cornerstone of this project's success.

2. Presentation to the monetary board

This provided the project with maximum exposure in the financial sector and ensured maximum commitment from all stakeholders. The presentation was a one-off, just 45 minutes during a broader monetary board session. My presentation was reviewed in advance both by the project leader and by the central bank director in charge of the project. It was supposed to be mostly a one-way presentation but it turned out to be very interactive, with the board asking a lot of questions and asking how they could follow up. The presentation was highly successful and a turning point for the project. Personally, I was treated with much more respect and given more credibility after the presentation, which supported my leadership.

3. Increased use of informal communication

It was my intention to maximize internal communication within the bank in order to speed up implementation time. I left formal channels more or less as they were before but I dramatically increased informal communication. I would drop by at least every other day to have conversations with all relevant stakeholders, just talking about both the project and in general about the national news etc. It became a habit to have lunch each week with people from various departments at least three or four times, and include in the discussion some critical issues of the project. The result of such action was that most of my counterparts became very responsive when something important popped up. As an example, when it turned out that the material for training presented by the software provider had to be strongly changed, it was not such a hard assignment to convince my colleagues at the central bank to do it themselves.

4. Communication with involved banks

This communication used three formal channels. First, there was top-down communication through the monetary board; second, there were formal training sessions that lasted about three months to teach banks how to use the new system; third, there was a regular communication bulletin (of eight pages) on the importance and progress of implementation, printed on a monthly basis for over a year, always formal, and used as a strategy to create awareness at bank level. All these channels contributed to creating awareness of the project with banks. As a result, at go-live, none of the banks initially participating in the project found major problems with the system.

5. Communication with the World Bank

This communication was fundamental as it allowed the project to connect with both one of its main sponsors (the World Bank was a key lender to the project) and a main adviser (the World Bank advised to proceed with this reform). I personally sat once a month with a World Bank representative in the country to explain progress and critical issues looking forward. Communication in this case was mostly formal and extremely effective, and as it was two-way, it allowed me to get insightful tips on how to move ahead. In addition to this informal communication,

I had to present regular reports to World Bank headquarters experts on a monthly basis in order to show progresses. Such reports were also very useful because they touched all relevant areas of the project and created the required level of documentation.

Project results

The RTGS system went live just one month behind schedule, with a first group of key banks as participants, constituting the main commercial banks. Since then, RTGS system participation has been extended to all commercial banks and to other major players in the financial sector.

The RTGS system is alive and well as of now, and various improvements have been made over the years to make it run even more smoothly and to better manage the main risks involved (mainly systemic liquidity and credit risks). A central bank team is currently dedicated to it as a system provider.

At the same time, the project has become the main pillar of the modernization of the payments systems in the country. Further improvements have come since then, in the area of delivery versus payments mechanisms for settlement systems, and in the strengthening of the oversight over payments and market infrastructures at the central bank.

'Key moments' during the project

For me the project became a special one due to the dynamics that developed with the central bank team, both professionally and personally. In the following paragraphs, I would like to single out some of the key moments to show how bumpy and at the same time how rewarding an international project can be.

First contacts and impressions

My arrival in the country was not particularly welcomed at the central bank. I think the main reasons for this were:

1 Previous overseas consultants had not made a great impression on the people I worked with.

2 I was probably too professorial (see also my later comments on this).

In any event, during the first days in the country, the following happened to me professionally.

Everybody was at the same time extremely courteous but also extremely distant, as if fearing I could only do damage to them if they opened up to me. After only a few days in the country, I had already made clear what I felt were the main actions to be taken, and I called a meeting with the central bank director in charge of the project and the core project team. The meeting was really very difficult. I presented my evidence and conclusions and was received with extreme hostility by the project director, who complained that it is easy to come and criticize, but it is difficult to really make things happen (something, by the way, in general, I tend to strongly agree with). I had not anticipated such a reaction, especially the feeling of not being welcome, which was really bothering me. In any event, the meeting ended with me raising openly my doubt about whether I should stay or not. Although I was invited to keep running my project, I still had real doubts due to the difficult nature of the environment. In my professional career, I had never started in such a difficult manner. Accordingly, I tried as hard as possible to change the situation, as shown over the next paragraphs.

Building key relationships and my presentation to the monetary board

After about six weeks my relationship with the core team had definitely improved. One IT expert, who was the liaison between business and the core team, was assigned to support me in anything I needed. It turned out to be an extremely good match, both professionally (as we had complementary skills) and personally.

At the same time, I was able to liaise well with the project leader (a senior business professional) and the IT directors, as well as the person responsible for the organization department. The latter set up a meeting for me with the general manager of the central bank. This was a key meeting, very informal (it was a lunch), but extremely important professionally, as I was able to make it clear to him that the project had insufficient exposure to be successful within the central bank and the banking sector. On realizing this the general manager set up the presentation that I had to make at the monetary board.

The mere fact that I had to make the presentation changed the whole dynamics within the project. The project director (who was not enthusiastic at the beginning, to say the least) helped me review the presentation and tone it in such way that it would maximize the probability of success. The core team helped by providing all circumstantial facts for it and helped to create a team spirit with me as well.

The monetary board meetings were divided into a number of sessions, and I was to arrive before the beginning of the first one. So I had to wait almost an hour before entering for my presentation. A detail I will always remember is that in the waiting room there was a painting with all kinds of brutal things you can imagine in human warfare. I did not dare to ask, but the person accompanying me explained that it was meant to describe all the horrors that happened during the civil war which had ended not so long before. I felt really sad in a way, thinking that I was trying to help in my 'normal' context of working, in a 'normal' institutional setting, when until very recently in this same place things had not been 'normal' at all. Perhaps this sensitized me, and the presentation went very well; I received positive feedback both during the session and afterwards from the general manager and the project director. After this, it was agreed I was to inform both of them on a monthly basis about the progress of the project.

Hepatitis

Unexpected events happen in life and certainly during international projects. When the project seemed professionally to be going well and heading towards a happy ending, although with still a lot of work to be done, I started feeling unwell, and after a couple of scary days, I was diagnosed with hepatitis A, the food version of hepatitis. As a result, I had to retreat to my hotel for a few days. It was truly horrible; I felt extremely weak and I could barely eat. At the same time, the response from my central bank counterparts was simply fabulous. First, they provided me with all the medical assistance I needed; second, they enabled me to provide just the necessary limited support remotely (it turned out I had to stay away for six or seven working days). Finally, I was called every day not only on a professional basis, but also to provide some human comfort. Before getting back to work, my central bank counterpart came to pick me up to stay with his family for an entire non-working day on a Sunday. It was the beginning of a great personal friendship that it is still ongoing (I have visited them after the project several times since then).

Goodbye and final acknowledgments

As the on-site part of the project came to an end, noting that I continued to assist the project remotely for four months, relationships and mutual respect with counterparts in the central bank improved further. The project was going well, activities were completed, and timelines (at least for my part of the project) respected. Before I left, I met all my counterparts, including the project director, who was not easy at the beginning, the general manager and all members of the core team. Everybody thanked me for the contribution, and I have kept in contact with most of them. What I was certainly not expecting was a goodbye chocolate cake for my last day on site at the central bank that was charming as well as delicious (see picture below)! The message was unequivocal ('May things go well for you Alberto'). I can never thank them enough for this wonderful experience (and delicious cake!).

Figure 11.1 Goodbye cake

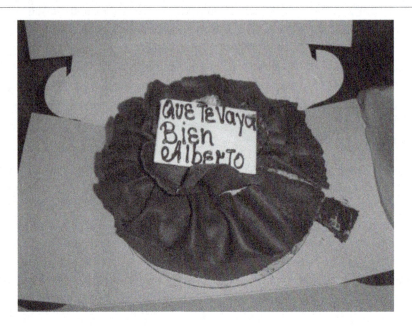

Project reflections

In my project reflections, I would like to look at what I see as some of the specific challenges of international projects, and think about my lessons learned during this project experience.

Working in an international context

This project was international for the following reasons. It was composed of organizations and individuals from different international environments (the World Bank supervisory team from Washington DC, the software provider, an American corporation, myself, from Italy, and the local team). It was about introducing internationally governing principles on payments and securities settlement systems in a specific country. The extra difficulties that I encountered due to this being an international project were the following:

1 I had to adjust to an environment with a challenging past with former international consultants and providers.

2 I had to make amendments to a project that was going relatively well, but needed several key adjustments in order to be able to go live and respect the relevant international standards, which were unclear to key personnel and, therefore, the amendments I was asking for were seen to be of little impact.

3 I found that I had to make four key adjustments to manage this international context:

a Engage and influence: I had to try to engage as many relevant stakeholders as possible, align them and bring them on board. I used formal and informal communication channels: bringing them to lunch, talking about non-project issues, having the will to work with them and making them have the will to work with me and amongst themselves. If it is possible, make them friends; if not, make them aware that you are happy to work with them, to understand their point of view and to sort out differences in case there are any. Be proactive with this.

b Be authentic: I had to try to be as honest as possible and as committed as possible to the success of the project. It's important not to mask what you feel too much, disappointment or happiness, because it will show up sooner or later. Of course, many other approaches might work; the fact that being dishonest after all can pay out is historically proven. Nonetheless, it does not work for me. In this project, the fact that stakeholders felt I was extremely authentic and committed helped dramatically in having great relationships and contributed enormously to the success of the project itself.

c Be highly competent: I think it is vital to be professionally impeccable. In this project, I needed to be able to draw lessons for the project from international benchmarks, from my past experience and from my education, and to have the ability to provide solutions through logic.

d Create clarity and transparency: I tried to be transparent with all key stake-holders. This involves communicating both agreement and disagreement with each one of them, using meetings to resolve more complicated matters, aligning stakeholders amongst themselves, and trying to get to a position where you can commit together to activities and goals looking forward.

Lessons learned

First, put simply, stakeholder management is key. My general rule for stakeholder management is to split relevant stakeholders into normal and difficult ones. With the former, be with them as much as you can and get the best out of it; possibly enjoy the experience with them as well. For the latter, do more. Be around as much as is allowed to you, and try to talk through points as much as they let you. In this project, I had an initial general resistance; the pressure was from all counterparts. I overcame negativity by taking all stakeholders one by one. Slowly, people became more aware of who I was and the relevance of the project. By the end, through perseverance, I had everybody on board.

Second, communication is vital – honest communication and sometimes key events are really important. On honesty, actually, this is not true for all type of projects. There are, in fact, projects where secrecy pays off, or where managing the truth helps. Not in this project: since all main stakeholders in the country needed to know about the project, the creation of transparency, with the bulletin, was a key major success factor. On important events, it was not foreseen but the presentation to the monetary board was really a key moment.

Third, a project consultant needs to have the right attitude. My general rule here is that – despite any initial idea one might have when arriving at a project – adjustments have to be made to discover the right attitude and the right approach. As an example, before this project, I was involved in advising another country's central bank where I had to be extremely pushy over almost every topic. I arrived in this project thinking that the same would apply. At my first meetings I was extremely straightforward over the needs for the project, without using any type of caution, probably somewhat reflecting the idea that it would be the same again as in my previous project. This helped generate the initial difficulty between the project director and myself. Fortunately, I was then able to rebalance the initial difficulty by developing the relationship with the central bank at general management level, something that at the end paid off even with the project director.

Fourth, the quality of the local team always makes the difference. In the case of the central bank, the initial people assigned to the project were very good, from the project leader through to all the team members. People were highly competent and very motivated. There was already an idea of being a team which would deliver. But with my presence, such awareness was strengthened because I helped people to succeed. All improvements I solicited were quickly introduced and implemented.

Importantly, external providers are not the only solution for implementation issues. A general rule that in my opinion applies to all implementations where an internal team needs to take over immediately thereafter, is that the more the internal staff are involved throughout all non-outsourceable issues from the beginning, the better. This was very much the case with the software vendor documentation issue. It turned out very advantageous to redo it internally. It helped create more awareness on the topics and reduced dependence on the provider. It doesn't always apply, but in this specific project it turned out to be a very positive event.

Finally, I would stress the need to focus on IT fundamentals and be flexible. Often IT architecture elements, once chosen, are deemed not changeable. This should not be the case. In this project, for example, we reviewed the business continuity strategy in place and found one major flaw. The central bank acknowledged it once we talked it through, and did not hesitate to resolve the pending issues effectively and efficiently. This is not a usual behaviour as there is often resistance to change once initial decisions have been taken, and there are many bureaucratic hurdles to overcome in order to change a project once it has started. In the case of the central bank, they saw (also because of my insistence) the advantage of changing, and decided that it was worthwhile to make an effort in this direction. In fact, they were able to negotiate some changes in the hardware and software provider contracts that even minimized the cost difference, and found a way to push to have all new hardware in place in a short time.

A few final words

It's always a good final exercise to think about what you might have done differently. In the case of this project, I would single out the following ideas:

1 I would have been more cautious at the beginning, with the central bank core team and the project director. I assumed the present was like the past, which was a mistake; I should have exposed weaknesses in a smoother way, and tried better to understand why some of these were not resolved or addressed earlier. I was not cautious at the time because of time constraints (the project was relatively short, and I felt I should not waste time in being indirect), and a bit of lack of experience in finding the right balance between a sound and transparent communication and the risk of appearing to be the good professor in a class of non-performing kids.

2 I should have tried to escalate key policy issues up to the general manager much earlier, something I have actually done immediately in later projects. I did not do it at the time because of the initial resistance of my counterparts to have me meet top executives of the central bank. I respected it, but by doing that I was not maximizing the project's chance of success. So in a sense, I should have been more of a 'rebel' from the beginning.

3 Related to that, I guess I see how important it is to insist more on involving all stakeholders, particularly very senior and strategic ones. Although my stakeholder management strategy in the country was quite aggressive, I still regret not having been able to hold a seminar with monetary policy economists in order to explain fully the potential benefits for monetary policy of an RTGS system. I did it elsewhere, later on, and it was clearly beneficial. It did not happen because – as I said before – it was out of the scope of my contract, and because at the time I was unaware that there could have been potential misalignment between the project (operational team) and the monetary department.

Part 2: Interview

The following is a short extract from a series of personal conversations between Bob and Alberto, which ranged across the specifics of this project and international leadership project management in general.

Q: I just want to pick out one thing with you, Alberto. You talked about influencing and the need to be proactive. What is proactive influencing?

A: I'm just talking about anticipating, anticipating moves. I was thinking constantly, what is going to happen next, what could happen next? I spent a lot of time sitting and thinking about scenarios – to create some form of plan, to be ready.

Q: So is that a kind of rule you applied?

A: No, I think rule is the wrong word. You need to understand the situation, to always have a smart look at what is around you, to have a sense of what happens. And then you test it, you do something. And then you can learn. There is no rule you apply before as such. Maybe I say, make it a rule not to have a rule. This for me is very, very important.

Q: So, this means you are quite cautious.

A: Again, it depends. If you can be cautious, be cautious. If you are too cautious, you can start to lose time, then you often can't recover in a project. So if you need to have results fast, you just have to go.

Q: When you go faster, I guess you use a kind of expertise to persuade?

A: I use logic, yes, talking people through very clearly the pros and cons, of course, if I want to convince. I also have many international references for what I say, so I can make people believe. I have experience.

Q: But you also get very close to people too. It's not just data. You blend a number of strategies.

A: Yes, I can get very close to people. I like that. I can go out and play guitar with a sponsor all night. We did that in my Brazil project and became super friends, in fact.

Part 3: Commentary

Here are some reflections on Alberto's case and interview.

Alberto's case is almost overwhelming in its appearance of 'mission impossible'. There are many valuable lessons to be learned. The key topic here is how important it is to have clear the initial situation of a project, the mandate, the understanding of the setting in the organization: how decisions run; how escalations are possible; the needs as regards stakeholder management; the communication necessary in a complex environment and the necessity of a dedicated and reliable core project team. All these topics should be on the list of a project manager of an international project, and he or she should be ready to find adequate tailored and creative solutions which may not be reflected in classical project management methods and tools. Clearly, external consultants also need to be sensitive to how externals may be seen in the enterprise, how much accountability and responsibility will be delegated to them, which organizational and legal frames they have that will enable and restrict their activity. It is also interesting to reflect that a project manager needs in such demanding environments to have the self-confidence that he or she will always find a flexible solution that fits.

Peter Wollmann

Part 4: Reflecting on international project management

Take time to reflect on the following questions to help you reach further insights and take practical actions to improve your own project management practice.

1 How is it possible for you to get a very rapid picture of your international project landscape – which decisions are possible, which escalations are possible, what communication is necessary and possible? Who might be able to help you with this?

2 How important do you think it is to make your international project colleagues your friends? Why? Why not?

3 How self-confident do you feel in the environment of a large international project? What would improve your self-confidence further?

Part 5: Putting it into practice

There are a number of very valid insights and ideas for project management present in this case which the reader can learn from and adopt, customizing for their own projects. Take a few minutes to note down your main learnings from this case, and note down some actions for yourself.

Personal insights, learnings and actions

Strategic business expansion

12

NATHAN LAMSHED

Profile

Nathan Lamshed is a project and programme manager with 15 years' experience delivering business and technology projects for some of the world's largest global investment banks as well as the airline and education industries. Nathan has experience delivering strategic business expansion programmes, organizational transformations as well as software and infrastructure technology initiatives. Nathan has experienced the project lifecycle from executive intent to business as usual and has worked closely with C-level executive sponsors and stakeholders around the globe.

Foreword

This case introduces a project breathtaking in the scale of its commercial ambition and complexity, looking to transform the capability of a bank to operate more effectively as a global player. The dynamics of this particular project introduce a number of important features which affect many projects, such as the relationship between IT and the more obviously commercial arm of the business. Planning and execution activities in this project, interestingly, were driven very much from a product management perspective, despite the project having the appearance of being an IT-driven exercise. The close relationship between IT and sales offers an interesting model for others. The issue of vendor management is important within this project, as is the challenge of over-promising and under-delivering across organizations involved in project work. Finally, the topic of scope creep, extraordinary in this case, is prominent, and provides salutary lessons on the need to be aware of the risks of over-ambitious estimations of organizational capability in the face of potentially huge commercial rewards.

Before reading on, reflect on a number of key questions addressed in the case. Then compare your experience and answers to the ideas in the case itself and the final commentary.

1 How effectively do IT and other arms of companies cooperate, in your experience, in projects which involve the roll-out of new IT solutions? What should be the model of cooperation?

2 What can be the challenges of using third-party vendors, for example from India, to deliver IT solutions for large international projects? Who is to blame if these vendors deliver late?

3 Which pressures can lead to 'scope creep' in international projects? How can these pressure best be handled?

PART 1: CASE STUDY Strategic business expansion

Introduction

The organization is a global investment bank with an expanding presence in Asia, looking to broaden its business portfolio with new liquidity and cash management product offerings for multinational clients in India and China. Big businesses buy a range of products from banks including, for example, overdraft accounts and ways to manage payments in and out of the organization. The bank wanted to target the treasurers of large multinationals with new products to meet these day-to-day corporate banking needs.

This was very much part of a strategic business expansion for my bank. After many years of investment in mergers and acquisitions, it wanted to develop the opportunity to invest in Asia and other emerging markets to increase revenue and balance revenue geography. The bank had run large projects before, but this was one of the biggest and most important investments in Asia. It was very much business driven, so much so that all functions of the organization were involved, as they were all affected.

The project outcome was not to become a market leader, but to expand the range of client products to attract new and retain existing clients. The aim was to offer the bank's client the opportunity to manage their finances globally from a single platform. To provide a scalable offering, the bank also sought to replace and enhance existing country-specific banking solutions with a single platform that provided treasurers with global visibility of cash and allowed easy management of day-to-day banking; so multinationals, rather than have a different local bank in each territory, could choose just one bank, my bank, making things simpler and saving on cost.

In terms of scale of project, if actual capability was 2 out of 10 in the bank at that time, then the planned end capability after the project was 7 out of 10. So this was a significant business transformation, which involved not only new products but also significant internal change. We had to create internal capability to deliver the products, which meant that we needed to create IT systems or deliver new technology, create sales and marketing processes, and ensure compliance needs and customer service operations – all internal processes essential to offer the product to the bank's customers. It was a major undertaking.

Project set-up and progress

The range of stakeholders was broad, across most functions of the bank's internal organization, and included:

- sales, product and country management stakeholders across Asia locations;

- regional product and operations management in Hong Kong;

- global executive sponsor and executive stakeholders based in the United States

- a vendor based in India

- development and operational teams in Hong Kong

The actual project was driven using a geographically diverse project team located in Asia, Europe and North America. I was the programme manager and had to coordinate all aspects of the project. A lot of it was internal, particularly around sales, coordinating local sales and product teams to agree on what clients wanted, what was in place, what opportunities were there – and then lots of assessments had to be run. We were very aware that what looked to be similar products in Malaysia and Singapore might be very different; regulations were very different. In China, banking is very much province by province; a deposit product approved to sell to clients in Beijing could not be offered in Guangzhou without appropriate regulatory approval in Guangzhou.

Product managers were really instrumental in all of this. Once we had determined the product, then we would contact the technical and subject matter expert teams and look at what was needed to operationalize the product, the procedures etc. Then we sought global financial platform providers to find a supplier or suppliers who may have software already developed which would accelerate time to market. And then, after a vendor selection, we started to build the platform itself. At the same time as that, we started to build up local operations, defining a strategy for sales and marketing, looking at what the local regulator might demand in order to offer the product. Sometimes, that was just some form of filing to the local banking regulator. In other situations, banking regulation officials would come to the bank, meet people and check that everything was in place to meet required regulations. So this was also very product driven, working backwards from demand, from sales to operations.

Project challenges

Key challenges

- Project scope expanded.
- Quality of technology substandard.
- Subject matter expert resource problems.
- Global financial crisis.
- New restrictions on travel and headcount.
- Project communication conducted via telephone conferences.
- Relationships imploding.

In terms of project progress, one of the most important things to happen was the rapid expansion of the geographical scope of the project. It was initially China and India. However, the scope subsequently expanded, only months later, to a global roadmap, excluding North America. In fact, before the contract was signed with our development partner, the initial project scope expanded to 10+ locations in Asia with 10+ locations in Europe to be negotiated as the next priority. In some ways, this just represented an awaking of the interest in the project, which was actually one of the advantages of the project, and people were at the beginning very willing to get behind and join it. Management teams in sales were finally getting the product they had been wanting to sell to their clients for years. But this 'creep' was a key factor in creating the challenges the project experienced.

Another major challenge was that the selected vendor for cash management systems, our development partner, agreed and committed to deliver technology for China and India within an unreasonably short timeframe. This is one of the major lessons of this project for me; to look for over-optimistic commitments that can impact on delivery if not fulfilled. Unfortunately, the early versions of the products that were delivered were just not working; that really brought things to a standstill. We were holding lots of eight-hour conference calls to try to get things back on track and working. And all of this began to snowball because we wanted to move on to the next location. Having completed the implementation in the current country, the intent was to leave the project outcomes to local teams to operationalize and realize the project benefits. But because operations were working with a bad platform or products, the whole thing began to grind to a halt as product subject matter experts had to go back and help resolve issues with the previous country. Eventually, there was reluctance to go live with the system anywhere as it was felt to be too unreliable.

Finally, and to cap it all, the global financial crisis hit, which meant headcount got frozen and travel budgets became restricted, which meant we didn't have the resources we needed to run the project, and communication went back to lengthy and sometimes not very efficient voice telephone conferences. This all impeded the resolution of the China and India problems and other Asia location deliverables.

Project results

In terms of outcomes, the project had to be reset in terms of scope, schedule, people and overall structure. There was a real scaling back of the product features and capability we had planned to offer. Strangely, this didn't create less work in an obvious way, as we then had to rework all the operations, legal, sales and marketing sides of things that had been done. In the end, the project team was eventually substantially disbanded and new resources were progressively transitioned in to re-innovate with regional streams established and managed independently.

Lessons learned

There are a number of lessons learned that are very apparent to me:

- First, if a project scope is to be expanded, and it may be necessary for all the right reasons, then it has to be handled carefully with an assessment of additional resources required, and a rigorous impact assessment on the then-current project timeline, scope, costs and any other constraints, particularly the availability of mission-critical subject matter experts, specialist vendors and key executives. Even highly paid executives have an upper limit of capacity. It can't be feasible to simply increase a project by x10. And a project manager probably can't plan and manage this by themselves; a proper impact assessment involves conversations with all project stakeholders and scenario planning to anticipate the unexpected as best as possible.

- Second, it is vital that vendors are given reasonable timeframes to deliver, regardless sometimes of what the vendor is telling you. If it feels unrealistic, then it probably is. It is important to review vendors' project plans to ensure dates committed have been planned, are realistic and contain contingency.

- Third, manage expectations of those who are not at the coalface of a project. What was striking in my project was that many aspects of the project's problems surprised the US executives. The lack of scalability of resources in Asia was not understood, for example.

Situation and future outlook

I think we have to say that this project failed in terms of the classical definitions of project success and failure. It didn't achieve on its own ambitions and was scaled back. However, I believe an experienced project manager will generally have experienced a failed project, so we should keep perspective. It provides valuable foresight for future endeavours and builds resilience. On the positive side, the bank's product portfolio was expanded. And with regards to projects, there was organizational learning, and a focus on not letting the same mistake happen again with respect to major international projects.

Part 2: Interview

Part I: Understanding the challenges

Q: Just going back to the very beginning, can you tell me why you were selected to take this very demanding role?

A: It was a combination of things. I had just worked on a general ledger replacement and established trusted working relationships with executive stakeholders. So someone knew me, trusted me and asked me to join the team to run projects in the Asian expansion initiative.

Q: How did it feel to be asked?

A: It was good. Funnily enough, one insightful executive actually advised me against taking the role because they could see that the project would most likely fail. But I had faith in the executive who was inviting me. Unfortunately, soon after I joined, he resigned, which was not only a personal disappointment but also a major contributor to the project's eventual failure. Loss of an executive sponsor for a project that is high risk can have a huge impact if the person is not replaced with an equally strong sponsor, particularly if the investment is not supported or political forces are in play in the organization.

Q: **You mentioned vendor management as a challenging topic, getting vendors to work with reasonable timeframes. Can you explain a little more about that?**

A: It's just a fact that some of the big IT vendors will overcommit when contracting project deliverables. It's not always for the same reason that they do this. Sometimes, it's about pleasing a client at a point in time, and they believe they will deliver even though they see problems. Sometimes, it is a lack of awareness and/or understanding of the client's expectations.

Q: **I've heard a lot from western companies operating with Indian vendors that this is a very Indian culture-specific problem – saying 'yes' like this. Is it a question of national culture?**

A: No, I wouldn't say I agree. I think it is more to do with vendor and sales cultures. Organizations from all backgrounds and cultures want to please clients and maintain solid trusted relationships. The same mentality existed with staff from my own organization in sales and relationship roles who overcommit to clients. I think it is more a topic of sales culture.

Q: **But aren't people aware of this issue? It's not new.**

A: Yes, it's a little more complex, as client organizations are also part of this problem. My own organization was missing project deliverable deadlines for the vendor to in turn hit their agreed target. In keeping a good relationship with the client, vendors are sometimes reluctant to push for the deliverable and hope time can be made up. Alternatively, vendors often know the client will struggle with their own side of the bargain and can then justifiably complain that they couldn't deliver because of the client missing dependency deadlines. So it sometimes works like a merry-go-round, which creates challenges for the project manager; executives set unrealistic deadlines, project teams on both sides hope for the best, and when we fail, it's not clear who is responsible.

Q: **How do you handle that?**

A: I think you need to lead in a very clear and strong way. You certainly need to be strong enough to call out your own organization's deliverables and accountability. I try to work closely with a vendor during the planning phase. Also, since this project experience, I see it as good practice to put into the contract what my organization needs to deliver for the vendor to deliver on their side of the deal – to connect the two. Internal stakeholders are often very focused on the vendor and pushing blame there. I think the project manager needs to be somewhat independent in the best interests of a project's success, and manage both sides of the deal. As a PM, if you do this, it builds trust with the vendor and can create internal momentum to deliver. On the negative side, it does contract your own organization to deliver.

Q: **Overall, this sounds like it was a tough project for you. Any regrets?**

A: This project was the hardest that I ever worked on. But I feel that I was as successful as I could have been. I also developed a lot from the experience. It's funny. If I look back, I'm not sure I would do the project now. But I was younger and greener, and maybe more resilient to the challenges, and not caring about risks to my career. Maybe you need that to run these projects. Maybe I would be too safe now.

Q: **But if you had to do it again, what would you change in terms of your project management practice?**

A: I think when I was young, I was a very entrepreneurial PM. I wanted results that mattered for the business; I was an advocate for the business and very close to the business leaders. I think now I would hold all stakeholders accountable for their part of the project's outcomes. I would better balance my role as PM and advocate of project outcomes. I would much more hold business stakeholders to account if there was a problem with the project and things were going to fail. I would tell people if they were failing.

Q: **Is that collaborative?**

A: Yes, this can be done in a collaborative way with the overall success of the project in mind. The project manager cannot substitute the expertise and scale of a diverse team. If the project is near-impossible to achieve, and there are weak links, it's important to step up and deal with that directly or the project will fail.

Part II: communication strategies

Q: How did you handle communication with senior stakeholders, particularly getting them to understand and appreciate all the problems?

A: There was no appetite in the organization at senior levels to invest time in that. You had your 15 minutes with the global executive project board, during which you had to update the global execs on what was going on and what you were going to do about it. You know, senior people, running global organizations, important as it was, could only give 15 minutes a week to balance their own priorities. It would have taken hours of face-to-face meetings to provide the context, to be able to get a deep understanding. This is just one of the problems I faced in terms of communication.

Q: And other issues? You mentioned that the global crash meant that you had to rely on telephone conferencing, as travel budgets were limited. What is your perspective on telephone conferencing?

A: Well, for me telephone conferencing – pure voice – is better than the written word. Good-quality video conferencing is better than just voice – but none of these replace the face-to-face meetings, and, more important, the subsequent discussions around the meetings. That's when you go and have dinner with peers, that's when you ascertain if they have the experience or not to handle the project, that's where you build trust and faith in other individuals.

Q: What makes you trust somebody? Is it about relationships? Liking people?

A: Actually, there are plenty of situations with peers where I visibly had friction and conflict. So I don't need to like people. My main need is for trust that the person will deliver. Personally, I can put dislike aside. I build confidence through seeing how others operate: their emotional intelligence, if they have commercial acumen, and technical ability, if they really have relevant experience. Trust also comes from hearing someone say I am going to do this and they do it without any problems. And they do it again and again. And I do that consciously with my sponsors, tell them what I am going to deliver, and then I deliver. And I talk to them if I have problems – well ahead of time – to manage expectations, but delay only as an exception.

Q: So you also need to be careful not to overpromise?

A: Absolutely. So if I am asked to do something complex or high risk, I always ask for time to let me think it through, and then I come back with a recommendation. It's a more measured and methodical approach. But you also don't want to be seen as deferring, or unable to take a decision. So it's quite a balancing act.

Q: **You talked at one point about a disconnect between the North American operation and Asia, that people in the US didn't understand the other context was different?**

A: Yes, maybe one fault of mine was I should have better managed the expectations of the global execs in the US so that risks on the ground were known. As an example, stakeholders in the US could not appreciate the resource constraints in Asia: teams of product managers were available in the US and readily employed from the market at short notice, but only four were employed in Asia with long lead times to expand the resource base and build knowledge of our operations and strategy. There just weren't that many people with the required skills and knowledge. Where the US could upscale easily and quickly if there was a need, this presented a significant challenge in Asia.

Q: **So dangerous assumptions were in play?**

A: Yes, people still don't realize that the world can be very different region by region, country by country. Often enough questions are not asked to understand the local environment and practices.

Q: **So asking questions is important?**

A: Especially at the beginning, asking lots of dumb questions – ask stakeholders and subject matter experts about project feasibility, resources required, and validate how you will approach a project. This also earns trust as you are engaging and not making assumptions. You get the benefit of aligning the extended team, and it pays benefits later, when everyone needs to deliver their part without your direct oversight, ideally on time and in formation!

Q: **So you need to be dumb sometimes as an international project leader?**

A: Yes, you need to play a bit dumb from time to time and be willing to expose yourself as not knowing in order to gain the required insight to set the project up and manage it to success. You need to quickly demonstrate that you have understood the project, and ensure that people start moving forward with clear direction, objectives and understanding of what they need to do and how this interrelates with other project team members. You need to bare your soul in a way that people don't lose confidence in you as the project's leader. It's difficult to re-establish lost confidence in leaders. You need to do it in a confident way – be explicit – so people get what you're doing.

Part 3: Commentary

Here are some reflections on Nathan's case and interview.

Nathan touches a very important point, namely, the cooperation and relationship between vendors and large enterprises. These days, large enterprises normally have central vendor management with sophisticated selection, approval and tracking processes. So steering a vendor in a project often has to reflect two dimensions: the general agreement of the enterprise with the vendor, and the concrete cooperation with the vendor on a concrete task and scope set by the single project. The probability of effective and efficient vendor cooperation in a project is, of course, influenced by the general relationship between the enterprise and the vendor and its culture. In the more demanding financial environment of a specific project, trust-based cooperation deriving from a general enterprise-wide agreement can be difficult.

Reflecting that a good balance of trust and control is crucial for productive cooperation, it does not make sense to formalize all the bits and bytes of cooperation during a project. On the other hand, it should also not become a pure relationship-oriented interaction which can be easily taken advantage of. So it is important to explicitly agree on cooperation principles with the vendor for the duration of the project, and review their application, and the general perception of the cooperation, jointly and on a regular basis. In this context, briefing and debriefing are vital: the enterprise's project (leader) briefs the vendor about the specific task and result strived for, and the vendor debriefs what was understood, to prevent any misunderstandings.
Peter Wollmann

Nathan's comments about communication are highly relevant to those working in an international project context. His stress on the need to ask questions, and questions which might at first sight appear 'dumb', is a strong driver of clarity, engagement and more effective collaboration in international projects. One of the major risks of working in international contexts is not knowing; not knowing the people you are working with very well, not understanding their real level of competence, their levels of availability etc. It is essential, therefore, to move into strong asking mode early in an international venture, so that hidden risks and opportunities can be surfaced, and false assumptions exposed. Whilst this is simple to state in principle, my observation of even highly experienced professionals is that people simply underuse questions. Of the three choices available to us as communicators – tell, ask, silence – people seem to favour tell and silence rather than, as Nathan suggests, 'expose' their ignorance in front of others. Getting brave and honest about one's ignorance is a key success factor when working in international projects.
Bob Dignen

Part 4: Reflecting on international project management

Take time to reflect on the following questions to help you reach further insights and take practical actions to improve your own project management practice.

1 How far do you agree that sales people tend by nature to overpromise? How might this cause problems in your projects, and how can you handle these problems?

2 Nathan discusses a very explicit trust strategy, namely promising and then delivering on his promise to build a sense of reliability. What other trust-building strategies are there, and which do you use?

3 Clarification, the asking of dumb questions, is recommended by Nathan. What kinds of clarification questions could you ask, and on which topics, in your project contexts to create better understanding for both parties?

Part 5: Putting it into practice

There are a number of very valid insights and ideas for project management present in this case which the reader can learn from and adopt, customizing for their own projects. Take a few minutes to note down your main learnings from this case, and note down some actions for yourself.

Personal insights, learnings and actions

Making the case for a coaching approach to IT projects that implement substantial change

13

BERNADETTE CASS

Profile

Bernadette Cass works with people and organizations who want to create change, often through challenging circumstances. She has a strong business and change delivery background, having held posts as IT director and programme manager for organizations including Gillette International, London Underground Limited, HM Treasury and BP. Her experience includes implementing major business systems implementations, including on one occasion new sales and financial reporting systems across 56 countries.

Bernadette now works as an organizational change facilitator and executive, board and team coach. She is an International Coach Federation accredited coach and is a contracted organizational transactional analyst. She is inspired by the power of teams and working with those who want to be at their best.

Foreword

Bernadette's case is not so much a traditional case study; she is more making the case for a coaching approach to become included in international project leadership practice. Bernadette is herself a coach, and slightly unusual in the sense that she has a very strong industry background as an international project leader. This makes her assertion to place coaching at the heart of project management a very credible one.

The meaning of coaching is still hotly debated among theorists and practitioners. Bernadette has her own approach, which she will outline in this chapter. Perhaps what is not in dispute is the rise in awareness of the value of coaching and the practice of leadership conversations with a coaching element: which seek to define clear targets, to inspire reflection in others, and to drive creative insights and powerful ownership of solutions to problems. This case offers up a coaching approach for those leading international projects as an additional tool which, as Bernadette says later, should be 'deployed' strategically as one among many communication tools at the disposal of a leader leading or a manager managing. This case offers you the opportunity to reflect whether this is a tool you should also embrace.

Before reading on, reflect on some key questions addressed in the case. Then compare your experience and answers to the ideas in the case itself and the final commentary.

1 What do you understand by the term 'coaching'? What do you see as its main value in a professional context?

2 How far do you think people are hard-wired to resist change?

3 How important is it for those leading projects to create a positive team culture? How can coaching support this process?

PART 1: CASE STUDY   Making the case for a coaching approach to IT projects that implement substantial change

Introduction

As a programme manager and IT director, I was responsible for introducing significant changes to ways of working within international organizations, where change was supported or often made possible through the introduction of new technology and business processes. Examples include customer relationship management, remote access to sales and financial information, and time-critical product availability. I became interested in understanding how the same new project could be embraced and received with excitement in one country or region and rejected or branded a failure in another.

On reflection, it becomes clear that some organizations are less open to changing the way that they work. There can be a variety of reasons for this. Often people have built up ways of doing things and relationships which serve them well, and which may be informal or outside approved policy. These can be difficult to translate into standardized processes. Sometimes there is a natural resistance to change where the benefits of the new project are not clear, and there is a reluctance to move to the new and untried.

Creating an environment for international project success

Implementing successful and sustainable international projects requires a variety of conditions, including well-defined business outcomes and benefits, business sponsorship and leadership, good organizational governance and collaborative working between technical, business and multi-disciplinary teams.

Whilst there are many sources of helpful project delivery guidelines, including substantive methodologies, the role of the project manager is critical. The project manager manages and delivers the technical elements alongside the business functionality, and maintains strong communication between the technical and business teams to ensure the project and business benefits are delivered on time and within budget.

My experience indicates that sustainable change is more likely to be achieved where attention is given by the project manager to supporting the recipients of change to *co-create* the future improved working environment, and where the project manager enables open communication to take place throughout the project. I describe this as a 'coaching approach'.

I propose that when the project manager takes a 'coaching approach', this supports the development of transparent and direct communication, and a no-blame culture of continuous improvement that enables all team members to work to their full potential.

Defining the coaching approach to project management

Set within the context of defined organizational benefits and effective team working, a coaching approach consists of a variety of behaviours, including:

- Setting clear personal and team objectives:
  - clarity on personal and team deliverables is essential.

- Inviting team members to make the commitment to participate:
  - is this a learning opportunity for the team member?
  - does s/he have the relevant skills and appetite for the work?
- Allowing individuals scope to determine how they can best deliver their objectives:
  - participant given the option to use all their resources and choose how they will personally deliver their contribution and achieve their objectives, within the wider team context;
  - project manager delegates authority where relevant;
  - ethos of personal responsibility and accountability created.
- Developing a 'no-blame culture' of continuous improvement:
  - sharing information and learning from mistakes is valued, not criticized;
  - people are appreciated for identifying and naming problems, and as a result, the project team is working with reference to operational reality and accurate data rather than a hypothesis;
  - project manager and teams offer support and assistance with problem solving;
  - all voices are heard so different points of view are taken into account and compromise or adjustments made on all sides.
- Aligning between local and international benefits:
  - clarity on where the local agenda and benefits are separate to the overall organizational goal.

Benefits of a coaching approach

Once the business objectives have been clearly defined, along with individual and team roles, responsibilities and outcomes, then the project manager can invite participants to be self-determining and choose how they will personally deliver their contribution and achieve their objectives. This approach enables people to consider if their values and beliefs align with the new direction of the organization, and to make a choice to participate or not. It is much more effective for someone to choose not to engage in the project than to have a dissatisfied or uncommitted team member.

This stage can be facilitated by coaching. If the leader provides a clear understanding of the responsibility and deliverables for the staff member, a coaching approach allows the individual to fully engage and take ownership of delivering their part of the project. The individual can work out their own route to success and liaise with others in the team, resulting in a creative and energized approach.

Team coaching and facilitation can also accelerate the development of effective ways of working together across organizational boundaries, particularly when transitioning to matrix organizations or other new ways of working. A coaching approach can enable the team to reflect on what parts of their working relationships are effectively supporting the delivery of objectives, and what requires attention and development.

The development of strong relationships enables a culture of open communication where doubts and vulnerabilities can be expressed. People can ask for and receive help from others within a framework of trust and respect.

Leadership

It's useful to consider the coaching approach within the context of recent leadership thinking, where there is a move away from the 'heroic' concept, based on personal attributes, towards a more relational concept that accounts for organizational context and challenges. Recent thinking (Turnbull, 2011) suggests leadership is:

- more than a set of individual competencies;

- multi-faceted;

- both formal and informal;

- about working collaboratively and learning;

- to be shared and dispersed away from 'the top';

- backed up by organizational practices;

- necessary to match organizational challenges.

Leaders need to make interventions which challenge the status quo.

Micro case: an international project 'near failure' turned to success

A local company complained that after the implementation of a new sales order processing system they were unable to locate and ship product and raise invoices. The organization had been working on pilot implementation for several months and encountered many issues and financial discrepancies in testing between the existing system and the pilot. Communications and governance were fragmented, and the go-live decision was taken with incomplete testing and without consultation with the software supplier or wider international group. This was a major crisis, with risk of company closure and financial failure.

A new project team was formed, consisting of members of the local organization, including IT and business functions, together with representatives of the software supplier and the international group finance and IT functions. The 'no-blame' approach invited all participants to share their findings, name the problems and offer their opinions.

This culture of openness enabled the new team to work together with confidence, knowing that all opinions in the room would be valued. As a result, the team was able to identify operational reality and work with accurate data to understand what was really happening, as opposed to what had been perceived. The complaints about inability to ship product were due to product not being physically present, because of errors in the data that was transferred from the old locator system. There were also some software bugs, which compounded the problems.

Benefits of applying the coaching approach in tough contexts

New business systems implementations can highlight uneven management, gaps in understanding and poor governance processes within organizations. If some of the participants have a different agenda or don't want to engage then it will be difficult for the project to be implemented effectively. This approach invites people to work to their full potential, and once trust is established within a team then my experience is that this way of working attracts in others who wish to participate.

Part 2: Interview

Q: Coaching is a word with many meanings and approaches behind it. Can you explain your own sense of the purpose and process of coaching?

A: For me, coaching is a structured process which enables participants to access their own resources to achieve their objectives, based on the principle that people can think, grow and develop and will find the best solutions for themselves. Coaching is often deployed in challenging and complex situations, where answers are not easily forthcoming. Team coaching is often introduced as a short-term measure to support the development of effective working relationships and high performance.

Q: So how do you coach in projects? One to one, in groups, a blend of these?

A: As you know yourself, coaching is a very diverse process. Getting the objectives is critical; so I may well do that one to one with a project manager or a business partner. But the coaching approach is more a philosophical way of working than traditional coaching conversations. It is about being open and transparent about the issues, and about inviting people to bring their thoughts and challenges, to see what is possible – so collaboratively and collectively the team can work out an appropriate solution. That's where the real power lies, in harnessing the problem-solving capability of a team, getting the team to participate.

Q: But what does a coaching approach look and sound like in daily project life? Do meetings run any differently? Do e-mails read differently? Are decisions made in a different way?

A: I think it's about asking lots of questions, and inviting the wider team to bring both the issue and potential solutions to the table, taking advantage of mutual problem solving. It's also going to look and sound supportive. A no-blame approach supports an environment of trust and mutual respect, and means that discussions are focused on seeking solutions and energy is not diverted into criticizing others. Open and honest conversations mean it's acceptable to challenge and disagree. This can certainly change the tone of meetings and e-mails. Decisions will still be taken within the framework of organizational authority, but the conversations leading to decision making can feel quite different. It's much more a process of co-creation.

Q: Co-creation of culture sounds, on the one hand, a very democratic approach. But it implies a high level of responsibility for project team members. Is this demanding for some to accept, in your experience?

A: Yes, this can be seen as a challenging approach, especially if teams are used to operating in separate units. However, there is a natural energy to human beings communicating and working together. My experience is that as people come together and engage in joint development and problem solving, they enjoy the shared energy, the sense of achievement and shared commitment to the development and performance of the overall organization.

Q: This sounds very positive. How far do you subscribe to the theory that people are hard wired to object to change? This is often quoted in change management.

A: I don't believe that this is the case. However, I believe that the benefits of change do have to be clearly identified for people to be willing to move away from existing proven patterns of behaviour to create new ways of working.

Q: Coming back to the coaching topic, does the coaching approach mean that project managers have to be good coaches? If so, what happens if they are not?

A: Managers do not have to be experienced coaches to take this approach, although a knowledge of coaching principles is important. Many managers are now trained in holding coaching conversations, where they follow key coaching principles to hold productive co-created conversations with others; that releases the energy of all parties to find solutions.

Q: But how many organizations that you see really provide the right conditions for a coaching approach to project management? Is it really encouraged?

A: Many organizations have embraced coaching, have internal coach teams, and support their managers to have coaching conversations in their work. I often work within organizations who seek to accelerate project team performance and consolidate strong working relationships by taking a coaching approach to creating and delivering major projects, and results are quantifiable. I recently coached a newly formed cross-organizational technology and change team to develop a new way of working and deliver a technology-based change and cost-reduction programme across Europe. Areas of work included changing historical hierarchical relationships to create cross-functional teams based on influencing, trust and collaboration. Having identified their own optimum way of working the team received praise from the wider organization about the way they partnered with local businesses to collaboratively address the challenging cost reduction agenda. This co-creative approach spread within the organization and formed part of a significant cultural change.

Q: OK, so finally, what practical advice would you give to a project manager on learning about coaching? Is there a 'must-do' qualification or book to read?

A: Internationally, qualifications vary a lot. Many organizations now offer managers access to coaching skills programmes, for example a two-day programme where you learn to work with a standard coaching model, learn key skills to identify the challenge, name the ideal outcome, use curiosity and questions to raise awareness, and then invite the client to find the solution best for them. So a two-day programme would be sufficient provided people get practice in the session and afterwards, and feedback on their coaching once back in the organization. It's not a huge investment of time for a huge potential reward.

Part 3: Commentary

Here are some reflections on Bernadette's case and interview.

Bernadette raises the interesting prospect that the definition and practice of leadership may finally be changing, away from the heroic models of the past to a collaborative and engaging model which seems to be more aligned to so much of the cross-functional and cross-border working we see in international projects. Coaching is part of this transition and, certainly in the UK, there are many who have been through some form of coach training, a rapid induction into the processes of goal setting and enabling of creative problem solving in the minds of others by conversing with questions. As a practitioner coach, I can only testify to the effectiveness of this approach with clients in a wide range of contexts, particularly where current assumptions may not be working. Second, the concept of 'co-creation' is seen as central, a concept which has been mentioned by a number of contributors in their diverse project contexts. However co-creation is practised, there does seem to be consensus among many of the contributors that open and explicit dialogue about communication, understanding the rules of engagement for interaction, and working with open and collaborative processes that get all ideas on the table, seem to be a recipe for success. It takes time, it takes patience, it takes the ability to listen; it requires curiosity in others, and a sense that they may be right and I may be wrong. All of this describes a rebirth of a very old concept, teamwork, which as Bernadette indicates, is a process that liberates more talent to solve problems than is available in separated and isolated minds. Personally speaking, the two-day training Bernadette recommends changed the way I communicated, and changed the way I interacted with everyone, inside of projects and outside. It might do the same for you.
Bob Dignen

Part 4: Reflecting on international project management

Take time to reflect on the following questions to help you reach further insights and take practical actions to improve your own project management practice.

1 How far do you believe that co-creation is the most effective form of teamwork in international projects? Why?

2 What would make you effective or ineffective when applying a coach approach? Why?

3 What is your own definition of leadership? What will inspire followership in the way you lead an international project?

Part 5: Putting it into practice

There are a number of very valid insights and ideas for project management present in this case which the reader can learn from and adopt, customizing for their own projects. Take a few minutes to note down your main learnings from this case, and note down some actions for yourself.

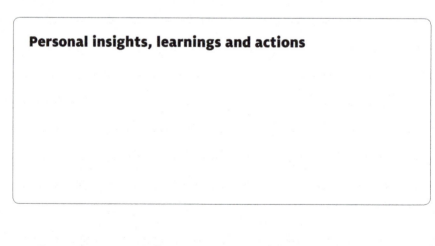

Personal insights, learnings and actions

Reference and further reading

Turnbull, James K (2011) *Leadership in Context: Lessons from new leadership theory and current leadership development practice*, The Kings Fund, UK

Berne, E (1963, 2001) *The Structure and Dynamics of Organisations and Groups*, Fremantle, Australia, Fremantle Publishing

Project fan club: an effective means to achieve a performance boost in projects

14

DAGMAR BOERSCH, FRANK KUEHN AND PETER WOLLMANN

Profile

Dagmar Boersch is a project, programme and consultancy professional with her own company. She has been successfully cooperating with Frank for years and recently also started cooperation with Peter. As a graduate molecular biologist and certified project manager, she has been involved in numerous projects with a focus on pharma and medical device development. Her working philosophy is to create successful projects – in time, on budget and to a high quality – with value-orientated leadership. She is very well known and appreciated in the German Project Management Association and is a jury member for the German Project Excellence Award. Her vision: 'Nobody talks about project management – we just do it naturally!' Peter Wollmann and Frank Kuehn are introduced elsewhere in the book.

Foreword

This case study is a more general contribution to the book sourced from the authors' extensive international and local experiences over the decades. It examines the growth in importance of projects for enterprise value creation. The corresponding methodological overkill started in response to this strategic recognition has not proved successful; the failure ratio of large projects (especially international ones) has not decreased but has, on the contrary, increased. One of the key 'soft' factors for this ongoing underperformance in projects is the lack of official and, particularly, unofficial support for projects in organizations. Projects with real fan clubs – a cluster of meaningful and committed advocates and followers – succeed more often in enterprises. Accordingly, one of the most important tasks for a project leader – beyond methods and tools – is to create a fan club for his or her project or programme.

The capability to create a fan club is highly dependent on the personality and skills of the project manager and the sponsor. This does not mean that the capability cannot be learned. In some instances, only marginally more attention is required, with a focus on thinking at a more strategic and systems theory level, and putting more priority on topics beyond what might be termed technocratic ones. However, project success is likely to depend on the presence of such skills.

Before reading this case, reflect on the following questions. Then compare your answers to the ideas in the case itself and the final commentary.

1 What are the main challenges of developing a so-called fan club for an international project in a very complex and diverse global company? Why? What is the best way to cope with these challenges?

2 What are likely to be important preconditions or success factors for a project manager aiming to create a sustainable project fan club?

3 If a fan club has been started, how can it be successfully maintained over the course of a project and even a longer period?

PART 1: CASE STUDY   Project fan club: an effective means to achieve a performance boost in projects

The practice of project management in the world today

Key developments are impacting upon the theory and practice of project management. On the one hand, we see the rise of digitalization and globalization, acceleration and volatility, and greater uncertainty as to how projects can be well designed and shaped in such an environment. Various developments, including agile project management, scrum, rapid prototyping, and minimal viable solutions, point to an emerging contingency and flexibility in planning. At the same time, we see the merging of project and change management approaches. Customer-based thinking is also driving approaches such as design thinking. In the background, there is an ongoing effort to professionalize the core of project management being driven by renowned international institutions such as IPMA, PMI and PRINCE2, competing to establish themselves as standard bearers and certification bodies for project leaders and organizations.

Figure 14.1 Market shares of leading project management institutions

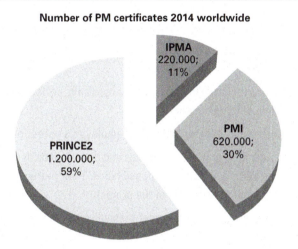

Number of PM certificates 2014 worldwide

The project portfolio of an enterprise is increasingly important for its value creation

As project management practice changes, it also evolves to occupy a more significant position within organizational strategy. An enterprise's success and value is increasingly determined by its project portfolio. According to studies, the share of this total added value is currently 36.7 per cent. In 2007, the project share of this added value in the German economy was estimated at just 2 per cent. This represents an increase of almost 35 percentage points in only 15 years with numbers forecast to grow at a breathtaking pace: by 2019, a share of 42.8 per cent is forecast. It is in projects that innovations are born and implemented; it is projects that shape the future of an enterprise. Therefore, it is absolutely crucial for the management of an enterprise to select the right projects, those suitable for the enterprise's strategy and organization, and subsequently to manage and run the selected projects efficiently. In theory, and in their public statements, companies set great store by their full awareness of the importance of this task, but their actual behaviour says more about their genuine priorities than public statements. Project management is often seen as a part of daily operations, driven by toolboxes and a checklist culture, rather than as a strategic leadership instrument.

How are projects embedded in your organization?

- Projects are a relevant component in the strategic and planning process.
- Project expenses are considered in the short-, medium- and long-term planning of resources.
- Project leaders appear in the organizational chart.
- Project budgets and resources are rarely altered. If they are, then the process is transparent and sustainable.
- Project work is included in annual staff appraisals, performance assessment and compensation.
- Project work is an obligatory part of an employee's career path.
- Owners of functions, processes, systems and data are included in projects, and involved with their actual responsibilities. Their performance is measured against the success of the project.
- All parts of the organization consider themselves to be service providers for projects, supporting, in this way, the success of the enterprise.

Projects must become the expression of an attentive and innovative enterprise

Projects should enable businesses to succeed, to secure competitiveness by optimizing processes or reducing costs, and to maintain operating ability by renewing and/or updating systems and modernizing sites, or by providing an enterprise with new strategic and economic advantages by means of product innovations, post-merger integration, or so-called 'excellence campaigns'. They cost resources as with other tasks in the enterprise and, therefore, require at least as much care and attention in order for them to succeed, from initial project idea to post-implementation. Strong attention has to be paid to the following three core dimensions:

1 composing and steering of the project portfolio;

2 setting up, steering and finalizing of individual projects;

3 implementing of project results into daily business.

The first issue is a primary task of management as a whole. The second is usually a job for project committees. The third is generally the responsibility of the benefit owners. All need to exercise and demonstrate care with respect to individual projects and programmes.

Project care quotient

There are a number of indicators that can highlight the degree to which appropriate and due care is being exercised in practice towards project portfolios. Three care categories – capturing features of fan club behaviour – can be surveyed and used as a checklist to test the 'care temperature' of a project landscape.

1. How is care for and attention to the project portfolio at management level be measured?

- The project portfolio is regularly discussed in management meetings with proper attention paid to detailed content, not merely form.

- All members of management are involved and engaged in discussions, providing their own input both beforehand and afterwards.

- Projects are provided with sufficient budget and resources.

- Management and direct reports make competent staff available for project work.

- Project-related decisions have a certain consistency and are not constantly amended ad hoc.

- Actions agreed in and arising from meetings are dealt with in a timely manner.

- Problems are handled constructively, especially at the 'seams' and interfaces between projects (no silo mentality is present).

- An enterprise-wide PMO is established which has appropriately high status in the organization with both budget and influence.

- The project portfolio is mentioned in relevant reports and presentations.

- Management makes itself available and is ready and willing to make decisions in the event of problems arising.

2. How is care for and attention to the project at sponsor level measured?

- The project has explicit priority #1 on the sponsor's personal target card.

- The sponsor is available quickly if necessary, and devotes sufficient time.

- Agreed input for the project is delivered by the sponsor in a timely manner.

- The sponsor is ready and willing to make decisions.

- The sponsor delivers agreed input for the project in a timely manner.

- The sponsor is reliable when it comes to complying with agreements, even in difficult situations.

- The sponsor treats the project members with respect, appreciation and esteem.

- The sponsor asks for an appropriate number of project briefings (in person, by e-mail or telephone).

- The project is mentioned in relevant reports and presentations.

- Project reports are sought in committees, at high-level meetings etc.

- The project is given appropriate support, even in the face of external criticism.

- There is proactive organization of liaison between organizational interfaces and seeking of relevant synergies with respect to resources, activities etc.

3. How is care for and attention to the project at project leader level measured?

- The project has explicit priority #1 on the project leader's personal 'to do' list.

- Agreed deliverables are provided in a timely manner both to the and/or in the project.

- There is reliable availability of budget and resources.

- Information concerning problems and variance is reliable and available.

- The project leader is available at appropriate times.

- Invitees attend project meetings and project presentations.

- Project leader schedules an appropriate number of project meetings (in person, by e-mail or telephone).

- The project is mentioned in relevant reports and presentations.

- Project members are invited to inform/brief on other projects and departments.

- Project members are approached by other projects to coordinate/agree interfaces and synergies.

- Decisions are made, even in unclear situations, Entrepreneurialism is evident.

Project communication focus – building care for and attention to your project

- Positive surprises cause positive attention.

- Extraordinary successes within the project can be very well communicated.

- Extraordinary measures might interest high-level peers.

- Gaining of award for project excellence and celebrating this with the sponsor.

- Rousing and inspiring meetings which become an enterprise-wide benchmark.

- Strong project leader who is perceived as a great performer in the enterprise.

Project management must become more dynamic

Today, in most organizations, resources are becoming ever scarcer, complexity is increasing, and more is required. Depending on the source one consults, 50–85 per cent of projects are deemed either not effective or not efficient or both (Hastie and Wojewoda, 2015; Gröger, 2004). Even when it is recognized that a project ought to be stopped, this only actually happens in 33 per cent of cases (Gemünden, 2009).

Overall, this signifies grave consequences for the efficacy of project portfolio investment. Interestingly, numerous analyses into the causes of this under-performance make clear the general reasons for inefficiency and failure. Yet, little has improved, as the causes of project failure remain complex and primarily systemic. Organizations continue to pretend that the issue is one of (incompetent) project leaders and leadership, even though project leaders are more qualified and certified than ever before, albeit in operative tools and not in dysfunctional aspects of organizational culture and practice.

If projects are not to remain underperforming, they need to borrow from the language of linguistics. The noun 'project' must be transformed into the verb 'to project' – into a so-called 'doing word'; projects must become more dynamic. The handling of moving targets entrepreneurially, and the embracing of a challenging and dynamic global environment that integrates difficult change request management, must become part of a project manager's day-to-day repertoire. In the project management of the future, beginning will be more important than securing, speed more important than completeness. The key challenge will be to combine the approaches and benefits of classic project management with more dynamic approaches and appreciation-orientated leadership methodologies.

Figure 14.2 Overview of low project performance and its consequences
(Evaluation of various sources by Project Solutions GmbH)

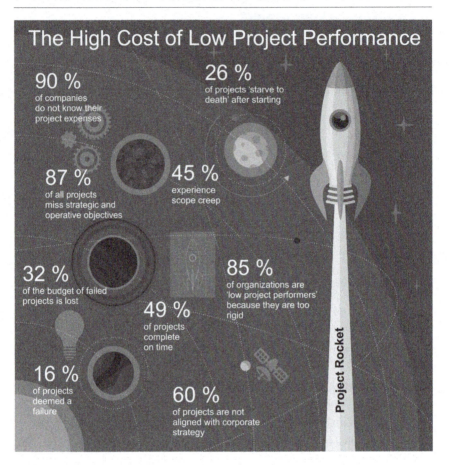

Projects need to gather support in their own organization

Projects do not succeed if they are not supported by the broader organization, if
they do not fit into the organization or if the organization is not able to cope with
them. Projects cannot succeed if they do not receive care and attention, if the
enterprise's management allows, for example, its senior executives to play politics
and secretly shift priorities, all of which undermines project efficacy. Such political
approaches to projects will differ between organizations, depending on the profile
of the host organization. Engineering firms or consultancies that live from their
projects tend to handle them more reliably. It is their 'daily bread' and in the event
of failure they will pay the price immediately and powerfully. At the other extreme,
large public sector construction projects may struggle to cope with a variety of

forces: financial crisis can quickly result in austerity policy and a focus on dividing the 'cake' of an already scarce public funding; a lack of political desire for transparency when it comes to actual total cost might mean resourcing becomes problematic; risks may be ignored over political expediency etc. Widely reported numbers indicate that costs in such public sector projects tend to at least double over their lifetime and completion may be delayed by many years. However, whichever organizational context a project finds itself in, the conditions are likely to be demanding and require a cohort of advocates.

Achieving project success in complex organizations

Enterprise performance derives largely from its many processes and projects, many of which, importantly, are driven by internal competition rather than collaboration. Paradoxically, while the primary task of the entire line organization is to make budget, competencies and resources available, it often behaves in its parts contrarily, often according to the logic of separated segments, divisions and departments, each with their own KPIs, which fail to align in ways that would make cross-functional project life straightforward.

Studies by Prof Gemünden of the TU in Berlin have profiled the characteristics of top-performing projects in demanding organizational contexts:

- Top performers have organizational forces in the company and its environment under control and align the project portfolio quickly to any changed conditions.
- Top performers are innovation leaders.
- Top performers are more entrepreneurial.
- Top performers integrate risk information into their project portfolio management.

Clearly, those leading large projects and programmes in the organizations of today need to assertive and tough, resilient and determined. But a superhero project leader alone cannot guarantee success in the face of complex and contradictory organizational dynamics.

Projects need the mobilization of a critical mass of 'comrades in arms': a so-called fan club.

Making the case for a 'fan club'

What is a fan club? It is a community of supporters and advocates with some importance who have relevant contacts in and interaction with official and unofficial contexts of the enterprise.

What is a fan?

- A fan believes in the project.
- A fan is loyal and reliable.
- A fan can be turned on in an emergency.
- A fan likes taking part.
- A fan gets involved in positive debate.
- A fan gives you his opinion.
- A relevant fan has an important, appreciated role in the enterprise and is perceived as important.

Why is a fan club essential?

Fan clubs contribute the belief, followership, energy and enthusiasm necessary for project work, for joint creation of tasks and for desired solutions. In addition, they expect and demand success and winners they can identify with.

How is a fan club created and sustained?

A fan club needs significant fans, people who are important for the topic of the project and its realization and eventual success. In short, this means a fan club comprises relevant stakeholders from all parts of the line organization including decision makers from development, production, procurement etc. Who these people are need not necessarily be described by the formal project organization. Indeed, the reverse is more the case.

How does one become a fan?

- Possesses enthusiasm for the idea.
- Idea and objectives are credible.
- The issue, the project and its club have a clear identity.
- Is passionate about project management.
- Wants a stake in a valuable outcome.
- Sees personal benefit.
- Moral values involved.
- Inspiration for own life.
- Higher personal profile in the corporate limelight.
- Deeper insight into a topic and its context.
- Has a sense of belonging to a group.
- Respects people in the project.
- Finds interesting people populating the project.
- Confirmed as a valuable part of the group.
- Finds pleasure in joint achievement and successful results.

How can the fan club have a full effect within the project?

This has to be discussed with the fans at their club meetings, at events taking place within the corporate limelight; there is participation in project events, inclusion in the project organization, and inclusion in the project process. Never forget that fans are more than stakeholders, they represent pure energy for the project. Fans sit in the front row of the project arena and stamp their feet in excitement; sometimes they even run onto the pitch. Of course, a fan club expects total passionate commitment in the arena. That goes without saying. A fan club should identify wholly with its project and – once it is formed – should never accept second best.

Can management board members become fans?

Members of a management board are also human, and enjoy enthusing about fantastic developments, not simply figures. As project leader, put yourself in a board member's shoes now and again, and engage them in conversations. Imagine their questions to you (below) and your responses to them which can excite and engage:

'Do you have any interesting insights for management?'

'With which great results can you brighten up my challenging day today?'

'Do you have anything new and exciting for my next board meeting?'

'Do you have anything that is going to move our enterprise forward?'

'What contribution can the developments in your project make to the issues that currently concern us in the enterprise?'

'Is this project going to give us a competitive edge?'

'Have you got another of your brilliant workshops scheduled soon?'

'These latest developments – Industry 4.0, Enterprise 2.0 etc – can you tell me anything about them? Are you also dealing with them?'

Leverage the play instincts of those in the boardroom to engage them in the fan club. Use unfamiliar facilitation methods or show them new 3-D technical gadgets, give them models they can touch and hold in their hands, noises they can hear. Engage their attention with all senses.

If you arouse their attention, they will join

If it is to work better, project management needs much more attention than it has had to date. Project management can only succeed if management gets actively involved. There are several examples of this from leading enterprises.

- *A German chemical plant.* Every project succeeds. Why? Because people's understanding of the projects does not only include correct order execution but also courageous decision-making that determines whether the project continues, changes direction or is stopped. Projects are discussed in weekly management meetings, with technical expertise, realistic estimations and real decision-making power.

- *An international chemicals company.* The CEO and the management team ensure that there is a high degree of consent and agreement on the project. Pragmatism instead of vanity: the project has to succeed. Small, swift decisions because it has to continue. Deadlines come before content-related formulations. We will find a solution that fits the timeline. Pressure won't make anything better.

- *A metalworking company.* The organization succeeds in doing the right projects. This is mainly due to a COO who takes time to get involved, to understand what is happening, to exchange expectations. In the major projects he makes sure that inspirational workshops take place. There is a striking degree of trust between COO, management and the team. Everyone creates time and space for good communication and joint success.

- *A global insurer.* Working as one team: department heads take on responsibility for steering the project portfolio together with true commitment from the board. The team takes one day per month to coordinate the project portfolio and to allocate resources. During one of those days the board takes the time to consider results and required decisions. Project management is a respected discipline within the enterprise.

What do energized projects have in common?

Fan clubs energize projects and inject them with a number of core qualities.

1. Care, attention and responsibility

Energized projects demand care, attention and responsibility. In the examples outlined above, this has less to do with refined project management methodology and more to do with visible and emotional identification, particularly from management. Care can easily be measured in terms of committing time and presence. How can projects succeed if the managing director declares a project to be priority No 1 and then sends apologies for absence at project meetings? Is the time of the top management in the organization so scarce that the official top priority no longer counts for anything?

2. Disentanglement

If project management is entangled and enmeshed by its organizational dynamics, then it is time for the project to take a step back and discover a way to navigate a clear pathway. Identifying pain points and asking relevant questions are essential for breakthrough. What insights do past project failures offer? What hinders excellence in everyday practice? How far might the ideas of agile project management support you in the future?

3. True joint understanding and commitment

In energized projects there is little wastage of time addressed to fixing what seem to be permanently different perceptions and evaluations of the project's status. There should be true commitment and singularity of vision from the beginning on how to develop the project and involve all parties. This joint view includes a common sense of fundamental success factors (clarity of roles, joint values, transparency etc) and the resources (skills, competences, capacities, position, reputation) that are needed to realize the project. There also needs to be joint understanding about the official and unofficial political environment for the project.

4. Top management presence

Top management shows commitment to surface themselves and data, providing transparency around official and previously hidden priorities. Management must assume full and active responsibility for the project and its goals and objectives, scope, procedure and the allocation and deployment of resources. The serious-ness of its commitment can be seen in kick-off workshops with the necessary presence of top management. These should number at least two three-to-five-day off-site workshops, allowing full concentration and time and space for personal responsibility.

5. Sense of opportunity

Significant and successful projects will have a beneficial effect on the results and culture of the enterprise. Those who have been enthusiastic about important developments in a company, who have demonstrated their engagement together with fellow colleagues and who have experienced the dedication and engage-ment of the project team, present together an opportunity to develop new standards for a dynamic enterprise, for future-oriented leadership and cooperation. Ultimately, projects provide a momentum for organizations to challenge themselves and their environment, to survive and succeed.

Lessons learned

Projects demand a fan club, particularly the more international and more complex ones.

Successful fans clubs, to be developed, maintained and improved, require a project manager with a strong personality and deep experience, alongside a supporting executive sponsor.

The specific form, purpose and life of any fan club will strongly depend on the character of the hosting organization.

Part 2: Interview

The following is the summary of a series of personal conversations between Bob and Frank, which ranged across the specifics of this proposal and programme management and international leadership in general.

Q: You mention that the skills needed to create a fan club are very important? What does this mean exactly?

A: It's really about honing into key stakeholders' happiness and enthusiasm in order to make them support your project with full energy; it's about making them make your project the priority in their life. The fan club must feel the passion; you must all have a shared level of passion. And all this presupposes a deep understanding of their pains, what they feel, think, say and do.

Q: How far is it possible to develop an international fan club for an international project in the world of travel restrictions?

A: I think social media is the key; using Facebook, YouTube videos, all this makes a difference. You need to make people feel proud to be part of the club. And it's interesting, if you see how people share YouTube videos, these videos become like the badge of a club. People get really emotionally involved and like the messages behind the videos; they become proud to be part of the community.

Q: How do you know which people to have in the project fan club?

A: Of course, you need to start with the organigram, top-down. Identify who are the drivers and owners of the topics that you will work on in your project, then ask colleagues of yours about who else could be interested in it. Identify people who are taken seriously in the organization, who have a good standing.

Q: Isn't this classical stakeholder mapping?

A: No, it's more focused. This is more emotionally driven. You need people you can excite and who can excite others. It's more passion mapping. And you need to see people beyond their role to see their passion potential. You need to know them and work with them in their full humanity.

Q: You talk about the organizational context a lot and mention the need to disentangle a project from that and navigate a way through. Can you say a little more about what that might look like in practice?

A: I think what I want to talk about is giving the project a profile of its own. You need to put your stamp on it – what is your specific approach to projects? What is spectacular in the project? Maybe it's just quick results that create this momentum. But fans need to know why they should love it.

Q: Finally, do you think that consultants have a role to play in facilitating fan club creation and maintenance?

A: I think it's a relationship between the external and internal. It's a challenge to facilitate the process if you are under pressure as a project manager. And an external is sometimes more skilled at unlocking and managing passion in others. Business people are often not used to thinking in terms of passion; they have passion in them but are not prepared to get it out of themselves or others. A lot of my work is spent moderating meetings, and my role is sometimes to stop people where whey are struggling with passion and conviction; they go too quickly or they get stuck in arguments. I am supporting projects a lot to optimise their passion.

Part 3: Commentary

Here are some reflections on this case and the interview with Frank.

> *This case resonated with me on a number of different levels. Overall, what struck me again was the very strong focus on the people side of projects; on the importance of engagement and ownership through an organization for a project to deliver. Some key words also stood out for me. The first was 'Care'. It's a driver for human behaviour. We do things we care about. We fight things that go against what we care about. If we don't care, we tend to do nothing. 'Passion' is a related but more intense word. Frank talks about the need to excite passions in people and how passions have somehow become diminished in business life; professionals are unsure how to deal with passions. I think he's right, and we need to learn to connect with our own passions and emotions again (self-awareness) and re-connect to the inner and often unseen passions of others to lead (empathy). The final word, and a more mundane word perhaps, is 'informal' in the context of 'informal organization'. I have an increasing sense that our understanding of the word and the entity 'organization' may contain many false assumptions deriving from an earlier industrial age. Curiously, the*

organization may not be led by those who organize it but by informal agents, those with high levels of expertise, those in the company for decades, those who are liked, who have a proven reputation above and beyond the latest CEO. Make these people your fans, and the winds of change will blow.
Bob Dignen

Part 4: Reflecting on international project management

Take time to reflect on the following questions to help you reach further insights and take practical actions to improve your own project management practice.

1 What could be the advantages and disadvantages of creating a fan club as we have described in global programmes or local projects? How could this be best organized?

2 How useful are past experiences and expertise for leaders of a global programme when coping with the challenge of developing a fan club in new contexts? Which 'old' learning will help and which will not?

3 How can building trust be sustainably used a constructive leadership tool for fan clubs in global initiatives?

Part 5: Putting it into practice

There are a number of very valid insights and ideas for project management present in this case which the reader can learn from and adopt, customizing for their own projects. Take a few minutes to note down your main learnings from this case, and note down some actions for yourself.

Personal insights, learnings and actions

References

Gemünden, H (2009) MPM benchmarking study 2009, quoted in MPM benchmarking study 2011 [online] http://mpm.tim.tu-berlin.de/fileadmin/docs/MPM-Studien-Expose_2011.pdf)

Gröger, M (2004) *Projektmanagement: Abenteuer wertvernichtung*, MBA, Munich

Hastie, S and Wojewoda, S (2015) Standish group 2015 chaos report: Q&A with Jennifer Lynch, *InfoQ* [online] https://www.infoq.com/articles/standish-chaos-2015

E-learning product development with a virtual team

15

MIKE HOGAN

Profile

Mike is an international team and leadership trainer and executive coach, and is particularly interested in the dynamics of working in cross-cultural and virtual teams. Additionally, he has many years' experience in e-learning development, virtual training and event live streaming. He is a licensed coach for The International Profiler (Worldwork), and accredited facilitator of both Team Management Profile (TMSDI) and Developing People Internationally (DPI – York Associates). He is currently working towards a diploma in executive coaching and leadership mentoring (ILM Level 7). Titles published by Mike include the *Global Business eWorkbooks* (Macmillan) and the award-winning *Basis for Business* (Cornelsen). Mike works globally and lives in York, UK where he enjoys spending time with his family, cooking and being outdoors.

Foreword

The case outlined is a product development project to create a digital educational product which was to be sold to the corporate market, either B2B by the publisher's sales team or to end users (B2C) through a global network of local in-country educational agents/resellers. York Associates was commissioned by a publishing partner (the publisher), located in eastern Europe, to develop the product through concept development to launch.

The case highlights well some of the general dynamics of international projects: the importance of a clear project brief and vision; the importance of effective planning and clear leadership at the outset; the issues surrounding leading virtual teams; and the challenges of bringing together industry-leading experts into a collaborative venture. It also reveals some of the specific dynamics of working in an educational publishing project: the impact of the particularly humanistic culture that underpins education and teaching, and the challenges for freelance writers involved in such projects.

Before reading on, reflect on some key questions addressed in the case. Then compare your experience and answers to the ideas in the case itself and the final commentary.

1 How might the highly people-centred culture of education and teaching impact (positively and negatively) on international project working?

2 What could be the challenges of managing a virtual team of freelance writers to deliver an e-learning product?

3 How might expertise be challenging to handle in the context of an international team?

PART 1: CASE STUDY
E-learning product development with a virtual team

Introduction

Increasingly, more global companies are leveraging the benefits of digital learning for their employees. The global corporate e-learning market for content, as opposed to technology or services, was worth an estimated US $12 billion in 2015 (Technavio, 2016), and the overall global e-learning market is expected to grow at a CAGR (compound annual growth rate) of 17.81 per cent during the period 2016–2020 (Research and Markets, 2016). It was in this context of such industry size and growth that this product development project was conceived and commissioned. The publisher is a leading player in this field, albeit for a non-corporate user base. They brought York Associates on board as an experienced partner in digital development and a leading player in corporate training and innovative publishing, to support with the product definition and lead on the design and content development of the product, as well as support with reselling into the corporate sector once the product was launched. The publisher's system technology is state of the art, and their in-house technical developers are able to programme a wide range of features on demand.

Project goals

The specific goal of the product development was to launch a leading and highly innovative digital learning product for the corporate sector, which would not only cover English language acquisition and development, but also intercultural and interpersonal communication skills topics. York Associates' remit and goal was to design and develop a multi-level e-learning course that could be suitable for autonomous self-study as well as a blended learning approach to go hand-in-hand with classroom training. The three leads on the development team would also be the faces of the product for marketing purposes, with their industry reputations and endorsement supporting sales and promotion.

The desire to launch this product was driven by the publisher's strong belief in its potential value to the corporate market, building on many years' digital product development and sales in the educational sector. There was growing interest in e-learning among corporates for all aspects of learning – hard and soft skills. Additionally, professional learners were (and are) under severe pressure not to travel to training, for cost and time reasons. However, specific market intelligence for this project was limited due to the fact that corporate was a new market for the publisher and the sales teams first needed a product with which they could approach, sound out and eventually enter the market. As a result, rather than being driven by researched market needs, the product was developed based on the general industry knowledge of the needs and interests of the target user base. Importantly, the partnership with York Associates was seen as adding this corporate knowledge and content development experience.

Project stakeholders

The major stakeholders of the project, with relative significance for each stakeholder, included:

- Project owner (publisher) – senior management of the holding company located in northern Europe (never met).

- VP of new products (publisher) – tasked with pushing the overall product line into new markets and sectors.

- Project leader (publisher) – the success of the project would be a career merit and lead to more responsibility and potentially higher profile projects.

- Content project leader and product ambassador (York Associates) – the success of the project would directly benefit the overall company revenue from publishing projects and reaffirm the content project leader's competence and reputation.

- Product ambassadors (*two further well-known professionals to work on design and content authoring, as well as to endorse the product and assist with marketing and promotion, one York Associates and one external*) – the success of the project would reaffirm their reputations on the overall market as well as lead to higher ongoing revenue following royalty agreements.

Technical development team (*internal at the publisher*) – this project was one of many for this team. Their task was to programme the content supplied by the development team.

- Content editor (*experienced freelance editor for both print and digital learning*) – the success of the project would be a good career merit and reference project.

- Content authors (*a freelance team of three experienced trainers with mixed publishing experience, and limited digital authoring experience*) – the success of the project would be a good career merit and enable the individual members to take on further similar digital projects having gained new experience in digital, as opposed to print where their experience already lay.

Project process

The project had four key stages.

1. Definition

During an initial kick-off with the VP of new products, the publisher project lead, the content development project lead, and the two product ambassadors, the overall goals were defined. In the absence of specific market intelligence, assumptions had to be and were made about the target-user needs based on the team's experience and knowledge of this sector.

The product was defined as a Business English e-learning course for non-native speakers of English with the aim of developing users' language, communication, and intercultural communication skills, at six linguistic levels, from beginner to advanced.

2. Planning

In this stage the overall syllabus across all six levels of the product was to be designed, as was a more detailed syllabus for the first level with 18 units. Two sample units were written for the authors as a reference point on the writing, and the following milestones were identified and set for them: a timeline for first submissions; final drafts; technical conversion; sign-off on programmed sections; and product launch. Initially, there was a desire to plan in detail the syllabi of all six levels of the product, though after some initial delays in confirming the planned topics for all six levels it was decided to plan each level as the content for the previous level was being written. This iterative process got around the challenges of mapping everything in one stage. Syllabus-writing responsibilities were assigned to one individual. However, the precise sign-off responsibility for the syllabus-writing work was not clearly defined. Differences in opinion regarding the syllabus then led to delays in its definition, even for the single level 1 stage. Overall, there was a general fuzziness around who was responsible for what. And we underestimated the differences in opinion among the experts even about the basics.

3. Execution

The process of writing was essentially an iterative one, a standard approach in such projects with unit (or module) drafts being sent back and forth between various parties for comment, approval and sign-off. First, the author sent a draft to the content editor and a stable draft version was agreed upon. This stable draft was then sent to the project leader (publisher) to sign off on the technological suggestions within the draft unit and ensure that the desired activities and approach would be programmable. The unit then came to me (the content project lead) to sign off on the content. Re-drafting was done as necessary. A final version was agreed upon and signed off by both the content project lead (me) and the publisher project lead. The unit was sent to the programmers. Finally, the programmed unit was cleared by the publisher project lead, and sent on to me to sign off.

Communication

In terms of communication flow, I was working closely with the publisher project lead located in Eastern Europe, while also leading an external team of writers – content matter experts who were developing the content for the product. We had little contact with the publisher's VP, past the initial kick-off.

The development team had regular virtual meetings to discuss the timeline, submissions and ongoing developments. E-mail was the main channel of com-munication across the project, for both the development team and the authoring team. In the end, e-mail became too much relied upon and lines of communication became quite fragmented. There was an online file system for the content authors to upload their drafts and final versions into various folders. However, it soon transpired that e-mail was being used instead to submit content drafts, which were subsequently uploaded by the publisher project leader to the online file system. It's difficult to establish why exactly the authors did not use the online system, though I suspect it was down to lack of knowledge of how to actually use it.

4. Launch and sales

We were working backwards from a very ambitious desired launch date to coincide with a major international trade fair at which a working prototype demo was needed in order to drive sales. The final working product was scheduled for first sales and implementation three months later.

Key project challenges

1. Target user

As we were developing the product without specific end-market intelligence, we needed to base the content and approach on our overall knowledge and experience of the Business English language learning sector. The product needed to be generic enough to serve multiple end-user types, from pre-work-experience learners in educational settings, eg university or vocational school, to corporate learners with many years' business experience.

2. Underestimation of timeline delays (decision-making process)

The project quickly fell behind schedule as there were delays in submissions of sample units, which can be tracked back to a lengthy decision-making process on the syllabus for the first level. This led to further delays in the iterative process and in signing off completed and approved content from each of the writing team, which could then serve as a model for each author.

3. Quality

At some point, we took the decision to start the product at the lowest level, for the lowest English level of students, beginner, and build up from there. This gave the project the advantage of not having to define the syllabi of all six levels at the beginning; we could design a level at a time more or less, writing one level and keep an eye on the next. The problem with this was that it meant that authors had to begin writing beginner-level material, which is actually more difficult than intermediate, and a level our trainers had much less experience with as trainers and writers. As the authors struggled to produce what the editors felt to be the right quality, it led to frustrations for everyone. Some authors felt their work was good enough. Some began to get irritated at the high numbers of redrafts, as the amount of time they were spending soon became uneconomical in terms of the monies they were effectively being paid for writing, as remuneration was based on a per-completed-unit basis rather than per hour. These delays led to some conflict within the team, stemming from expectations around quality, the need and also availability of support, and the timeliness of communication or lack thereof.

4. Communication

As mentioned, there were instances on all sides of slow communication when delays became inevitable. This led to further delays. Also, the impact of delays was significant with everyone so busy. If a delay meant that a window of work for one person was missed, this might then have a domino effect with other windows for others being missed. This became really very tricky to manage. On the file sharing, or non-use of it, little training was given on the actual online file-sharing repository, and so this led to it subsequently not being used as intended, with authors instead reverting to e-mail for file sharing. While not a major challenge, it was something which did contribute to delays and overall lack of clarity on the progress of the project. It also made it difficult to keep track of the latest version of a given draft or to be sure that all associated team members had seen the latest version or were even working on the same version. Again, in publishing projects with multiple parties, if you lose track of the latest versions and people start editing already-old versions, relationships can become strained.

Project results

The project fell behind schedule, though the eventual quality of what was completed in a highly innovative project was good in some areas. After a slow start, all team members gained a greater understanding of the approach and standards necessary for the product development and a revised overall timeline was created. In order to still meet the original launch deadline, it was decided that further levels would be worked on in parallel by a second content development team that had greater levels of experience and would be able to benefit from a greater body of completed modules that could act as models.

Ultimately, though, the project was put on hold due partly to a scrutiny of the original business case and a scepticism as to forecast demand, and partly also to a shift in portfolio focus and priority by the publisher, with development and also sales resources being re-allocated to existing core products. It is planned to review the project status, and adapt the syllabus accordingly in advance of a restart.

Lessons learned

1. Team strengths

We started writing content for the lowest linguistic level rather than choosing an intermediate level where the team's strengths lay. Starting with an intermediate level would have enabled the authors to familiarize themselves with the content features, approach and technological limitations, while working on a level they were particularly strong in. The lesson here is to play to the team's strengths, especially early on in a project, to ensure high levels of success from the beginning. After an initial phase of success, it is then possible to re-assign project members based on observable strengths and performance.

2. Timeline

A lesson learned was to build more buffer time into a schedule that may seem unrealistically tight. Use this to plan people resources accordingly, and if necessary bring on additional support in order to still reach timeline goals. Do some contingency planning in case there are delays or quality concerns.

3. Project drivers

A greater understanding of market drivers in the design phase of a project can support efficient progress through a planned timeline and development of a market-ready and market-focused product, leading to easier sales and market penetration. The lesson here is to take time to do market research even if it seems to put original deadlines under pressure. In many cases, greater understanding of the market will enable us to create more relevant development plans, ultimately leading to a better product and, most likely, making up time during the execution phase anyway.

4. Communication

An over-reliance on e-mail communication should be avoided through regular team and individual meetings, either face to face or virtual. Greater levels of openness among team members about ongoing difficulties they may be facing can enable support mechanisms to be put in place and actioned, and minimize the need for escalation or delay. Finally, as lack of personal contact can be a key issue in virtual teams, I would schedule more regular virtual group meetings. Even if diaries are full, these have to be made a priority.

5. Roles and responsibilities

The involvement of multiple experts in this project led to some confusion and disagreement as to individual roles, specifically with regard to defining syllabi and signing off on quality. With multiple stakeholders in such an educational development project, the roles and responsibilities need to be clearly defined and accepted by all in advance. This will provide everyone with a greater sense of clarity, while reducing perceived complexity and ensuring higher levels of engagement.

Summary

While the project got off to a slow start and fell somewhat behind schedule, we got things back on track and brought in more team members to enable us to complete the project on time and on budget. The completed content, as well as the overall design, were highly innovative and if I had to redo this project I would spend more time on the conceptual development phase and the proposed timeline. I would ensure greater clarity of roles and responsibilities, especially around syllabus design and quality assurance. Finally, I would start the content authoring on an intermediate level and move on to the higher and lower levels after the intermediate levels were complete.

Part 2: Interview

The following is the summary of a series of personal conversations between Bob and Mike.

Q: You mention that a number of assumptions were made at the outset of the project, even basic ones concerning the target audience for the project deliverable. In the end, the project was actually put on hold as this business case did not convince senior management at a decision-making meeting. Did your early assumptions strike you as problematic at the beginning?

A: In fact, at York Associates we were very aware both of the assumption and the risks of the assumption. We tried to flag it very explicitly at early meetings – this whole issue of a lack of market intelligence. In the end, I think there was a desire on both sides to get started. Financially and strategically it was good for both parties and I guess we collectively decided to overlook the risks. On a more positive note, you could say it was entrepreneurial.

Q: It sounds a mix of detailed planning but still some fuzziness?

A: Yes, that's true. We did actually plan a certain level of detail; so six levels, each level had 18 units, each unit had six lessons, each lesson had three screens of learning content. We got quite granular in some ways. But when we tried to populate this framework with, for example, themes for the units, we immediately saw differences about what was appropriate – was it high-level 'global marketing' or more everyday 'a problem in the office'? And then we had different views of what grammar to teach, which intercultural skills to teach – the meaning of culture etc. There was the assumption that experts hold the same view of content and approach, which was not the case. And as they were peers, it was difficult to say one had more authority over the others, so deciding was not easy. And then it was such an innovative product and project, there were few ground rules to refer to. It made it all quite challenging.

Q: Why did you rely so much on e-mail?

A: It was really a problem of availability. It was nearly impossible to get everyone on the phone at the same time, let alone together for a face-to-face meeting. Just to give some background to this, the project was originally planned to start at the end of November, during the quiet period for the York Associates' people involved. As the project was delayed to March, both York Associates' people were involved in heavy travel for their work; for the first eight weeks of the project, one was present in the UK for one week, the other for three weeks. So the project became highly virtual in character and very e-mail reliant, partly due to circumstance.

Q: Why were false assumptions made around author quality? Could authors have been supported and mentored better?

A: The challenge was not just around level, although that was an issue; it was also about writing into a new and very innovative e-learning template that was not easy to visualize or master. So, yes, in retrospect, you cannot assume that great trainers make great writers. It's a different skillset entirely. But the writers were not helped by the template challenges, the fact that the syllabus was not very clear, and the fact that the sample units, just two, did not give enough orientation as to how they should write.

Q: You mention conflict in the case. What kinds of conflict arose?

A: Well, just frustration on all sides, to a degree. Authors felt they were getting information late. They began questioning the role of leadership, the timeliness of feedback; they felt the quality was better than the editors thought. And this issue of feedback is always a sensitive one with writers; some writers can be incredibly sensitive when their work is critiqued, and that is something that publication projects really should flag up and deal with openly in advance before writing starts, or it can really lead to bad feeling.

Q: Looking back, if you were to give someone one key piece of advice, what would it be?

A: I think you need to plan properly, in different aspects. You need to plan the course structure and have syllabus fixed before starting, or 90 per cent fixed – you can allow some flexibility so you can adapt to lessons learned. So 90:10; we were more like 10:90, it felt at times. You need to plan to have more clarity on what to do when and how and who. This would have allowed the leadership to be less fuzzy. And have better sample units. The planning around sample units was for us a little bit like pilots for our project, but we didn't create enough material with our sample, or enough good material, so the authors didn't have enough orientation. It was difficult for them to succeed.

Q: It's interesting, as you deliver intercultural training as an organization, how come you didn't establish the right culture in the team to overcome these issues?

A: The culture topic is interesting. I think in this project we all came from a very specific professional culture, a teaching industry culture which is very collaborative, very indirect, where feedback tends to be supportive, and where consensus and involving everyone is valued. I think this influenced the running of this project as a very open process, with not everything defined, roles overlapping, little hard critical feedback etc. These are all good things, but when working in this type of project with time pressure, quality pressure, virtual working and high levels of innovation, with freelancers, that cultural baggage became a liability.

Part 3: Commentary

Here are some reflections on Mike's case and interview.

Mike's case highlights the fact that projects tend to become challenging not simply because of one reason, but because a multitude of factors come into play at the same time in unexpected ways. The multifactoral nature of problems is something that needs to be anticipated and planned for more consciously in complex projects where not everything may be visible. Even scenario planning, a 'what if' approach, may be necessary to put in place contingencies for the unexpected. Secondly, Mike's case reveals how financial structures play a large role in project dynamics. Both the publisher and York Associates wanted the project to happen because it represented a financial opportunity. This led to a relatively light business case analysis, which ultimately led to the project being withdrawn by the sponsor organization. And within the project, the tight margins on payments to contributors, although not an issue at the outset, quickly became a major issue with rewrites of content necessary, as the authors quickly began to feel that their participation in the project was not financially viable given the number of hours involved. Finally, and very significantly, is Mike's reflection on how the cultural value the individuals brought into the project actually became part of their problem. The tolerance for fuzzy collaboration, flat hierarchy and indirect feedback, to name a few issues, became a source of project weakness and not strength. It provides a timely reminder not to assume that the values, experience and expertise that we bring into a project are always enablers.

Bob Dignen

Part 4: Reflecting on international project management

Take time to reflect on the following questions to help you reach further insights and take practical actions to improve your own project management practice.

1 Brainstorm the types of risk that can impact on an international project: intercultural, financial, political, technical etc. Think about what measures might mitigate these risks.

2 Which aspects of you, your personality and your cultural values might be problematic for others in an international project context? Where might you need to be flexible?

3 What are the particular challenges of running innovation projects? What impact might these challenges have on project planning?

Part 5: Putting it into practice

There are a number of very valid insights and ideas for project management present in this case which the reader can learn from and adopt, customizing for their own projects. Take a few minutes to note down your main learnings from this case, and note down some actions for yourself.

Personal insights, learnings and actions

References

Research and Markets (2016) Global e-learning market 2016–2020, *Research and Markets* [online] http://www.researchandmarkets.com/research/7k5tzl/global_elearning

Technavio (2016) Global corporate e-learning market 2016–2020 report, Technavio [online] http://www.technavio.com/report/global-education-technology-corporate-e-learning-market?utm_source=T4&utm_medium=BW&utm_campaign=MediaFirefoxHTML\Shell\Open\Command

Global wine and global leadership: a striking analogy

16

CHRISTAL LALLA

Profile

Christal has been working as a certified sommelier in Italy, Germany, France and the United States since 2012 and has built up a fast-developing, innovative business around wine, wine services and wine education under the name VinAuthority. Christal is, from my perspective, one of the rare people with 'absolute tasting skills', not only in the wine context but also in its combination with all sorts of food. She follows a holistic approach which understands wine as an event for all senses including music, the winemaker's philosophy and approach, the visual and haptic sensations of the vineyards, and the cellars with their barrels

Based on her extensive travels, Christal has developed a broad understanding of the cultures of the world, and the diverse understandings and interpretations of wine making and wines in different countries and regions.

Foreword

Christal's case study explores the striking analogies between the development, production and management of wine internationally, and leadership in global projects. As core theoretical items for (global) programme/project management such as philosophy, methods and tools have always been interpreted, adopted and tailored to local and specific contexts, so has the interpretation, adoption and development of special international grapes. However, whereas nobody is surprised that Chardonnay will taste different in different countries, even professionals are sometimes surprised that global concepts of programme or project leadership and management are interpreted differently across continents, countries and organizations. A PMI-certified project lead can behave quite differently if they are working in a more relationship-oriented continent (like in Latin America or Asia) or in a more objective-oriented environment (like in the United States or the UK). So a Chardonnay grape will behave differently as it grows in diverse and special *terroirs* (soils, micro-climates). Exploring these differences – where they come from and why – whilst exploring the analogy between wine making and programme/project management, will reveal fundamental truths about the challenges facing those leading international projects in the world today.

Although the intention is not to develop the reader into a wine specialist, the case takes a short detour into the technicalities of wine production in order to allow the aromas of the analogy to stimulate the palate. We have marked these passages, which you may want to skip if you do not wish to go too much into detail.

Before reading this case, reflect on the following questions. Then compare your answers to the ideas in the case itself and the final commentary.

1 In which ways might wine production and project management have similarities? Which learnings might the practice of wine production have for project leaders?

2 What is the special *terroir* of your project? In which way is it specific in comparison to other global initiatives? What is the best way to cope with the special *terroir*?

3 What are likely to be important success factors for the special *terroir* you are in and for the person leading a programme in it? Why?

PART 1: CASE STUDY
Global wine and global leadership: a striking analogy

Introduction: the development of the wine business

The theory and practice of wine production have developed significantly. The processes of preparing the vineyards and working in the cellars have improved substantially. The entire business has, in recent years, been greatly professionalized, with a growth of low-priced drinkable wines one the one hand, and on the other, more sophisticated productions to increase the number of wholly amazing high-quality wines. In some ways, the growing professionalization of the project management industry mirrors this development.

This all means that the wine business is today a mature and very differentiated market. Its rapid development and ongoing globalization, and influence from the ecology movement with its awareness of biological and sustainable economy, have returned wine making to the value of an innovative, artistic and fast-developing expertise.

Mature markets are subject to a so-called value migration, which means that a sophisticated, individualized, high-end area is formed on the one side and a thoroughly upscale standard convenience on the other side. The non-profiled average disappears.

Particularly in the high-end range, the original product – the bottle of wine – has to be linked and combined with other products (such as special food) and with services (such as wine education/information and access to the producer) to form an individually tailored, comprehensive customer experience that is 'unique'.

This requires specific personal expertise, experience in different countries and various *terroirs* and access to comprehensive and sustainable networks of professionals and customers, as well as a reasonable number of cooperative partners. These general success factors of the high-end wine business have some immediate similarities to global programme and project management.

The *terroir*

It is of great importance to clarify the meaning of *terroir,* a critically important term in wine production, before proceeding. The *terroir* summarizes in one term the climate, soils, terrain with flora, elevation, slope and traditions of a defined wine region or part of a wine region. It is a unique combination of atomic factors from the categories mentioned above (eg the blend of the special hot and humid micro-climate, the minerality and age of the soil, the steepness and height of slopes, with their particular trees, flowers and microbes, and the traditional handcrafted way of wine fermentation there).

The number of these atomic factors is nearly infinite – and so the variety of the wine produced is too. The range of factors that define the identity and character, the flavour, of a local business unit in which a project takes place are comparably infinite, deriving from beliefs and direction, structure, roles and responsibilities, understanding, defined and lived processes, cultures etc. The result is also a complex and unique biological organism. The interesting question for you to consider is the specific identity of the *terroir* of your project. What does it look like? In which conditions does it prosper? What does it typically yield? What in your project could be the analogy for the soil, the climate, the rain, the farmer etc?

Global and local wine production

There are a significant number of grapes cultivated worldwide. Prominent examples include Chardonnay, Sauvignon Blanc, Pinot Blanc, Merlot, Cabernet Sauvignon, Syrah, Sangiovese and Malbec. Increasingly, we are also finding interesting Rieslings outside of Germany, in Italy, and even in Australia.

On the other hand, the interest in the autochthonous is fast increasing, and a lot of such local grapes are being rediscovered and redeveloped these days. In fact, their number is much higher than those of globally planted grapes. What they have in common is that they fit perfectly to a special region with its soil, micro-climate and other preconditions, and there is an old and often unique knowledge about how to treat them. A lot of these wines are against 'standardized common taste preferences', so they have to fight for acceptance outside the region where they are produced.

However, the focus of this case study will not be about autochthonous grapes, even though this would be a very interesting subject. Instead, this case study is about internationally used grapes – just as we focus in the book on international projects and their specific nature and character. Importantly, although the autochthonous wines are unique and focused on their region, it must be taken into account that international grapes, which seem to be more standardized, also produce different wines in different *terroirs*. The Chardonnay from the Mudgee Region in Australia tastes significantly different from the Chardonnay from Napa Valley or from the Burgundy Region. We will go through some examples in the following section.

A dive into the diverse wines of two international grapes for the reader with a thirst for more background

Chardonnay

Chardonnay is a green-skinned grape variety which produces a lovely medium- to light-bodied dry white wine. Originally Chardonnay comes from Burgundy in eastern France, where it has been famously known as Chablis, but it is planted internationally and has become one of the most planted cultivars in the world. Currently, it can commonly be found in all important wine regions of the world: North America (especially California), South America (Argentina and Chile), Europe (France, Italy, Spain, Portugal, Germany, Austria, Slovenia, Greece and even in England), South Africa, and Australia and New Zealand. So Chardonnay is a well-known world wine and has an easy entry into the international wine market. The Chardonnay grape strongly reflects the character of the *terroir* and way of production. The flavour profile of Chardonnay is strongly influenced everywhere from the *terroir*, vinification, micro-climate, yeast, barrel use or malolactic fermentation. All these variables play a big part in how the final product will taste. The Chardonnay grape can pretty much adapt to any different soil but tends to thrive in chalk, clay, limestone, or kimmeridgian marl soil.

As mentioned above, the Chardonnay grape strongly reflects the character of the *terroir* and way of production. So let's now have a look at some famous examples to understand the variety of Chardonnay wines. Take California Chardonnay for example. It is famous for using oak barrels and malolactic ferment-ation, which gives creamy, oily or nutty notes. A totally different style can be found in Burgundy, where the famous Chablis, a very elegant, lean, crisply mineral wine, has been produced for centuries from Chardonnay grapes. In Champagne, Chardonnay is one of the three grapes allowed in the making of what we know as the famous champagne.

In general, the production in cooler climates such as Burgundy, Champagne, or Alto-Adige, gives Chardonnay wines that are more mineral driven, with crisp apple and pear flavours. In the warmer areas such as Australia (Mudgee in New South Wales), New Zealand (Marlborough), California (Central Coast) or South Africa, Chardonnay shows more tropical, honey, and citrus flavours.

Consequently, the same grape produces totally different, successful wines dependent on *terroir*, production methods and philosophies, timing etc. The comparison to project management is obvious if we think of the different styles, methods, and tools in organizational and cultural contexts (the 'enterprise *terroir*'). There is no easy 'one size fits all' recipe. The different influencing factors have to be carefully analysed and the right combination out of a mass of options has to be chosen.

Merlot

Merlot is a dark blue grape variety that originally comes from the Bordeaux region in the south-west of France. It is a cross between Cabernet Franc and Magdeleine Noire des Charentes. The most famous locations, where Merlot was first cultivated, are Pomerol and St-Emilion. One of the primary grapes used in Bordeaux, this grape has medium tannins. Merlot has become one of the most important and often-used grapes worldwide – called an international grape – as a great blending grape. It also makes one of the most expensive monovarietal wines in the world, if you think of France's Petrus from Pomerol or Italy's Masseto from Bolgheri. You can find Merlot everywhere in the world, with some focus on France (Bordeaux), Italy (Tuscany and Campania), Chile (Apalta), Switzerland (Ticino and Valois), the United States (Washington, California with Paso Robles, Napa Valley, New Mexico Deming), and Australia and New Zealand. Merlot grows best in clay and sandy soils.

As mentioned above, Merlots are a medium-tannic grape variety that can soften even the hardest tannic grape varieties such as the thicker-skinned Cabernet Sauvignon, which makes it an ideal blending grape. Since the merlot is grown all over the world, there are many influences on the result of the wines, not just only *terroir* or especially climate. Various factors play a huge role, such as vinification, viticulture, wine techniques and the creativity of the winemaker. For example, climate and wine techniques influence different flavour profiles of the wine. In cooler climates, you will find especially red berry flavours such as raspberry, strawberry, plum and leafy green vegetal notes. In warmer climates, you experience dark berries such as blackberry, warm dark plum, black ripe cherry, and blueberry. However, chocolate, vanilla, cedar, tobacco, toffee, coconut or marshmallow flavour profiles do not come from the climate or the grape itself but from the oak barrels. Nevertheless, they can be definitely predominate flavours in a monovarietal wine when it is aged in oak.

In general, barrels really play a strong part in wine production, but especially for the Merlot as it is a thinner-skinned grape and has softer tannins. If you want to make a more structured wine and give the tannins a bit of a boost, ageing in barrels is a good way.

Similar to Chardonnay, a large number of influencing factors are essential to finding the right combination. The great blending capabilities of Merlot offer unique features. The high art of French wine making is significantly based on the right mix of Merlot, Cabernet Sauvignon and Cabernet Franc to form a harmonic product.

Insights into international project management from the world of international grapes

- The same grape (the same project management concept) looks very different when applied in different *terroirs* (environments).

- As a wine maker (project leader), it is imperative to explore and understand your *terroir* very well.

- As project leader or wine producer, you have to choose your philosophy, your methods and tools to make the best in your *terroir*. There is no 'one size fits all' recipe.

- The right blend of diverse capabilities needs to be carefully mixed to get a harmonious product.

- Proceeding in an experimental way to find the right mix is advantageous, as there is a huge range of influencing factors

- You must always to be prepared to change or re-calibrate.

Lessons learned

Wine production is a fascinating exploration of nearly infinite options and opportunities. A good wine maker is a person who is in a learning process all their life, trying to push the limits of their knowledge and/or expertise. Innovation can result from applying very old and nearly forgotten methods, as well as from working with a very new development in another wine region. It always gets exciting when the old methods – like harvesting according to the moon cycles (biodynamic method) – are combined with new insights such as those from modern chemistry. A very professional and successful wine maker in Montalcino plays Mozart to his vineyards all day, with universities confirming the positive effect on the grapes and the produced wines. Today, organic wine makers use old methods to successfully prevent grape diseases. The good wine maker knows that he or she will never be at the end of his or her learning curve.

A good leader of global programmes or projects should work with the same mindset. In today's globalized world, a lot of foreign continents and countries seem to be familiar but this might be a misperception. To really understand another 'system' – if it is a continent, a country, a company, even another a function in the same company, a diverse *terroir* – is a challenge. The danger for professionals in programme/project management and in wine making is that there seems to be a common set of standardized methods and tools to be applied. The wine maker, who is in the vineyard and/or in the cellar, knows that there will always be surprises. So too, the programme or project manager will often have to adjust to variables and uninvited surprises. This is a key component of international project leadership.

The number of important influencing factors for wine making and programme/ project management seems to be similarly huge. The role of natural factors in wine making, like bad weather, hail or diseases, is played out by human factors in programmes and projects. Heavy storms are like teams that do not work; the sudden loss of sun like the absence of top management. It is much more effective to be aware of the ever-changing environment and to be ready for permanent evaluations and calibrations, including innovations from all perspectives, adopting a continuous learning approach.

Part 2: Interview

The following is the summary of a series of personal conversations between Christal and Peter, which ranged across the nature of this analogy.

Q: Which are the success factors for wine making with international grapes in special local regions? What has to be reflected?

A: Oh, this a very broad question to be answered on an abstract level firstly. You should know and deeply understand your *terroir*, what is similar to other *terroir* sand what is different. And then you have to experiment a bit, being aware that you will experience a lot of surprises. There are too many influential factors to be thought about, so you cannot predict or calculate the result. If you have a lot of experience in different contexts, you will have built up a certain intuition, which helps, but in which you should not trust 100 per cent. You have to know that you do not know everything, that you can learn, that you have to apply in practice to know more, that you will have errors but that you can learn from them.

Q: What is your recommendation for a leader of a global project who has to apply an international standard locally? How should he proceed?

A: I think that the diversity beyond global standards is tremendous. The best wine makers planting an international grape know exactly how they should proceed in other regions of the world. They decide what they should do similarly and where they want to be different or unique. And – that is my experience – they can explain what they do and why.

They are very conscious of what they are doing. A good programme or project manager should do the same. If you are a professional, if you evaluate your initial situation very carefully, if you are confident enough to take a decision and document it – and to defend it – then you are, from my perspective, on the right path.

Q: What is the key difference between wine making and programme/ project management?

A: Wine is – together with food, the philosophy and history of the wine maker, the natural environment of the vineyards – the animation of all senses, a central part of life. It is something absolutely close to your physical existence, which is for most of the programmes and projects not the case. So learning from wine production means, from my perspective, learning from real life.

Part 3: Commentary

Here are some reflections on Christal's case and interview.

Christal has developed an exciting and striking analogy. My key takeaways are three insights. First, nobody should ever think that he or she is able to reflect all influencing (atomic) factors for a programme or project (the terroir*).*
It is impossible, which means that there will be surprises. This should reduce all potential arrogance, and it should make us ready for life-long learning in a creative mindset. Second, there is a need to focus. If you are not able to reflect all influencing (atomic) factors, you have to decide on which abstraction level you will focus, which factors should be regarded. This might be a systematic or intuitive exercise. Both are fine, but the result should be documented with the reasons for the focus. All people evaluate a situation coming from a 'standard model for judgment'. This is fine, but one should check whether it fits or whether the gaps are too large for the real situation. Third, and connected to the previous insight, take your time to explore the situation and be aware that it will take time. Don't let yourself be put too much under time pressure. And, perhaps, take the chance sometime to work with a wine maker to get a new perspective from a new experience. In general, I would like to stress that this brief view of a different world is intended to support the development of creative ideas for your project through alienation. Alienation is sometimes needed to make things in a well-known environment very clear and understood in a new context.
Peter Wollmann

Part 4: Reflecting on international project management

Take time to reflect on the following questions to help you reach further insights and take practical actions to improve your own project management practice.

1 What could be the advantages and disadvantages of using similar iterative proceedings to those described in wine production for global programmes or projects? How could this be best adapted?

2 How useful are wine production experience and expertise for leaders of a global programme?

3 What do the *terroirs* of your programme/project look like? Which factors are defining it in detail? What is the impact of this on you? What are your management strategies?

Part 5: Putting it into practice

There are a number of very valid insights and ideas for project management present in this case which the reader can learn from and adopt, customizing for their own projects. Take a few minutes to note down your main learnings from this case, and note down some actions for yourself.

Personal insights, learnings and actions

Dialogue in Montalcino

17

In early April of 2016, a group of contributors to *Leading International Projects* and its two editors meet at Il Cocco in Montalcino. The objective, beyond enjoying the beautiful wine, food and landscapes of Tuscany, was to exchange thoughts and experiences around their diverse experiences of international project management. The result was a dialogue, much of which is captured below, whose content reveals insights and suggestions on how to lead projects. Perhaps more importantly, the commitment to discussion and dialogue itself, is a call to action to those involved in complex international projects to dialogue more with stakeholders, to exchange and learn – to tell and to ask – with extensive dialoging itself a key component of successful international leadership. Last but not least, the experience of this event proved again that an animating and relaxed atmosphere, a number of experienced and open experts and leaders, and the parallel learning about a different but somehow related topic (wine and how it best fits with different foods) nearly always produces creative insights, which is perhaps a good recommendation for project initiation and kick-off workshops.

Contributors in Montalcino: Bob Dignen, Peter Wollmann, Alberto Casagrande, José Moreno Codina, Sharon Lalla

Figure 17.1
Il Cocco in Montalcino

Part 1: Reflecting on international project challenges

Alberto	Let me start. For me, the most tragic mistake to start with, at the beginning of a project, is to think that this thing is going to be similar to the things in the past. In developing countries, I have so many examples. I can tell you about so many companies that do this; they show up, go to good restaurants and hotels and have absolutely no impact. I keep seeing people arrive who think they can apply the past. They achieve nothing.
Bob	To echo that, I always remember one guy who in a seminar in Zurich stood up and said, expertise is my greatest handicap.
Peter	This is also known in knowledge management. You have to learn from experience, but sometimes you have to cancel expertise.
José	There are two aspects to this. Most projects have two assumptions: first, that the people who sign off the project know the most important things around the project. Usually, this is wrong. It's not the case. The second assumption is that nothing is going to change, which, of course, is not true. Certainly, these two came very strongly in my experience. One was in Poland: the company was convinced of the way to go, and completely disregarded the emergence of a new channel. Second, there was the assumption that Poland would take a long time to adopt western ways, which was totally wrong. Generally, I don't have an answer to this. But big companies are not very good at it.
Bob	It's curious. It's not a very complex insight. It's obvious, isn't it?
Peter	Yes, but it's complex in this way. A sponsor must be sure he can complete something. Yet if you have a sponsor who is too sure, then the probability of failure is very high. That means you need to have a consistent and powerful person, but also a person who has a lot of doubts, and knows that what he thought yesterday might not fit the day after. He needs to be open to learn something. You need to be able to recalibrate, not every day because it's not possible, but on a regular basis. Maybe your assumptions are wrong, or what fitted in the past will not fit now in this situation. This combination is quite difficult. You have a lot of people who have no doubts at all. To cope with those sponsors is a little bit problematic.

Alberto	I totally agree. There are two aspects. You need people with vision, but you also need elasticity. Vision and elasticity. I have a vision that I want to have a bigger company in this direction. Then I have three or four ways to go. Let me give you an example. A software in Brazil was chosen by a client, actually for the wrong reasons. They kept going. They kept designing it wrong. They kept saying, 'No, this is the right thing to do'. The budget just increased dramatically. And it still doesn't deliver. It still affects the operations of a multinational in the region today. So, what happens, probably the high-level decision was right. But somehow, they got stuck on a wrong solution.
José	One common problem which is difficult to solve is that there is often more focus on the tasks and problems in the project than on the objectives. Not enough time is spent on objectives. In other words, you are saying, what was the objective? We want a very good system: flexible, quick, easy to manage and cheap. These were the objectives. But maybe the objectives were not embedded into the decision and so it went rapidly into two or three options, and then the process, and then hundreds of PowerPoint slides and boxes to be ticked, and tasks, and all that stuff. But the root problem, the objective that they wanted to achieve, was lost, and it's actually a moving target because technology is always moving, and so are the business requirements.
Peter	I have some background to this. I have seen a situation where a senior sponsor says, I have a solution for all the regions, many countries. We take a very cheap system with an amazing business case. Only I could have thought of this. Now, if you start like this, it's very difficult to say after one year, oh, this was a mistake, because your reputation is linked with this. And that's why you go on, or you really put your position in the company in danger. This person is today in an even more important role. So, you see, a lot of people know this in the company, that it was a significant mistake. And mistakes are not bad. The question is, how does the company cope with this? How easy is it to say that the whole project was a mistake; the investment of some millions was a mistake? People don't do this.
Bob	Yes, I would say that many large organizations are in a very real way irrational in some way, toxic and subject to powerful personal agendas, or powerful people.

Alberto	OK, but assuming there is some toxicity, you still have to believe that by designing the project in the right way, you can achieve the results. So you need to have a big objective, you need a vision, you need a way of managing uncertainty, and then you go down into the organization, and you realize the project.
Peter	It depends. It's what you said, the project sponsor has to have a vision, particularly for big transformation projects. But you have to realize that your vision to realize the project has quite a high probability of mistakes, between 30 and 60 per cent. This analysis comes from studies showing that one-third of the large projects fail, one-third are so-so. and one-third are successful. This has not changed over the last 30 years. You know this. Of course, you get sponsors who believe they are better than everybody else, and they see others fail with a large project type, and they believe they can do it better, and then they fail too. It's not wrong to try it but you have to be very careful.
Alberto	Let's try to split a little. There are projects where the entrepreneurship factor, the risk, is high, and then you can accept failure. There are projects where this entrepreneurship is not so high. It's business as usual.
José	Yes, the distinction is important.
Peter	I am totally with you but if you have this large vision project then you need to run the preparation or investigation phase in a very careful way. You have also to be ready perhaps to change the ambition. One platform for Europe is the goal, then some countries are difficult, so you change. This flexibility in design should be there because you need to reduce the risk. I've seen some companies over a 15-year period lose over two billion euros with projects. You need to know if you are not good, and plan accordingly.
Bob	How does this sound to you, Sharon?
Sharon	Oh, yeah. I've done project management for years. This is nothing out of the ordinary at all.
Bob	Isn't all this a question of project capability? And what strikes me when I look at large companies is that they never seem to focus energy on building up skills internally, the capability to run large projects.

Peter	That's very true. So you often come to a situation like this; you know you are not the best in international project management, and you can say, we need to invest in people. And then what happens, there comes a focus on costs, and so you cut these because you need quick wins; it's a dilemma situation for managers. It's a systemic problem which prevents the company from building up sustainable capability if the company is listed on the stock market. If the company is owned by a family with beliefs, and they don't care what is written about them, they have time, then you have another logic in the system.
Bob	I remember sitting in a meeting with a senior manager in a huge family-owned company. He was talking to his senior guys and saying, we need to think long term. I asked him what he meant by long term, and he replied 25 years. In these family companies, long term is really long term.
José	Yes, mutual companies are also like this.
Bob	And do they do projects better?
José	I think so. I know one mutual company. The president is 81 years old. He signed off the strategy 25 years ago. And it's very successful, very consistent.
Peter	So, it shows, when leading projects, you need to analyse the system. What is the philosophy, how strongly is the company long- or short-term oriented, how does the company learn, how easily can the project cope with changes, is there a need for quick wins?
José	There is a way around this, to report to the stock market value creation. So you can say it doesn't matter what we did this year. What we did this year is going to materialize in the P&L in 10 years. So let's report an increase in value created. This is supported by the actuarial profession, in fact. It's a way to get around just profit reporting, talking around value.
Bob	Ok, but just to bring it back a little. Understanding the system and thinking of new systems is good, but how does this help the people I work with? The system is given to you. You can't change it.
Peter	But if you don't understand the logic and culture of the system, it's difficult to run the project successfully. It is given and you can't change it. But you can better decide how to cope with it.

Bob   So what you recommend as coping strategies?

Peter   The understanding of the system decides 50 per cent your communication strategy. If the project is under short-term pressure, then you need to look at your quick wins. You have to decide on which quick wins, even selecting those that are not optimal for the project in some cases. But just so you have something after three, four or five months which is tangible.

Alberto But Peter, you are describing a sick environment, I'm sorry to tell you. I have been in much better environments. But you cannot write a book about sick environments. There are environments, good examples. We need to make this transformation, from this to this. We need to arrive there. And then if you come to politics, I say, either you do it or you are out. Very simple.

José   From healthy to sick environments, you have everything in between.

Alberto Yes, but the truth is that if you have a good top management, then you should have as much a top-down approach as possible.

Peter   Yes, if this company with a good top management has a clear sense of the priorities, then it works.

Bob   It's interesting. You are classifying organizations as single entities, either sick or healthy. My sense of organizations is that they can be highly fragmented. There are islands of health and islands of sickness. And in a healthy environment, you suddenly run up against a senior leader on an island of sickness, and things get difficult.

Peter   Good point. That's normal.

Bob   And the other tricky thing is that it's often not clear if it's sick or healthy. So one company I work with, it's structured globally as a series of manufacturing sites. These sites are silos, and all have world-class expertise. And you have people at headquarters looking at this and asking themselves, can we drive cost savings and synergies? Can we not optimize production across the sites in some way, to coordinate this all? The guys locally feel that if they transform, they risk the quality of the product. Globally, the desire is focused on cost, and running operations top-down with transparent coordination. So there are just different views about how a large organization should be run. Should you remain specialist, local and drive quality? Possibly you embed higher cost. Or should you go for a global organization with a matrix mechanism which theoretically delivers on cost, but the numbers are quite shaky and high level? So I can sit with two clients in the same company with two entirely different but valid views about how the business should be run. And some people who resist international projects, often authentically driven, well, they may be right.

| Alberto | Yes, ok, and sometimes there is no clear best. But as an organization, if you decide, then that's the decision. |

Alberto Yes, ok, and sometimes there is no clear best. But as an organization, if you decide, then that's the decision.

José And part of managing a project is clarifying the benefits.

Peter Yes, it's about coping with doubts. And the sponsor is important for that.

Alberto You cannot afford doubts. If the doubt is valid, you escalate the doubts. You have to communicate the doubts but keep working. The moment that you have the doubt, communicate it to a higher level. If you have to deliver against a deadline, you have to do it.

Peter So, the sponsor has to manage things like this. He has to go in front of his team and say, we have this and this situation. We need this; there are some doubts but nevertheless we have to do it. It's communication and alignment. If you have a sponsor who disappears when it gets difficult, then you have a problem. You can be honest with doubts as a project manager, but you have to deliver. If you are not able to handle such situations, then you are really lost as a project manager. You need to be competent.

Bob I think competence is also an interesting thing in projects which often leads to unexpected issues. I am working at the moment with a world-leading German engineering company that is working with its American subsidiary to co-build a new production site in the US. On the German side, you have an organization populated with world experts, the best in class in the world. In the US, they are good but there is a history of bringing in expertise from outside consultancies to complement in-house staff. So the German guys tend to view their American counterparts as lacking competence, which is true to a degree. The American guys feel devalued and untrusted by their German colleagues, and are having problems with their local consultants (also friends) who are upset when challenged by the German side. So uneven competence levels can sometimes really cause issues in international projects.

Peter   Yes, that's something that happens a lot.

José   Yes, as a consultant myself, none can claim to be the best. You always need to get knowledge from other people, other parts of the organization. But that's also the explanation for why consultants exist, like me.

Part 2: Strategies for dealing with international project challenges

Bob   So, we have been talking a lot. Now tell me what I should do one afternoon as an international project manager to handle my situation. What strategies do I need to employ? For example, what should I map if I look at my environment?

José   The culture of the sponsor; am I encouraged to take risks, to innovate.

Peter   To make mistakes ...

Bob   So what is this as a dimension of culture?

José   Risk aversion. I don't know exactly how to phrase it. How people behave with risk aversion. And is the environment short or longer term. Is the company focused on quick wins, or value orientation?

Peter   The problem is that you can never fully demonstrate the impact of a project on the value of a company. I have seen this before in companies, having a belief that we needed to modernize the company by investing in project management. We invested a lot of money in this. The CEO believed in it and it sounded quite convincing. But we could never prove that x per cent of profit of the company came from it. You have some indicators but they are partly soft, not hard. They are qualitative and not quantitative. So it's always a question of how a company works with these two dimensions. You cannot always be qualitative. You cannot also be only quantitative.

| Bob | There are also many non-human aspects to this. There can be really technical constraints which make projects difficult. My case is about an engineering project where the unknown behaviour of electricity on site, and the threat this posed to human life, slowed everything down. And then there's environmental issues; devaluation of local currency can make operations in a local environment really challenging, for example. |

| Peter | Yes, I saw this with a major German chemicals company. |

| Bob | And bringing it back to the human, there are the psychological dimensions that impact how people behave. |

| Peter | There are system theorists who do not believe in this. I have a colleague; he argues that the system produces human behaviour and thinking. The environment influences the person. His wife is a psychoanalyst and she is always reluctant to believe that the system is so strong over the individual. The scientific research on this is very clear; the system is much stronger. |

| José | They must have interesting dinners together (laughs). |

| Sharon | But isn't it about the team skillset? You see individual leaders who are successful in some contexts and not in others. The difference is the team skillset. |

| Bob | José, you mention this in your case. That it's the constellation of team members which is important and sometimes you just get lucky. |

| José | I was in a lecture the other day and was listening to someone saying there are four models to this team thing. They were using films to illustrate. One was using Henry V to illustrate, leading in a big battle and motivating the troops. The second model was The Three Musketeers; all for one and one for all. The third model was the Pirates of the Caribbean; no matter what happens, you try to survive and take the ship towards something. The fourth one was Gladiator; in a very difficult empire you still do something but you act alone against the establishment. |

| Peter | I think this is very valid to make things transparent. I think it's good to work with film or theatre, Shakespeare. It gives another perspective. |

Bob   So it means that as a leader, you need to shape to different environments, and that even teams might mean something different, or have to be constructed in different ways. I always remember an American working in Germany who said that teams don't exist in Germany – he said it to me in a training course. I asked him to explain and he said what he meant was that roles and responsibilities in a German context, for German colleagues, always needed to be clearly defined, and with a clear leader. And the US guy had a problem with this. He wanted roles and responsibilities always to be overlapping and intersecting, people collaborating and supporting, and actually sharing leadership. And around the world, there are very different preferences about this.

Peter   Yes, so now we come to a scenario that as a project leader you are in a company which works with fixed roles. And you start your project and you have a team with a different belief. You have no chance. You can achieve a little bit perhaps. This is what I meant with system, and how strong the system might be. But you need to know how much flexibility the system has. Then it's an individual decision to manage the system – how much do I deviate? You can do something, but you cannot do everything. The gladiator cannot kill the emperor. No way.

Bob   In my case, this became a very significant dynamic. You can have a multinational working with a kind of rigid and defined team dynamic, but operating in a country with a flexible team dynamic. The results, as my case shows, were pretty disastrous. The defined role guys saw the others as chaotic and unprofessional. The flexible guys saw the more rigid guys as hierarchical and authoritarian, lacking trust in the more flexible guys. This produced an enormous amount of conflict.

Peter   I can imagine.

Bob   So, let me just summarize these dimensions that project leaders need to look at in their environment, to map in some way. We talked about levels of risk aversion, time orientation, the overall clarity of project value, decision-making styles – beliefs or data driven – levels of commitment from sponsors, tools and resources available, technical challenges, psychological issues and team and leadership styles.

Peter	Yes, and you need to work on these things in a focused way. And always be a little critical with your assumptions, and very open to have them contradicted and to find ways to prove them. You need to be very aware of the rules around you – the culture, the organization. And you need to be clear how much space you have.
Bob	Can I raise the issue of communication? And if we want to challenge assumptions and check where we are, we need to regularly clarify what is happening around us, why something is happening, and what people mean when they say something. Clarification is needed, but is strangely very rare as a behaviour.
José	Clarification is essential; asking questions to understand.
Bob	I always remember with you, Peter, once when we had a meeting in Bonn and we took a decision. I called you the next day because I had a few more ideas. But you said that we had taken a decision. I said I knew that, but kind of dismissed it. I had new ideas for a new decision. But Peter said a big 'No', a decision had been taken. I then realized that we were using the same word with different meanings. For Peter a decision was something binding; for me, a decision was far more iterative. Both were fair and reasonable, but not the same at all. And this can cause a lot of issues in projects across cultures too.
Peter	Yes, I am quite sensitive to this. If a decision is taken in a group of people, I hate it when people come and say they think in another way. I don't change a group decision because one person says it is not right; I then have to involve everybody. Otherwise, there is no trust in the meetings.
Bob	Yes, so for you, decision making is a group-orientation, trust-based and binding process. For me it is iterative, entrepreneurial and creative. Both valid.
Sharon	Aha, I'm more like you, Peter.
José	I'm more like you, Bob. (laughs)
Alberto	Just tell me, where are you in the project? Are you the steering committee?
Bob	No, just in the project team.
Alberto	The project manager decides. It's your decision. If anyone else is there, we can talk, but it's my decision. It's very simple.

Bob   But that sounds very hierarchical.

Alberto But you need structure. Who takes responsibility for the project, the project manager? If you are in the steering committee, you need a mechanism to decide. To decide, you need a machine that works.

Bob   I don't disagree. I spend my life having these conversations. One person will say A, and the other person will say Z. And that's the problem. There's often no consensus on basics. There's such diversity on these basic things, it can really unravel projects. What I see is, whatever you say, someone will disagree with you.

Alberto OK, let's say you are in the steering committee, and two people disagree on something that is fundamental to the project; the project is locked, because you need the approval of the two. Let's go in the team. If you want to create a total disorganized thing, you say you can go against the project manager, I'm allowed to do that. That also is a cause of locking the project. This would be weak leadership inside of the team. That is a question to be answered.

José   I think it's a question of finding the right balance, the right governance.

Alberto I think there is one person responsible for the actualization of the project; it's the project manager. This guy needs to take responsibility. If the guy is not able to sort things out, he cannot manage this type of project. If you are on a deadline, there is no other way. You need to find agreement as soon as possible.

Peter   I would not disagree. I think it's important to have the way decisions are made transparent. And this has to be documented, and the principles behind the decision making.

Bob   Yes, and this is interesting as a competence, documenting, and making explicit, surfacing the rules by which teams interact and take decisions. It's rule setting. This is important because very often, we think our behaviours are clear to others but they may be very confusing. I always remember a German team member being given lots of positive feedback by the British project team leader, and she came to me and complained. 'Why did he give me positive feedback? Didn't he expect that I could do the job?' For her, no feedback was actually good feedback. You only get feedback in her context when things have gone wrong. So positive feedback was highly confusing. And this I see as a real dilemma. People thinking positively but others viewing the behaviours as negative.

Alberto   But what you just said is irrelevant. As long as the project delivers the objective, it's finished. People can disconnect and say you are an idiot but if the project delivers, it is a performing team. You know, if I go to Sao Paulo, do you know how many people want to give me a knock in the head? But I don't care. If you deliver, finished!

Bob   Interesting. I sometimes see line managers who work in projects working with a very different logic – their own logic more around sustainable relations, because that matters in the line organization.

Alberto   I would expect to see some correlation between line management in projects, and leadership style.

Peter   I think bad line managers generally make bad project managers. But good line managers do not always make good project managers. If they have a directive style, then working with people who do not report to them on a legal basis can be difficult for them.

Bob   José, as a consultant, you go into organizations and then exit.

José   Yes, and my experience is completely different because of the nature of the project mainly. I work much more with sustainable relationships.

Alberto   I can have a very good relationship but destroy your project. No. First, I deliver. If the team is happy, I'm happy. If the team is not that happy, I still deliver, which is the goal.

Bob   I guess there may be highly relationship-driven leaders out there who, if asked to step into a project which needs robustness and directness, may have to question if they can adapt, if they are the right person. I don't see that reflection happening very much, and also people's flexibility to shift from a democratic to a directive style can be limited.

José   Just to say, the deadline is important but it's not always true. Quality may be a higher value. So you need to also bear in mind the quality–time dimension. Which also relates to the issue of cost.

Peter   OK, so sorry to interrupt. But it is time for a wonderful lunch and some wine from Il Cocco. (laughs)

A word on Montalcino

The authors' meeting at Il Cocco was not the first successful workshop at this place. Il Cocco has been the base for a sequence of very creative and productive workshops of different groups since the early '90s. Il Cocco is a very old estate near Montalcino on a 600-metre-high hill with a breathtaking view at the Val d'Orcia (world heritage) and the Monte Amiata (a former volcano and the highest mountain in Tuscany). Since 2002 Il Cocco has also produced the famous Brunello wines. Christal Lalla has lived and worked for some years at this estate and in its vineyards. Peter met Christal there in 2012 and decided to start VinAuthority with her, in addition to his job in the insurance industry.

If you want to know more about wine and Christal's and Peter's wine business VinAuthority please visit www.vinauthority.de or contact Christal (vinauthority@gmail.com) or Peter (vinauthority@gmx.de). If you want to learn more about Il Cocco please visit www.ilcocco.it

Conclusion: looking to the future of international project management

In the Introduction we promised some concrete insights from a bundle of detailed case studies representing diverse international projects, giving some (new) direction, animation and ideas for readers on how to design their existing or future projects. The format we used – a case author introduction, a case analysis with lessons learned, an interview, commentaries from Bob and Peter and proposals for takeaways – was intended to produce more than only data or information, but knowledge in its best sense. The aim was to integrate into the reader's intellectual and emotional horizon an imagination of how the cases' insights might be adapted for themselves. We hope that this ambition was successful, and we hope for further personal interaction to deepen this stimulation, as real knowledge is always built up by application and interaction.

The range of insights and recommendations is quite broad. Therefore, we only want to touch on some of them here to prevent too much repetition from the individual articles. One key topic is the need to fully understand the context or constellation around the project, which means to understand, from a system theoretical point of view, the official and unofficial rules, roles and processes, the level of trust, the reliability of decisions etc of the organization around the project, and what the real attitude of the organization and its key persons is towards the project. This analysis, honestly and carefully done, is a good basis on which to decide how to proceed. A second key point is around leadership and how this is situational; it has to be adapted to the type of international project and its surrounding organization. Finally, there are the topics of stakeholder management, communication and intercultural understanding. The imperative is to develop a broad knowledge about people – the relevant stakeholders for the project and their cultural backgrounds – as well as setting priorities for information, motivation and development of the project core team. Fundamentally, this requires allocation of sufficient time, and never being in the situation of not having enough time.

Peter Wollmann

One of my objectives in writing this book is actually shared with those reading it, to encounter experience of international projects, learn and develop one's own practice. As a trainer, coach and facilitator of international project teams, I had a sense I understood some of the key challenges but I was always struck by the multi-layered nature of the challenges facing those I was working with. I always used to pitch my objectives for any training session as 'understanding some of the challenges of working in international projects'. I now see that I was right to add this disclaimer. The cases so wonderfully elaborated by the contributors to this book have given me many lessons. First, it's necessary to generalize but it can also be dangerous. This goes to the heart of human knowledge: we build expertise with our experience but any current or future reality may disprove all that hard-won expertise, so openness needs to sit alongside confidence. This is partly why I enjoyed Rana's and Alberto's cases so much, and also Nathan Lamshed's recommendation to ask dumb questions in order to check assumptions. Christal's *terroir* analogy makes, if I may say, crystal clear the complexity of our surroundings and the multiple influences that can impact on the formation of a wonderful wine or a successful project. Perhaps, as Peter Wollmann suggests, we will always need a little bit of luck.

And what about the future? Well, I imagine globalization will begin to stretch into new geographies, particularly in Africa if the economies of Asia, LATAM and Eastern Europe begin to falter. This will create an even greater imperative to develop cultural intelligence, for want of a better term. In other words, we will need to be looking at those different to us fairly and intelligently, harnessing, as Bernadette says, the resources which large multinational teams present to international project leaders. Unfortunately, this is not as straightforward as it appears. Much of my training in the last 10 years has been focused on helping very competent professionals recognize the limits of their openness, their tendency for intolerance, and the strenuous effort they need to apply to work with an open mindset. For anyone about to finish this book who has an interest in the topic, pick up Craig Storti's *The Art of Crossing Cultures*. It will help you become excellent with emotional intelligence.

A central theme of the book has been the context of the project, not so much the national cultural context but more the organizational context. One increased awareness for international project managers is understanding of organizations as in many ways disorganized, non-aligned, clunky and quite political places, full of disagreement and under-resourced to do what they want to do. This is not the 'sick organization' described in the Montalcino dialogue; it's simply the reality of many international organizations migrating along the pathway of enterprise maturity. Managing one's own organization and the multiplicity of organizations that intersect a project, each with its own history and story (see my case), has to become part of the project manager's daily to-do list. Will this organizational disfunctionality lessen in the future? For some organizations yes, for some no. The future is likely to be very uneven.

To close, I would like to bring us back to the core of international project management, from my perspective, and that's people. We do projects with people. We need people to do projects. Projects are essentially human undertakings and those leading them need to acquire and demonstrate human skills. Essentially, this means the ability to speak clearly, to explain what has to be done, with the control to get across a message in a way that the other understands and finds engaging. It also requires the ability to listen, to check what has been said has been heard, which implies empathy, curiosity and openness – others may have better ideas. It means having high-quality conversations again and again and again. Susan Scott, author of *Fierce Conversation*, and a former CEO in her own right, hints at the power of conversation in her book with a simple statement:

No conversation is guaranteed to change your life, but any conversation can. (*Fierce Conversation*, Susan Scott, Berkley, 2004)

I like the statement because it alerts us to the opportunity but also the obligation that each and every conversation presents us with. Susan Scott's appeal is to become more conscious, to live in the moment with and for the people around us. We need to shake ourselves from autopilot mode and abandon the inhabit the safety of our own world of concerns and prejudices. If we can become more aware of others, of the need to both manage and empower people through effective conversation, realizing the deep complexity of conducting even simple conversations, we give ourselves the chance to create more meaningful and impactful projects.

Bob Dignen

APPENDIX 1
Global Offensive: project management within 150 days

FRANK KÜHN

The detailed timetable

How did the project management capabilities develop in the company? The following description includes three paragraphs: (a) the main course, as planned in the beginning, (b) a practical application that emerged underway, and (c) the continuous improvement.

The main course

Timeline	Content	Involved
Week 1	Contact to external consultant (phone call).	HR, consultant
Week 2	First meeting with a delegation from the executive team, nominated to drive the initiative. Implementation strategy defined: common development of the standard, documentation in a handbook, training and feedback, consolidation step by step. The executives taking part in this meeting defined themselves as 'Core Team'.	Executives, HR, consultant
Ensuing	First outline of a possible standard, with various options. First draft of a training workshop design.	Consultant

Timeline	Content	Involved
Week 4	Content of the future standard fixed. Final decision in favour of a train-the-trainer approach. The trainers (still to be nominated out of the staff) should feel free to further develop the content. Criteria for identifying internal trainers fixed, first ideas of candidates.	Core team, HR, consultant
Ensuing	Next outline of the future standard. Second draft of a training workshop design.	Consultant
	Nomination of internal trainers.	HR, heads of divisions
Week 8	Final discussion of standard, handbook and training approach. Short list of internal trainers.	Core team, consultant
Week 12	International train-the-trainer workshop. Parallel processes: (1) discussion and further development of the standard, (2) practising and reflecting the training design.	Internal trainers, HR, consultant
Ensuing	Updating handbook and training design.	Consultant
Week 14	Review of the train-the-trainer workshop. Lessons learned. Feedbacks from the wider organization. Training schedule.	Core team, HR, consultant
Week 17	First training delivered by a team of three trainers from Germany. Supervision by consultant. Participants: experienced staff members, works council representatives. Core team members joined the evening session, feedback and discussion.	Internal trainers, participants, core team member, consultant
Week 19	Second training in a European site. Mixed trainer team. Supervision by the consultant. Participants from different countries. Started with factory tour. Evening session with core team.	Internal trainers, participants, core team, consultant
Week 21	Third training oversea. Mixed trainer team. Supervision by the consultant. Participants from different countries. Started with factory tour, country manager taking part.	Internal trainers, participants, country manager, consultant

Timeline	Content	Involved
Ensuing	Roll-out	Internal trainers, participants worldwide
In parallel	Three workshops for superiors and upper management: their role in project management, lessons learned to date, further development	Superiors, internal trainers, core team

Rapid practice

An urgent infrastructure project was to be supported. This included three steps with the project manager, the project team and the external consultant as expert and facilitator:

1 **Prep talk and one-day workshop.** Application of the new project management standard to the project. Clarification of Project Charter, customer requirements, SWOT.

2 **One-day workshop.** Further elaboration: Project Charter, customer requirements, SWOT, stakeholder analysis, work breakdown structure, project organization, next steps.

3 **Half-day workshop for decision preparation.** Project status. Capacity plan. Design of management kick-off.

Continuous improvement

The following measures have been planned by the trainer team themselves:

- Rebuilding the training design, splitting the three-day training workshop into two, two-day parts. Part 1: Fundamentals and support for smaller projects. Part 2: Managing larger projects, financial steering, critical project leadership situations.

- Learning on the project.

- Trainers' experience exchange every six months, including further development of training and coaching skills.

APPENDIX 2
An iterative evaluation of an online class to increase inclusion of international learners in an online forum

SHARON LALLA

The following are documents used during Sharon's facilitation of her online educational community. The first is a worksheet to help the online group define its expectations and norms of online collaboration – the Pledge. The second – Group Preferences – is a worksheet to help students reflect on and identify their preferences for working in online groups.

1. Take the Pledge

Please rank the expectations listed below in order of importance to you but add ONE additional expectation to the list. Put your expectation in ALL CAPS so we know your contribution, and place it in any ranking order you wish. Your reply to this message thread indicates your commitment to the expectations mentioned in this netiquette pledge. If you do not agree to these expectations, consider taking another class.

Netiquette Expectations

- I will never resort to personal name calling.
- I will welcome disagreements or questions as an opportunity to learn more about the topic or about myself.
- I will be respectful of other people's opinions.
- If I am replying to a post, I will select the post to which I want to reply before making the reply (this makes it easier for others to follow the trail of thought).

- I will not be afraid of asking a 'dumb' question.
- I will challenge my peers with thought-provoking ideas.
- When posting a new message thread, I will spend time thinking about a descriptive title for my new thread.
- I will be succinct but complete in my responses.

2. Group Preferences

Answer the following questions:

- Do you consider yourself an introvert or extrovert?
- Do you like to lead or follow in a team?
- Can you meet synchronously (ie meeting at the same time)?
- What time zone are you in?
- Do you prefer to have a group that meets only asynchronously? (ie not meeting at the same time)?
- Do you handle conflict well? How so? If not, why not?
- What skills can you offer to a team?
- Are you a perfectionist or pragmatist or other? Explain.
- Do you consider yourself a fair, good, or excellent writer? Planner? Explain.
- What do you like least/most about working in a team?

APPENDIX 3
The Nordic Leadership Study Tour to India

RANA SINHA

In his case, Rana refers to a tool for exchanging learning insights used within his project. Rana summarizes his use of the tool below.

The weekly/monthly insight exchange tool

As a project leader, I used this practice of encouraging everyone to contribute weekly insights related to the project. These observations could also be tangentially related to the project, for example something related to the organization, their experience of cultural differences or even how people reacted and related to the ever-changing and challenging weather of the day.

To encourage people to reflect and find insights, I pointed out that the core difference between sheep and humans was our intellectual curiosity – observing, cogitating and deducing meanings from our observations. Participants on the programme seemed inspired by my appeal.

There were only three ground rules:

1 When sharing reflections, no one was to criticize another person's observations just to point out that someone was wrong, though adding knowledge was encouraged.

2 The same observation could not be used more than once, if nothing was added.

3 Everyone had to contribute something.

This practice really caught on and a quick round at the beginning of our weekly/monthly meetings acted as a positive warm-up. It took only a few minutes and often functioned as a convenient bridge to the topics on the agenda. One huge benefit for the project was that it served as a way for people to voice some of their concerns and worries as 'observations' or 'insights', as well as learn to reflect and share experiences. I believe this form of reflective practice can be very productive in a range of project contexts.

FURTHER READING

Anderson, F F and Shane, H M (2002) The impact of netcentricity on virtual teams: the new performance challenge, *Team Performance Management*, 8 (1/2), pp. 5–12

Argyris, C and Schön, D (1966) *Organizational Learning II. Theory, method and practice*, Addison-Wesley, Reading, Mass

Barakat, L L, Lorenz, M P, Ramsey, J R and Cretoiu, S L (2015) Global managers: an analysis of the impact of cultural intelligence on job satisfaction and performance, *Internatnional Journal of Emerging Markets*, 10 (4), pp. 781–800

Barinaga, E (2007) Cultural diversity at work: national culture as a discourse organizing an international project group, *Human Relations*, 60 (2), pp. 315–40

Binder, J (2007) *Global Project Management: Communication, collaboration and Management Across Boarders*, Gower Publishing Ltd, Hampshire/Burlington

Bourne, L and Walker, D H (2004) Advancing project management in learning organizations, *The Learning Organization*, pp. 226–43

Cascio, W F (2000) Managing a virtual workplace, *The Academy of Management Executive*, 14 (3), pp. 81–90

Cisco (2012) Power of in-person: the business value of in-person collaboration [online] http://www.cisco.com/web/telepresence/economist.html

Comfort, J and Franklin, P (2011, 2014) *The Mindful International Manager. How to work effectively across cultures*, 2nd edn, Kogan Page Limited, London/Philadelphia

Creswell, J W (2009) Part ll. Designing Research, in J W Creswell, *Research Design: Qualitative, quantitative, and mixed methods approaches*, 3rd edn, SAGE Publications Inc., California, pp. 145–203

De Bono, E (1976) *The Use of Lateral Thinking*, Penguin, Harmondsworth

Druskat, V U and Wolf, S B (2001) Building the emotional intelligence of groups *Harvard Business Review*, 80 (3), pp. 81–91

Eberlein, M (2008) Culture as critical success factor for successful global project management in multi-national it service projects, *Journal of Information Technology Management*, XIX (3) pp. 27–42

El-Sabaa, S (2001) The skills and career path of an effective project manager, *The International Journal of Project Management*, pp. 1–7

European Commission (2016) Lifelong Learning Programme [online] http://ec.europa.eu/education/tools/llp_en.htmc

Fiol, M (1994) Consensus, diversity, and learning in organizations, *Organization Science* 5 (3), pp. 403–20

Fisher, E (2011) What practitioners consider to be the skills and behaviours of an effective people project manager, *International Journal of Project Management* **29**, pp. 994–1002

Goleman, D (2004) What Makes a Leader, *Harvard Business Review*, pp. 1–11

Goncalves, M (2005) *Managing Virtual Projects*, Mc-GrawHill, USA

Grisham, T W (2010) *International Project Management: Leadership in complete environments*, John Wiley & Sons, New Jersey, pp. 2, 391

Guba, E G (1990) *The Paradigm Dialog*, SAGE Publications, Inc., Newbury Park/London/New Delhi, pp. 19, 20, 25

Günter S K, Maznevski M L, Voigt, A and Jonsen, K (2010) Unraveling the effects of cultural diversity in teams: a meta-analysis of research on multicultural work groups. *Journal of International Business Studies*, **41**, pp. 690–93, 702–05

Hakonen, M and Lipponen, J (2009) It takes two to tango: the close interplay between trust and identification in predicting virtual team effectiveness, *The journal of eWorking*, **3** (1), pp. 17–32

Hambley, Laura A, O'Neill, Thomas A and Kline, Theresa J B (2007) Virtual team leadership: the effects of leadership style and communication medium on team interacting styles and outcomes, *Science Direct*, **103** (1), pp. 1–20

Hirzel, M, Kühn, F and Wollmann, P (2002) *Multi Projekt Management*, FAZ Verlag, Frankfurt am Main

Hofstede, G, Hofstede, G J and Minkov, M (2010) *Cultures and Organizations: Software of the mind. Intercultural cooperation and its importance for Survival*, McGraw Hill, New York/Chicago

The Hofstede Centre (nd) National culture, [online] http://geert-hofstede.com/national-culture.html [accessed 23 March 2015]

Horwitz, F M, Bravington, D and Silvis, U (2006) The promise of virtual teams: identifying key factors in effectiveness and failure, *Journal of European Industrial Training*, **30** (6), pp. 472–94

IPMA (2006) *ICB – IPMA Competence Baseline, Version 3.0*, International Project Management Association, The Netherlands, p. 56

Jónasson, H I and Ingason, H Þ (2012) *Samskiptafærni – samskipti, hópar og teymi*. JPV útgáfa, Reykjavík:??

Jonasson, H I and Ingason, H Þ (2011). *Leiðtogafærni: Sjálfskilningur, þroski og þróun*, JPV útgáfa, Reykjavík

Jullien, F (2004) *Treatise on Efficiency: Between western and Chinese thinking*, University of Hawaii Press, Hawaii

Jullien, F (2011) *The Silent Transformations*, University of Chicago Press, Chicago

Jullien, F (2014) *On the Universal: The uniform, the common and dialogue between cultures*, Polity Press

Kerzner, H (2005) *Using the Project Management Maturity Model* John Wiley & Sons, USA

Kühn, F and Wollmann, P (2012) *Interaktion als Organisationsstrategie*, Integrated Consulting Group, Berlin

Larson, E W and Gray, C F (2011) *Project Management: The Managerial process*, Mc Graw Hill, New York, pp. 534, 540

Lewis, Y R and Boucher, L (2012) PM: people management or project management, *PMI Global Congress Proceedings*, PMI Global Congress Proceedings, Vancouver, British Columbia, pp. 1–11

Mayer, M (1998) *The Virtual Edge: Embracing technology for distributed project team success*, Project Management Institute, Pennsylvania, USA

Mendenhall, M E, Osland, J S, Bird, A, Oddou, G R, Maznevski, M L, Stevens M J and Stahl, G K (2013) *Global Leadership*, Routledge, London/New York

Molinsky, A (2015) the mistake most managers make with cross-cultural training, *Harward Business Review*, **1–2**

Moon, T (2013) The effects of cultural intelligence on performance in multicultural teams, *Journal of Applied Social Psychology*, **43** (12), pp. 2414–25

Nonaka, I and Takeuchi, H (1995) The knowledge-creating company. How Japanese companies create the dynamics of innovation. New York, Oxford, Oxford UP

Pant, I and Baroudi, B (2008) Project management education: the human skill imperative, *International Journal of Project Management* **26**, pp. 124–28

Paul, H S and Ruchinskas, J (1995) From face-to-face meeting to video teleconferencing: potential shifts in the meeting genre, *Management Communication Quarterly*, **8** (4), p. 395

Pauleen, D J, ed (2004) *Virtual Team: Projects, protocols and processes*, Idea Group Publishing, UK

Pétursson, A (2016, april 6) Senior Adviser. (I Jónsdóttir, Interviewer)

Piante, J D (2010) *The Soft Part is the Hard Part*, PMI Global Congress, Washington DC, pp. 1–11

Project Management Institute (2013) *A Guide to the Project Management Body of Knowledge*, 5th edn, Project Management Institute, Inc., Pennsylvania

Ramsoomair, F and Howey, R (2004) The hard realities of soft skills, *Problems and Perspectives in Management*, **4**, pp. 231–39

Schmidt, J B, Montoya-Weiss, M M and Massey, A P (2001) New product development decision-making effectiveness: comparing individuals, face-to-face teams, and virtual teams, *Decision Sciences*, **32** (4), pp. 575–600

Siebdrat, F, Hoegl, M and Ernst, H (2009) How to manage virtual teams, *MIT Sloan Management Review*, **50** (4), pp. 63–68

Skills You Need (nd) Interpersonal Skills Self-Assessment [online] http://www.skillsyouneed.com/ [accessed 12 April 2016]

Søderberg, A and Holden, N (2002) Rethinking cross-cultural management in a globalizing business world, *International Journal of Cross-Cultural Management*, **2** (1) p. 104

Strang, K D (2003) *Achieving organizational learning across projects*, PMI® Global Congress 2003, Project Management Institute ,Baltimore, Maryland, USA

Thamhain, H J (2004) Linkage of project environment to performance: lessons for teamleadership. *International Journal of Project Management*, 22 (7), pp. 533–44

Wenger, E (1999) *Communities of Practice: Learning, meaning, and identity*, paperback edn, Zuerst 1998, Cambridge UP, Cambridge, UK

Willke, H (2006) *Systemtheorie 1*, UTB, Stuttgart

Willke, H (2011) *Einführung in das Systemische Wissensmanagement*, Carl-Auer Verlag, Heidelberg

Willke, H (2014) *Systemic Risk: The myth of rational finance and the crisis of democracy*, Campus Verlag, Frankfurt am Main

Willke, H and Wollmann, P (2012) Multi-level interaction, resilience and cross-cultural learning, in *Interaktion als Organisationsstrategie*, S 57–74, Integrated Consulting Group, Berlin

Yammarino, F J and Atwater, L E (1997) Do managers see themselves as others see them? Implications of self-other rating agreement for human resources management, *Organizational Dynamics*, pp. 35–44

INDEX

Italics indicate a figure or table

CPSIA information can be obtained at www.ICGtesting.com
Printed in the USA
BVOW04s2155280916

463641BV00016B/123/P